THE SIGNAL APPROACH TO CHILDREN'S BOOKS

THE SIGNAL APPROACH
TO CHILDREN'S BOOKS

*A Collection edited
by Nancy Chambers*

SCARECROW PRESS

Text Acknowledgements

The compiler and publisher wish to thank the following authors for the use of their copyright material in this collection: John Adams for *Dark Rainbow*; Anthea Bell for *Translator's Notebook*; Aidan Chambers for *The Reader in the Book*; Jane Curry for *On the Elvish Craft*; John Donovan for *American Dispatch*; Eleanor Graham for *The Puffin Years*; Peter Hunt for *The Good, the Bad and the Indifferent*; Robert Leeson for *To the Toyland Frontier*; Julia MacRae for *Amateur Joys*; Brian Morse for *Poetry, Children and Ted Hughes*; Elaine Moss for *The Seventies in British Children's Books*; Lance Salway for *Pathetic Simplicity*; Charles Sarland for *Chorister Quartet*; John Rowe Townsend for *Standards of Criticism for Children's Literature*; Alan Tucker for *Learning to Read*; Irene Whalley for *The Cinderella Story 1724–1919*; Mrs Barbara Williams for Jay Williams's *Looking for a Pattern*; Alan Garner and Aidan Chambers for *An Interview with Alan Garner*; Faber and Faber Ltd. and Harper and Row, Publishers, Inc. for permission to quote Ted Hughes's poetry from his books: *Crow* copyright © 1970, 1971 and 1972 by Ted Hughes, *Lupercal* copyright © 1960 by Ted Hughes, *Wodwo* copyright © 1967 by Ted Hughes; Faber and Faber Ltd. and Viking Penguin Inc. for *The Earth-Owl and Other Moon-People* copyright © 1963 by Ted Hughes, *Season Songs* copyright © 1963 and 1976 by Ted Hughes and *Moon-Bells and Other Poems* copyright © 1978 by Ted Hughes (published in the UK by Chatto and Windus); Viking Penguin Inc. for *Moon Whales and Other Moon Poems* copyright © 1963, 1976 by Ted Hughes; and Faber and Faber Ltd. and Bobbs-Merrill Co. Inc. for *Meet My Folks!* copyright © 1961 by Ted Hughes.

(Illustration Acknowledgements on p. 11)

Cover design and lettering by Michael Harvey

Library of Congress Cataloging in Publication Data
Main entry under title:

The Signal approach to children's books.

Originally published: Harmondsworth, Middlesex : Kestrel Books, 1980.

Includes index.

1. Children's literature—History and criticism— Addresses, essays, lectures. I. Chambers, Nancy. II. Signal.
PN1009.A1S392 1981   809'.89282   81-8824
ISBN 0-8108-1447-1   AACR2

First published in 1980 by Kestrel Books/Penguin Books Ltd

Collection Copyright © 1980 by Nancy Chambers

The Scarecrow Press, Inc., Metuchen, N.J., & London
Manufactured in the United States of America

Contents

5

Contents

PUBLISHER'S NOTE

The illustrations placed with the *Signal Quotes* throughout this book represent a number of British artists who have been honoured by the Library Association's Kate Greenaway Medal for distinguished work in illustration for children, either as Medal recipients or as runners-up.

SIGNAL magazine
is published by
Aidan and Nancy Chambers
Lockwood, Station Road, South Woodchester,
Stroud, Gloucestershire GL5 5EQ, England

List of Illustrations

List of Illustrations

Introduction

Since January 1970 SIGNAL: APPROACHES TO CHILDREN'S
BOOKS has been published three times a year by Aidan Chambers
and me, as The Thimble Press. We intended it to provide a publishing opportunity for people whose ideas about, and interests in,
children's books could not be contained in brief articles or reviews.
We wanted to encourage critical writing as well as to reflect the
world of children's books from a variety of viewpoints. And we
hoped to develop a manner that did not assume an audience of
parents or teachers or librarians in their vocational roles (as,
necessarily, do most other children's book periodicals) but that
spoke to individuals who were more than fleetingly attentive to
the subject. Since we believe that such individuals will want to
read about activity in parts of the children's book world other
than their own, we have always aimed to include articles that touch
on historical and international subjects. Our main line, however,
is the thoughtful consideration of children's books, their authors
and their illustrators.

Aims like these do not produce high circulation figures, of
course; but SIGNAL survives and, to our eyes, flourishes largely
because we have been so fortunate in the people whose writing
appears in our pages. We rely utterly on our contributors, several
of whom have become friends even though we have never met.
Their goodwill and expertise have been and continue to be signal
in every sense.

An impression of all our contributors' work is, I hope, conveyed
truly in the present collection, which reprints articles chosen to
demonstrate SIGNAL's range. The writers have had the chance
to update or otherwise improve the original texts. Where there were
gaps in representativeness, I asked for new material: from Anthea
Bell on translating; from Peter Hunt on a critical mode that differed
from others treated in the book; and – not a gap, this, but an

imperative, given the dates of our existence – Elaine Moss on the many developments in children's books during the 1970s.

Of course it was much harder to decide what to leave out than what to put in. I began by excluding articles that had subsequently grown into books themselves (there are two such titles: Dorothy Butler's *Cushla and Her Books*, Hodder; and Lance Salway's *A Peculiar Gift: Nineteenth Century Writings on Books for Children*, Kestrel) or had been reprinted from SIGNAL elsewhere. Then, because they were largely ephemeral, I decided not to extract either of the two continuing back-of-book features that have drawn considerable response from subscribers over the years: *Pelorus*, an in-house comment column, and *Book Post*, an informal correspondence about new books between Lance Salway and me. I also left out most of the material that focused strictly on an author's work (the articles on pages 101–125 are, to my mind, "the poetry articles" not "the Ted Hughes articles"), as that would have made a book or two on its own. The "Subject Guide to Ten Years of SIGNAL" on pages 329–339 indicates which authors and illustrators have been written about, or have written for, the magazine. Finally, I have not represented the Signal Poetry Award, first made in 1979, or the publishing that is closely allied to the magazine: our booklists – on poetry books, humorous books, and learning to read with picture books – which are not so much lists as testaments of individual experience with books.

A lot of people have been important to SIGNAL during its decade, but these are the ones we simply could not have done without: Alan and Joan Tucker, with whom we first talked about our publishing notions; Lance Salway, whose practical advice about and distinctive work in the magazine we were lucky enough to have from the very beginning; Elaine Moss, whose regular writing for SIGNAL is for many readers its chief attraction and whose constant support has been indispensable to our progress; John Donovan, whose *American Dispatch* enlivened our pages for more than six years; Judy Taylor and John Ryder, who guided our efforts to improve SIGNAL's look; Alex and Marie Langley and Gerald Cole of the Downfield Press, who have done all our setting and printing from the first issue; and Patrick Hardy, who paid SIGNAL its best compliment by asking for this book.

Introduction

The first-person plural pronoun used during this short introduction is sometimes actual, sometimes editorial. The other half
of the literal "we" made SIGNAL possible in the first place, and
has never failed to be the best board of directors an editor could
have: helpfully critical, optimistic, and generous.

January 1980   N.C.

Illustration Acknowledgements

The publishers wish to thank the following for the use of illustrations in this
collection: Penguin Books Ltd. (Kestrel Books), and David McKay & Co.
Inc. (Henry Z. Walck) for an illustration from *Paul the Hero of the Fire*
written and illustrated by Edward Ardizzone, copyright © 1963 by Edward
Ardizzone; Macmillan Ltd. and Atheneum Publishers for an illustration from
Mr. and Mrs. Pig's Evening Out written and illustrated by Mary Rayner,
copyright © 1976 by Mary Rayner; Jonathan Cape Ltd. and Holt, Rinehart
& Winston for an illustration from *Mr. Gumpy's Outing* written and illustrated by John Burningham, copyright © 1970 by John Burningham; Helen
Oxenbury and William Morrow & Co. Inc. for an illustration by Helen
Oxenbury from *Cakes and Custard* compiled by Brian Alderson and
published in the UK by William Heinemann Ltd., illustration copyright ©
1974 by Helen Oxenbury; Penguin Books Ltd. (Kestrel Books) and Pantheon
Books for an illustration by Charles Keeping from *The Golden Shadow*
written by Leon Garfield and Edward Blishen, illustration copyright © 1973
by Charles Keeping; The Victoria and Albert Museum for all the illustrations
reproduced in the article *The Cinderella Story 1724–1919* – that on page 147
being Crown Copyright; The Bodley Head Ltd. and Macmillan Publishing
Co. Inc. for an illustration from *Rosie's Walk* written and illustrated by Pat
Hutchins, copyright © 1968 by Patricia Hutchins; Hamish Hamilton Ltd
and Thomas Y. Crowell Publishers for an illustration from *War and Peas*
written and illustrated by Michael Foreman, copyright © 1974 by Michael
Foreman; Penguin Books Ltd. (Kestrel Books) and Viking Penguin Inc. for
an illustration by Janet Ahlberg from *Each Peach Pear Plum* written by Allan
Ahlberg, illustration copyright © 1978 by Allan and Janet Ahlberg; The
Bodley Head Ltd. and Farrar Straus & Giroux Inc. for an illustration by
Maurice Sendak from *The Juniper Tree and Other Tales from Grimm* trans-
lated by Lore Segal and Randall Jarrell, illustration copyright © 1973 by
Maurice Sendak; Penguin Books Ltd. (Kestrel Books) and Holiday House
Inc. for an illustration by Edward Gorey from *The Shrinking of Treehorn*

Looking for a Pattern

JAY WILLIAMS

Jay Williams was a novelist and storyteller for both children and adults. He wrote the first article in the first SIGNAL ("Children's Books and the Humanities", January 1970), and that is the reason I am beginning the book with him. He was an unusual person: a writer who was genuinely interested in the work of other writers, as his SIGNAL pieces on Peter Dickinson and John Christopher show. Until his death in 1978 Jay Williams was a constant friend; and the following article (published in the January 1975 issue) is, I suppose, as much about friendship as about writing children's books.

Not long ago, I drove up to the small Connecticut fishing village of Stonington to visit two old friends of mine, Dorothy and Robert Newman. They are both professional writers – she writes under her maiden name, Dorothy Crayder – and for some years both have been drawn more and more deeply into writing for children. Dorothy is a very slow and meticulous worker; her first book, *The Pluperfect of Love*, took her two years to write. It was widely hailed, while her second, *She, the Adventuress*, was a nominee for the 1973 Newbery Medal and was an Honour Book at the Children's Book Council Spring Book Festival. Its sequel, *She, and the Dubious Three*, was published in October 1974. Bob's books for children include *The Japanese: People of the Three Treasures*, which has become a standard reference on the subject, *Grettir the Strong*, *The Boy Who Could Fly*, and the much-praised *Merlin's Mistake* and its sequel, *The Testing of Tertius*. A new fantasy, *The Shattered Stone*, will appear in the fall of 1975. Both Newmans have long experience in the adult field as well. Dorothy started selling her stories to magazines more than twenty years ago, and has written for radio and television. Bob began earning his living by pulp fiction as early as 1936, ran up a staggering list of credits for radio shows such as *Inner Sanctum*, *The Thin Man*, and *Big Sister*, and then an equally long one for television daytime serials. Among his adult novels are *Corbie* and *The Enchanter*.

I planned to interview them in a more or less straightforward way, asking such non-controversial questions as "How do you work?" and "Can two writers live in the same house without explosions?" Almost from the outset, the interview became a discussion and took a quite different turn.

We sat in a large, light-filled room, furnished simply but with fine pieces. One wall was covered with books and faced another of glass, which looked out towards the water. The Newmans are both tall, slim, and youthful although they are in their mid-sixties; they have a complementary elegance and grace which is very striking, and they do not interrupt each other, as married couples often do, but supplement each other's conversation with an amusing and affectionate deference – "Bob, may I tell that story, please?" Dorothy will say, and Bob will listen as if he had never heard it before.

On this occasion, she began by describing how they had visited a friend in Woodstock, who had taken them to the local library. Dorothy had asked where the children's section was, and the friend said, incredulously, "Do you read children's books?" When Dorothy said that they both did, the friend cried with astonishment and some disdain, "My God, you're really serious about this stuff!" "I blew my stack," Dorothy said, going on to state that the writing of a book for children was as profoundly difficult and serious a task as any other branch of literature, perhaps in some ways, more so.

We talked about that for a bit, and about the kinds of children's books they read, and then Bob remarked that he had been looking at some books about contemporary problems. "In Dorothy's phrase, which I think is an excellent one," he said, "so many of these books deprive a child of its childhood. I'm speaking of books about abortion, books about drugs, things about which they should know but not at the expense of other kinds of reading. After all, adult books on these subjects are available and by the time the children are in their upper teens they can and usually do read those." Dorothy agreed, but added, "It isn't that I think children should not be reading problem books; they should read anything they can read. A teacher I met in Philadelphia had a charming way of putting it. She said she had a bookcase for her own children that went from the floor to the ceiling and any shelf that a child could reach – " We laughed, and she went on, "But last-time we were in London, we met a young librarian in Chelsea. At that time, the whole concentration was on books for children of the inner cities – the idea was that they had to give these children a mirror image of the life they were leading. She herself came from a working-class background and she was working with and reading to such children. She said, 'They don't need that kind of thing, they're *living* it. What they want are stories about princes and princesses.' "

I said that seemed to be borne out in England, at least, because the fantasies of Alan Garner were so popular among working-class children. There was, however, some question whether the same thing might be true for, say, black children in America. Dorothy said that she had been interviewed on the radio, in a programme sponsored by the New York Public Library, by some young people, both black and white, about *The Pluperfect of Love*. "I had been told by everyone that the book was really for upper middle-class children," she said. "It couldn't be further from the black experience. One of the children talking to me was black, she had been beaten up, I can still see her – she had a mark on her forehead – and she was talking about the character Jabez the magician, a most unsympathetic character; she said, 'I feel sorry for him because I think he acted the way he did because he didn't have enough love, that was his problem.' The other kids agreed. They had gotten the essential thing about the book, its dark side, that the whole thing came out of lovelessness. My view is, yes, there are unquestionably children who sadly, tragically, are in need of books about the Pill, about drugs, but they're flooded with such books so that the kinds we write sometimes have a struggle to surface."

Bob nodded. "Publishing is a business, as we all know," he said. "There are an enormous number of *made* books, non-books – you know, the story of *Jaws* and how it was put together. There are children's book writers who sit down in the same way and say,

'I'm going to do a book, now what's there to write about? Chicanos, the plight of the Indians, those have got to have appeal. I'll do a couple of weeks of research and write the book.' Then librarians and teachers say, 'Yes, this is the newest thing, it's true, I've read it in the papers and it's a book I have to have.' I don't work that way. I can only write a book when it means something to me. I make pages and pages of notes, ideas for a scene, for a character, and I have to ask myself, What does this mean? What does the story want to say? Why does it interest me? I start exploring it, and I can only write it when I discover what it does mean."

I remarked that most of his children's books had been fantasies, and that his adult novels, too, contained fantastic elements, and asked him why his tastes ran that way. He thought for a time, and replied, "You know that one of my basic interests has always been myth. Why is there a similarity between myths throughout the world? My theory is that the rituals on which myths are based are similar because people are similar all over the world, with the same needs, the same drives, the same conflicts which they resolve in similar rituals. Now, in my book, *Merlin's Mistake*, there was an Oedipal conflict between the hero, Brian, and an unknown Black Knight, who turns out to be his father. In *The Testing of Tertius*, there's a scene where Merlin is in Annwn, the hell which I took out of the Mabinogion: Nothingness, the place of No-Being, and this to me was the unconscious. I had the three main characters going down into their own unconscious, in which place they each faced their greatest fear and overcame it. What I was doing was using myth, and behind the myth using what I know and believe about psychiatry and its contribution, and these were what I found necessary to give a kind of substratum to the story."

I said, "Then in effect, you *are* dealing with real problems. Your fantasies are allegories about life. You're not just writing interesting tales – " Dorothy broke in, "Wait, Jay. When I say that problem books deprive a child of childhood, I don't mean that I think children should not be presented with problems. I think the best, truly felt, should – and do – contain children's problems: children are frightened, they are lonely, they have tragedies. . . ."

"What about your books?" I asked. She said, "I think *The Pluperfect of Love* certainly reflected – " she hesitated, made up her mind, and continued, "its origin was out of a deeply felt problem of my own. I had been reared in an atmosphere of lovelessness between men and women. The book came out of that. Even *She, the Adventuress*, which I regarded as an entertainment, came from my own way of trying to handle anxiety. That is to say, when I was scared as a child, sometimes I would pretend that I was the heroine of a tragic novel. Removing myself to the safety of an unreal third person seemed to help. So it was somehow only natural for Maggie, when she was scared out of her mind, to turn herself into She, the Adventuress. You asked Bob, Why do you think that your books are fantasies and about magic? He gave you a very full answer, but I think that behind it is still another answer. You once said you felt that the kind of books you wrote were the kind you wanted to read as a child. I think that's what I try to do, too, reach back into that past and try to find the things I was longing for in the books I read, that met some need in me. I think that Bob's engagement with myth and fantasy stems not from an intellectual thing but from a deeply felt emotional need as a child. He was a child who had to fill a very frightening real life with an adorned, imagined, unreality. He was always reading, reading – he couldn't bear to face what was happening in his own house. He had a mother who was no mother, and a weak father who didn't know what the hell to do about it."

We were all silent for a moment, reflecting on what she had said. Bob murmured, "You're right." I said, pursuing my own thought, "But why do we write for children?" "I think one is writing for oneself," said Bob, "trying to re-create what one was looking for at that age." "I think that's true," I said, "but I still haven't satisfied myself on the point. Why start in the first place writing for children? Why does it possess us to write for kids rather than just to write books which may find their way to children, as *Gulliver's Travels* did?" Bob said, "But Dodgson wrote for children." "He was addressing a child directly, telling it a story," said Dorothy. "Kenneth Grahame wrote *The Wind in the Willows* in letters to his son," Bob said. We all seemed to be groping towards something else.

I said, at last, "A lot of children's writers begin by telling their own children stories and then writing them down. All right, maybe that's how it seems to start. But there's something else – well,

Dodgson wrote *Alice* not just because he was telling stories to little girls, but we know he liked little girls, he felt safer with kids than he did with adults. I wonder if some of us feel the same way?"

"I do," Dorothy said, bluntly. "I say to myself, What am I trying to do now, in my autumn garden? Why am I not even attempting an adult novel? You used the word 'safer'. I think I am trying to return to the emotional world of my childhood, where indeed I do feel more at home. Not that that world was ever always that gorgeous. To me, it is a more appealing world at this moment than this distorted – than the real world outside, that I would have to enter to write an adult novel. I think that's beyond me. I'm dipping into another well from the one I would dip into to bring up an adult novel, and it's a place I feel safer in."

That was candid enough. I said, "Something else occurs to me. Do you remember, Padraic Colum said long ago that he wrote children's books because the child's world was full of wonder? That quality, the quality of wonder, is something that vanishes from the world when you're an adult, and I think all of us want to recapture it to a certain extent. That's why most of the best kids' books have something a little eccentric about them, they look at the ordinary world from an extraordinary position. It is the vantage point of *wonder*. Garner's books, although they may contain working-class children, put them in strange situations. E. Nesbit did the same thing." "Introduced magic into the real world – *Five Children and It* is essentially the same as *Elidor*," Bob put in.

"Yes, and not just magic, but something a little out of the regular orbit," I went on. "The Newbery winner, *From the Mixed-up Files of Mrs. Basil E. Frankweiler*, has the eccentricity in the situation, the locked museum. In *She, the Adventuress*, you put an ordinary child in a strange situation, alone on an ocean liner, and surround her with eccentric characters. And the world of Bob's Tertius is not just medieval but full of unexpected magic. What we're really objecting to when we object to books about abortion or the problems of blacks is not what they're about but the fact that they often lack this eccentric quality. One of the best books about blacks I know, Virginia Hamilton's *The Planet of Junior Brown*, is an absolutely real book about real characters, but it's got a strange, eerie quality, dark streets, empty buildings with lost kids living in the cellars – the reality is shot through with wonder." "I met Virginia Hamilton at the Spring Book Festival," Dorothy said, softly. "She is an enormously dedicated writer. She said to me, 'That's really all I want to do and think about, children's books.' She is obsessed ...." "We're all obsessed," I said.

Dorothy went downstairs to make some coffee. And Bob, looking out at the plane of intensely blue water on which a small white sailboat could be seen, said, "You know, I am essentially a storyteller. Dorothy starts from her characters. I work with character, of course, but essentially it is the story and what it means. But there's nothing specific I want to teach. Do you remember James Stephens writing about *The Worm Ouroboros*? He said Eddison's book was not an allegory, that he was a poet too busy creating to have time for schoolmastering. I think I suddenly realize what lies behind my stories; I don't start out to indoctrinate children. But what I suppose I do is try to give them a sense of how I feel about things I've spent my whole life learning."

I understood what he meant; the symbols and myths on which he draws are not consciously manipulated, but come to the surface of his mind as he works on a story. I said, "I'm a narrative writer, just as you are, and the thing a lot of people don't realize is the fascination narrative exerts on the writer of it. We both told ourselves stories when we were kids, in which we were the chief actors. The story becomes a refuge from the world, the narrative itself protects you and draws you along with it, and after a while becomes almost indistinguishable from reality. That compulsion can be worked out almost better in children's books than in any other form I've tried."

He nodded. "What the adult has is the ability to peel this onion, to realize that there is something under the skin. What does it mean? Why is it important to me? And then without being too explicit, to come out with it, to relate it to other things." He changed his tone and said with more intensity, "This you must know as a writer – the lost feeling we have as children that the world is too big and complex, too many things are happening, and there is no way that we can ever understand it. I remember one strange moment when I was a kid on a ship in the Mediterranean, a trip we took. I had crawled out around a lifeboat and was trapped for a minute, wasn't sure whether I could get back or would fall overboard. I was looking up at the stars and they all fitted together – " He made a circular gesture with one hand. "For the first time I felt that there was a pattern there, and that there must be a pattern in life. And then, when I started writing, I felt the sense of structure, the sense when something comes together in a story and you can see the pattern emerge. At least you can handle *that* amount, and that's what you work for in a story. You know that there are a certain number of elements, but something may be missing and you can't start working until the thing fits together; it's not until you've got all the elements for the structure and it has a pattern that you can start. It's this looking for a pattern, looking for a structure – I suppose that's still a defence for us. We can't structure our lives that carefully, but in this small segment we can control the material, give it structure, have it mean something. That's also why, when you've finished a story, you get a sense of loss until you can find another structure that you can immerse yourself in, create a new envelope in which you can live."

I said, "I feel a spasm of sadness for writers who want to get away from childhood, who make fun of it, who pretend that all children are monsters. I mean, it's true that children are capable of all sorts of monstrous behaviour, that they can be demons; nevertheless, the way children look at the world, it's always new. Anything is possible – even that you may get *out* of a lousy and terrible situation – and every day is full of surprise. That's the thing I attach myself to – it would be ideal, if somehow when you're grown you could look at the world that way every single day."

Bob laughed. "You know what that is? It's that great story, the one Mary Aswell told in the introduction to a book on the psychology of children. It's about a child who is drawing a picture of a horse, and it's purple. His parents said, 'Why did you make the horse purple?' and he said, 'Why not?' They said, 'We've never seen purple horses.' And the kid said, 'How sad for you.'"

Postscript: When I had written the above article, I showed it to a friend, an editor in the children's field. After some talk, she said, "I wonder if people may misunderstand what you and the Newmans are saying. It sounds a little to me as if you were claiming that you write only for yourselves, without regard for the fact that children are a different audience from adults. After all, the question of *whom* you are writing for – at least in the case of children's books – is at least as important as why you write. Surely one must take the children and their special needs and tastes into account?"

I thought about that for a while. The best illustration of whether we – Bob, Dorothy and I – exclude our audience can be found, of course, in our books. But that isn't really the problem. It seems to me that the alternatives, "Do I write for children, or do I write for myself," which have been talked of so often by authors, are not mutually exclusive. A serious and honest writer does both. The question really is: Where does a book come from in the first place? We have tried to describe, in this discussion, why we write for children (although we all three write for adults as well), but the impulses which produce any novel are surely the same: they emerge from the author's unconscious mind, at work in his imagination. They are dreams, the images of possibility, the endless stories we all tell to ourselves: What if such-and-such a person were to find himself in such-and-such a situation? They are the formulations of questions we ask ourselves about the act of living, and sometimes the answers to those questions, or only the realization that another and different question has to be asked.

Is there an audience, ever, in the mind of the writer? In my own case (and in that of the Newmans, as well, I must add) when I write for adults the audience is in my head; it consists of myself and a few intimate friends. When I write for children, it is for the child I once was, along with a few children I know now. I cannot write· for a vague, faceless audience – the audience to which a hack addresses himself – I can only speak to real people. Neither can I write propaganda pieces, manufactured to fit the political or social requirements of the moment. As Bob says, in our discussion, "I can only write a book when it means something to me."

What we discuss is what our books mean to us. We are, as thoughtful professionals, concerned with trying to look beneath the surface of what we write. But this does not and cannot mean that we aren't interested in, or sensitive to, the children we write for. The matter rests on this: how do we know what children are interested in and what they want? Our honest answer can only be that we were children once, ourselves, and it is to that root within ourselves that we must return, when we write for children.

Learning to Read

ALAN TUCKER

Alan Tucker is a bookseller and poet. His long surveys of poetry
books for children – one in the first SIGNAL and one in 1973 –
are among the most important and, to some people, infuriating
things we have published. Because the surveys are so tied to their
time of publication, however, I have chosen to represent Alan
Tucker with an article published in the September 1977 SIGNAL,
the text of which originally appeared in 1973 in a slightly longer
form in a private-press broadsheet that accompanied photographed reproductions of various teaching-reading aids (*Reading
Games: Some Victorian Examples with an essay on The Teaching
of Reading*, Brewhouse Press).

Learning to read is a once-for-all skill, like swimming or riding a
bike. Once you can do it you never forget. Perhaps that is an indica-
tion of how difficult it was to acquire. Like most people, I have
forgotten how I learned to read, or what the experience was like.
I wonder whether at that age one is able to retain self-consciousness
while giving close attention – to learn to read while at the same
time standing aside in one's consciousness thinking, observing: so
this is what it's like then, learning to read. We will not be able to
recall what we never thought to think at the time. In my own case
I do remember learning to swim, and watching myself failing to
achieve progress despite furious arm-flailing and throwing myself
on the water. After two years of sporadic visits to the baths I
was still incapable of two strokes together. One night I dreamt
I was swimming effortlessly. The next day I went to the pool
quite confident that now I understood the trick – that it was
a trick, not a hopelessly complicated set of physical movements.
Even so I was startled to find that I swam a length, and only had

to give up because I had no breath left. Is learning to read like this?

First the mind must be presented with enough information to work on. Then it needs to be left alone to work. In *King Solomon's Ring* Konrad Lorenz describes how shrews painstakingly learn paths until able to move along them with the thoughtless speed of habitual reflex action. By chance Lorenz moved two stones which lay on these paths. His shrews jumped into the air at the place where the stones should have been, and landed with a disconcerting bump.

They then did a most interesting thing: they went back the way they had come, carefully feeling their way until they had again got their bearings. Then facing round again, they tried a second time with a rush, and jumped and crashed down again exactly as before. Only then did they seem to realise that the first fall had not been their own fault but was due to a change in the pathway, and now they proceeded to explore the alteration, cautiously sniffing and bewhiskering the place where the stone ought to have been.

Lorenz then writes that this going back to the start reminded him of a small boy reciting a poem, getting stuck, and going back to begin again at an earlier stanza.

Lorenz's analogy is particularly apt to the mechanics of learning to read. As a physical skill, reading is a kind of path-finding. The written signs have to be followed, just as a tracker follows and interprets the clues of a trail. Children reading need to recognize what is significant, and they must have a sense of sequence, so they can hold in their minds their own progress so far down the page, setting it against a history or total picture of the piece. A primer is not a totally abstract puzzle. Children can find their way through it in precisely the way they would find their way home from school: by observing the topography, by looking for signs and features they can recognize. Little has been done (for the teacher) to isolate the critically significant detail of letter forms. Tinbergen's *Herring Gull's World* and Lack's *Life of the Robin* describe how birds respond to trigger mechanisms. There is an intriguing similarity between the way we learn to recognize, say, the letter *t* by its high cross, and robins' recognition of each other by the precise shade of red of the breast feathers. We now have the example of the difficulty of designing a compatible computer alphabet to remind us of the importance of topology in the business of learning to read.

A Gloucestershire headmistress, Miss Kelsall, now retired, taught individual letters by making a special event of coming in to take a class once a week, and telling a story about each letter. Letter *a* was an apple which was cut in half, and says *æ*. In the printer's *a* the stalk curls over to make sure you recognize it. The letter *e* was an old man bent almost double. He wears glasses to help him read. You draw him like *c*, then put in his glasses as the cross stroke. He says *eh?* The same technique can be used at later stages: the difficult word *eye* is like a nose with an eye on either side, the eyelids half closed. Such fancifulness works simply because it keeps the attention of the class on the matter in hand. It is neither the story nor the presence of the headmistress alone, it is the total event which ensures memorability.

Reading begins with spoken vocabulary. Children must not be expected to read words they do not habitually use and recognize and understand without hesitation. The first path to learn is the path that leads home. Nursery rhymes introduce new words and the idea of a more formal idiom. Also the rhythm of nursery-rhyme phrases makes a foundation for a later appreciation of poetry. (Even as inventive a poet as Donne has nursery equivalents; for example, the famous opening "Busy old fool, unruly sun ..." echoes "Here we come gathering nuts in May", while the "I'm sure I don't know" phrase from "Oranges and Lemons" reappears as a glorious melody in a late Beethoven quartet.)

Vocabulary is followed by pictorial representation, then the sense of story and continuity as in Bruna books. Recognition of form can also be learnt from picture books – e.g. *But Where is the Green Parrot?* or Scarry's dogs which recur in every drawing – and then soon leads to recognition of first-letter forms in notices and advertisements. Children have to learn that English is read from left to right, from top to bottom, and that pages turn over. Remember that the Chinese "naturally" read "backwards". At last comes reading proper, "the cat sat on the mat", learning letter and word patterns, lexicon shape, and experts begin to disagree.

The introduction of *The Golden Primer* by Prof. Meiklejohn and Walter Crane, published in 1884, states in bold type, "The only advice to be given to the young teacher is: TEACH ONLY WORDS, AND TEACH THEM AS WHOLES. NEVER MENTION THE NAME OF A LETTER UNLESS A CHILD DEMANDS IT."

And yes, surely this is sound and sensible. And then there are phonics and i.t.a., and no end of systems. And they all work if the teacher believes in them, because teachers, not systems, teach reading. The joy of reading games is that they have no opinions to canvass. They work on the assumption that reading is a mechanical skill. Of the paraphernalia of the Dame School, the best known is the hornbook, which was a single sheet with alphabet and a prayer printed on it, and protected by a thin sheet of horn. In the later form there was a handle to the frame, and it could be used as a bat, the "battledore". The commonest surviving game is the simple set of alphabet bricks, still fairly easy to find. Unlike the hornbook they have been in continuous production for the last two hundred years or so. Also still in production, though modified in form, are the complete letter sets. Old examples are uncommon and expensive, now being collectable antiques.

Most primary schools today use Breakthrough to Literacy, which is a further development of these games. Letters made of cardboard fit into the slots in a cardboard wallet, or into a plastic rack. The children have small wallets and cards, while the teacher has a giant version for demonstration and class use, also a magnet board and letters. Among other advantages, Breakthrough enables children to handle words physically before their co-ordination is adequate to enable them to write other than slowly and crudely.

The apotheosis of the reading game is an American device for speed-reading. It makes an ideal present for parents who have been talked into buying a set of encyclopædias. The pupil sits with a plastic box on the table in front of him. In the box is a slit, at the side a lever. When you press the lever a line of print flashes past the slit. You read it, and later answer the questions to ensure you have understood. Each day you increase the tension of the spring. The American comedian Woody Allen says, "I took one of those read-faster courses. I read *War and Peace* in four hours. It's about Russia." End of digression on reading games.

Once the child can read half a dozen primers it is all too easy to assume that now world literature will simply open up, readily

26

accessible, just waiting to be read. On the contrary, it is at this point that world literature closes up for most children, who will certainly never get inside one book of it. At this stage spelling has to be learnt, year after year, using whatever grace and enthusiasm the teacher can cling on to for the drudgery of it. There have been great men who couldn't spell – Napoleon, Beethoven, Yeats, Bernard Shaw. I think it must be marked down as a sure sign of lazy teaching, no more and no less, for many stupid people spell very well.

Shaw of course blamed the superficial illogicality of written English. He produced the gem *ghoti* – *gh* as in laugh, *o* as in women, *ti* as in station – spells *fish*. It is Irish logic, deduction by exaggeration and ignoring context. It does not allow for the complexity and sheer untidiness of things. I foresee two parties in the world state: the tidiers and the rioters. Those frightened by the multiplicity of demands life makes on us will sustain themselves with standardized pills, sleep in plexiglass cells and spend forty-two hours a week cleaning, pruning, cutting, preventing and putting in order. Those who are "for life", as they would put it, will live in environmental broken plexiglass packing-cases off rainwater, nuts, honey and drugs, talking for eighty hours a week (leaving no time to read) probably in Welsh, and, with any luck, in Wales. If only people weren't so clean and so dirty and so obsessed with whether it matters. What a wonderful thing it is to be normal.

Whether language is reality, or represents, or describes reality, it is inevitable that it will match the civilization of which it is part in nicety of form and structure. Shaw could have found himself faced with learning to read classical Chinese, with a character for every word, and a social decorum of equivalent subtlety. English orthography is not more difficult than is called for by the nature of our society. Every child has, and should have developed, a different background of spoken and literary English. Each should be accustomed to a slightly different rhythm and sense of idiom and vocabulary. Within the language are local and regional dialects, overprinted by class/occupation jargon and usage. From the cross-weave of these influences each of us produces a unique individual language, a dialect spoken by one person only, the idiolect.

We are beginning to share, all of us, the same few phrases and conversation counters. It is not a growth of mutual understanding.

Language is becoming so restricted that, unable to say precisely what we mean, we are reduced to the meaning look, like old women over a back wall. And the meaning look is impossible in written English. So some of our best writing is in the theatre, by Beckett and Pinter, unwritten, unspoken even, lying between the lines. Which is fine in the enclosed darkness of the theatre, but in daylight literature requires detail, endless hard factual firmly grasped explicit detail, before we're all reduced to nodding, winking, rib-digging idiocy. We are landing with a disconcerting bump on an inadequate vocabulary. My own instinct is to return to the start, try the path again from the beginning to see where it goes wrong.

I believe it goes wrong at the stage following first reading success. Children do not hear the words they must be able to handle with ease if they are to be able to read fluently. Established local idiom is dying. It is neither suitable nor adequate for most of our lives, but it was the foundation of idiolect, just as everyday home life is still the basis of personality. Schools tend to be two-faced about dialect, either subduing it, or treating it as an end in itself. Two faces, one mind: the aim is conformity, whether to B.B.C. English, or to home-rule regionalism. We have a national league table, regional brogue playing noughts and crosses with U and non-U. It is fine to speak broad Devonshire – rather quaint. The B.B.C. favours a Yorkshire accent (provided the man isn't going to talk about Italian painting in it). But Cockney, a far livelier dialect in the context of city life, is common, and to be prevented. Birmingham and Nottingham alone have produced a literature which will stand comparison with that produced by the whole of Wales in this century. But who wants a Birmingham or Nottingham accent? English is being ironed out from the centre. Only the edges crinkle and won't lie down.

When learning to talk children produce all kinds of neologisms. Many are listed in Kornei Chukovsky's book *From Two to Five*. A few I have noticed from my own children: "You carry me because I've got bendy legs". "Look at my decoration!" (vaccination), and "This is my mastic fand" (elastic band). There is the story of a class reciting "Little Miss Muffet sat on a tuffet eating her curls away." The inventive mind has the ability to relate what it knows to what it is sure is waiting to be discovered. Children "learn to read" but there must be no full stop. Learn to read what? They need to learn to read words they have never heard spoken expressing ideas which are totally new and strange to them. If we teach against a background assumption of a total landscape of English, and beyond that world literature, they will find their way constantly opening in front of them.

At one time, in fact always in the past, spoken English was sufficiently various to provide new openings into literary English. As dialects have come into contact with more universal usage, and a wider society, writers have been able to produce masterpieces. Wordsworth's use of rural speech can be compared with Browning's modern urban English in *Men and Women*. Dickens's novels spring from Cockney as surely as Hardy's spring from Wessex. Lawrence used Nottingham; Yeats, Joyce and Shaw used Irish, Dylan Thomas used Welsh, and today Macdiarmid is using Scots. Moreover the same pattern can be detected throughout the world, perhaps most beautifully in Heian Japan, when all the greatest literature was written by women – Lady Murasaki, Sei Shonagon and a number of others. It cannot be coincidental that these leisured ladies were the first ever to write native Japanese using Chinese orthography. The literary productions of the more educated men of the day were in pure Chinese, and have been totally forgotten.

Writers work at the edge of the possibilities of language. For them language must be new, capable of development. But there is no edge without a centre. The writers I have mentioned wrote in the literary language of the day, changing it, but utilizing it in order to set their personal experience against, and in terms of, general experience. They were alike in looking back. They are in fact the opposite of the solely regional writer, who sees the world in terms of the parish pump. Clare, perhaps the most sensitive English writer to attempt to start at home and work outwards, wrecked his life and talent in the process. There is scarcely a successful writer of the past hundred years who has not taken care to leave home as soon as possible.

The business of the school is not to give children a place to get away from – our parents do that for us – but to give something to get away with. Imagination, judgement, creativity cannot be taught. What time we waste on "creative writing" – surely it could more accurately be called "imitation journalism"? The mind must be presented with material, then left alone to work. Reading is a more physical skill than we allow. Just as we learn the vast complexity of English from two onwards by listening and talking, and the mysteries of orthography from four onwards by learning to read, so we can assimilate world literature and take it in our stride from eight onwards only by reading and reading, patiently and methodically, with a little enlightened encouragement and guidance.

Children get lost in tunnels of literature. Books open and swallow them whole. It's like taking them for a walk. Unless you keep them gently but firmly on the move, they will hang about, get lost, and in the end drop out with fatigue. We lose a large proportion of readers in the naughty pigtails and picnic fields at eight, many more in Narnia and Middle Earth at ten. How many literate students moon around in the half-light minds of Mervyn Peake and Hesse at University? There are those who can read, those who can't read, and those who get lost in a book. The vogue for fantasy indicates how many readers cannot or will not relate literature to life.

A sixth form boy complained to me that his English master told him Keats's odes were the finest in the language. "After all," he said, "that's just his opinion." As it happened the boy couldn't think of any other odes in English. "But one could easily be written tomorrow...." At this rate history teachers will have to avoid giving dates, since it is well known that history will be rewritten tomorrow. It is important to get across to children that English literature is a pattern of historical fact, to be learnt, not a quagmire of opinion where nothing is certain. In another local school a master has rebuked his third form for latinate usage. This is another nonsense. How can anyone with sensitivity to English wish to limit style and vocabulary in such a manner?

Teachers are frightened of being made fools of. In part the demand for plain English springs from a fear that, unless checked, a child might be so presumptuous as to mean more than he understood himself to mean (though that's how Shakespeare works – through the genius of the language). When we ask questions about recent reading, are we really testing comprehension? Or are we half afraid the child is lying, and never read the book at all? When we ask for opinions of books, is it genuinely to discuss response? Too often it is to check that the opinions are the right ones, that is to say, the same as everybody else's. Fear of being made a fool of is precisely the block to learning which the child has to overcome. Children must be trusted and given confidence. Above all let them read in peace. If a varied diet of English classics doesn't give them taste and judgement, no school teacher will manage it.

SIGNAL QUOTE

Edward Ardizzone in "The Born Illustrator"
(Signal 3, September 1970)

It might be truly said that the born illustrator is not very interested in life as it is. He likes to create his own version of the world around him. Actuality is not pointed enough for him.

Just in the same way that the author, in writing a work of fiction, creates a world which is not reality but has a life of its own, so the illustrator, if he is a good one, creates an imaginary world analogous to that of the author's. He creates a visual world, which looks real and which can be believed in. Yet it is not the real world but, like the author's, a fiction.

At his best, the good illustrator does more than just make a pictorial comment on the written word. He produces a visual counterpart which adds a third dimension to the book, making more vivid and more understandable the author's intention. In fact he makes a visual interpretation of the author's text....

From *Paul the Hero of the Fire*
written and illustrated
by Edward Ardizzone

Painting is the fountain-head of all the visual arts, and some knowledge of it is necessary for all who practise these arts.

The illustrator, however, besides a sensitivity of eye, and a feeling for colour and design, has to have his own special skills, which are:

1. Inventiveness.

2. The power to draw away from life, or, in other words, to make up.

3. The power to draw small.

4. The ability to use a pen and that intractable fluid, black ink, which is a craft in itself.

5. The ability to read, which is by no means so common as one would think. All can read and understand the words, but how many fail to get the meaning and implications of a book.

6. The ability to compose with figures and place them together in space.

Pathetic Simplicity: Hesba Stretton and Her Books for Children

LANCE SALWAY

Lance Salway writes and translates stories for children. In 1970 he was a librarian, however, with a particular interest in early children's books, one of the several aspects of the children's book world I wanted SIGNAL to reflect. His knowledge of the subject led to his editing for SIGNAL a series of reprints of nineteenth-century essays on children's books, which in turn led to the gathering and publication of his collection *A Peculiar Gift: Nineteenth Century Writings on Books for Children* (Kestrel, 1976). Nowadays his regular writing for the magazine comes in *Book Post*, an informal correspondence-style feature about new children's books. "Pathetic Simplicity" appeared in the first SIGNAL; it has been revised for this republication.

"I've just been reading *Jessica's First Prayer* to my maid," E. Nesbit once wrote in a letter to a friend, "and I felt my eyes smart and my throat go lumpy towards the finish. Pathetic simplicity is a grand gift in writing."[1]

It may at first seem strange that E. Nesbit should have been moved by *Jessica's First Prayer*, for this celebrated example of evangelical writing for children was exactly the kind of story which the Bastables heartily despised. But the books of E. Nesbit are themselves not entirely free from moral intent – *Five Children and It* can be read, after all, as an entertaining sermon on the foolishness of human vanity – and so perhaps we should not be surprised by her admiration for Hesba Stretton's "grand gift".

Today, *Jessica's First Prayer* and similar stories by other writers of the nineteenth century tend to provoke laughter rather than tears, but the story made a phenomenal impact on critics and readers when it first appeared in book form in 1867. It sold over two million copies and was translated into fifteen European and Asiatic languages. Contemporary opinions of the book were unanimous in its praise. Lord Shaftesbury wrote of it:

As a literary effort, it will hardly find a rival for nature, simplicity, pathos and depth of Christian feeling. The writer is doubtless a woman – no man on earth could have composed a page of it.[2]

Sunday at Home, the journal in which the story first appeared in 1866, reported that the effect of the book upon sailors "was marvellous" and went on to quote a surprisingly sentimental nautical critic:

Every word went right home to our hearts all soft as they were, and I am sure if Miss Hesba Stretton had seen four rough young sailors choking red-eyed over the story she has woven round *Jessica's First Prayer*, she would also have been compelled to allow her eyes to overflow with sympathetic joy.[3]

More convincing reports noted the enormous success of the book in Budapest – three hundred copies sold in 1901 alone – and Beirut, where missionaries found the Arabic translation to be an excellent inducement to conversion. Tsar Alexander II ordered copies of the book to be placed in all Russian schools, but his successor was less susceptible to the lachrymose attractions of the story and ordered them all to be burnt.

Jessica's First Prayer is a simple account of a girl waif's realization of the significance of religion. Jessica, the daughter of an alcoholic actress, is befriended by Daniel, a coffee-stall keeper, who is also an official at a local Methodist chapel. She follows him to the church and attends its services but, because of her ragged appearance, she is forced to observe the proceedings in hiding. Soon she is discovered and befriended by the minister and his two children, and it is they who encourage her to make her famous first prayer: "O God! I want to know about you. And please pay Mr. Dan'el for all the warm coffee he's give me." Jessica's conversion is unjustly rewarded by a severe illness, but she survives to be adopted by Daniel.

The plot is simple enough and the message unmistakable, but Hesba Stretton's story also examines the hypocrisy of some Christian attitudes. Gillian Avery has said of this book that "Hesba Stretton would have us believe that she was indifferent to how cold the poor were in the streets, so long as their appearance did not offend the wealthy in church."[4] This observation reveals a curious ignorance of both the character of the writer and the text of the book. Hesba Stretton explicitly condemns the attitudes of those who might be offended by Jessica's appearance, and she supports this censure with a Biblical text:

> "You shall come with us into our pew," cried Winny, in an eager and impulsive tone; but Jane laid her hand upon her outstretched arm, with a glance at Jessica's ragged clothes and matted hair. It was a question difficult enough to perplex them.... But Winny, with flushed cheeks and indignant eyes, looked reproachfully at her elder sister.
>
> "Jane," she said, opening her Testament, and turning over the leaves hurriedly, "this was papa's text a little while ago: 'For if there come into your assembly a man with a gold ring, in goodly apparel, and there come in also a poor man in vile raiment; and ye have respect to him that weareth the gay clothing, and say unto him, Sit thou here in a good place; and say to the poor, Stand thou there, or sit here under my footstool; are ye then partial in yourselves, and are become judges of evil thoughts?' If we don't take this little girl into our pew, we 'have the faith of our Lord Jesus Christ, the Lord of glory, with respect of persons'."

Hesba Stretton was born Sarah Smith in 1832 in Wellington, Shropshire. Her father was a bookseller and publisher, and his house became the centre of the intellectual life of the town. Her mother held strong evangelical views and imposed a daily routine of strict religious instruction on her children. The literary interests of Sarah's father and his friends encouraged her to begin to write while she was still in her teens and, in view of the puritanical religious views of her mother, it is not surprising that her writings should exhibit a fervent evangelical bias. Her first story, *The Lucky Leg*, was written with no thought of publication, but her sister Elizabeth sent it to Charles Dickens, who agreed to publish it in *Household Words* in 1859. The fee he paid was five pounds. Dickens encouraged Sarah's writing and a strong friendship grew between them. He continued to publish her stories in *Household Words* and the Christmas numbers of *All the Year Round* until 1866.

Despite the encouragement of Dickens, Sarah's work attracted little notice, and she decided to adopt the pseudonym Hesba Stretton in the hope that a more distinctive name might help her career. "Hesba" was composed of the initial letters of the names of her five sisters in order of age, and Stretton was taken from the village of Church Stretton where her younger sister Ann had property. Her first book, *Fern's Hollow*, was published in 1864 but it was not until 1866, when *Jessica's First Prayer* appeared in *Sunday at Home*, that she achieved critical and financial success. At least a million and a half copies of *Jessica's First Prayer* were to be sold by the end of the century but Hesba Stretton's share of the proceeds was limited by the fact that the Religious Tract Society owned the copyright. "Truly all men are cheats, especially publishers," she observed with justification.[5]

The story was based on her own experience of the existence of slum children in Manchester in the 1860s, and the horror which she felt at the conditions of these children was to influence the nature of her writing and her own efforts to implement social reform. The success of *Jessica's First Prayer* not only established her as chief chronicler of social iniquity but also encouraged other writers, whose intentions were perhaps less philanthropic, to imitate her. Few of her contemporaries, though, were able to match either her success or her skill at describing the sufferings of the poor. She was to write over forty books, but not all of them were about what Eliza Keary sternly called "ragged London depravity".[6] She wrote several novels for adults, among them *The Doctor's Dilemma* (1872), a title which Shaw used, with the author's permission, for one of his plays.

Few writers on evangelical themes matched Hesba Stretton's success, perhaps because readers were quick to distinguish between a sermon and a story. Although country vicars and elderly ladies produced tracts exhorting the poor to follow the Christian virtues, their main concern was not to induce sympathy for their condition but rather to encourage them to endure their misfortune with Christian fortitude. In *Joe and Sally; or, A Good Deed and its Fruits,* published anonymously in 1876, two waifs are befriended by a middle-class family whose motive is not to relieve the homeless state of the children but to encourage them to attend Sunday School. After a meal (in the kitchen, of course) and a prayer and Bible reading, the children "were dismissed".

As they trudged along through the cold, damp streets, leaving that place of warmth and comfort farther and farther behind, one thought filled their minds and became the theme of their talk: it was the happiness ... in having such a place for their home.

These children are kept firmly in their place, and the author implies that their attendance at Sunday School and their appreciation of the Christian message will provide adequate compensation for their poverty and homelessness.

Unlike the unknown author of *Joe and Sally*, Hesba Stretton garnished her own sermons with the realism of first-hand observation, and decorated her message with lively characters, theatrical plots, and a vein of humour that was distinctly lacking in the work of her rivals. The children in her books are not innocents ripe for conversion but distinctive symbols of social injustice. Jessica herself is no lisping infant, and she is at times engagingly pert:

"I'm just going, sir ... only it's raining cats and dogs outside; and mother's been away all night, and she took the key with her; and it's so nice to smell the coffee; and the police has left off worriting me while I've been here. He thinks I'm a customer taking my breakfast!" And the child laughed a shrill little laugh of mockery at herself and the policeman.

But then she has, after all, appeared on the stage:

"Mother used to play Jessica at the theatre ... and I used to be a fairy in the pantomime till I grew too tall and ugly. If I'm pretty when I grow up, mother says I shall play too, but I've a long time to wait."

Jessica's mother does not appear in the book, but we are given intriguing glimpses of her:

"Where is your mother?" he asked.
"Out on a spree," said Jessica, "and she won't be home for a day or two. She'd not hearken to you, sir. There's the missionary came, and she pushed

him down the ladder, till he was nearly killed. They used to call mother the Vixen at the theatre, and nobody durst say a word to her."

In 1893, Hesba Stretton published a sequel to *Jessica's First Prayer* in which the parent of her famous waif plays a larger part. But in *Jessica's Mother* the vixen has become a sad vagrant, anxious to exploit the new happiness and prosperity of her daughter. In the end she kills herself and, in his efforts to save her, Jessica's old benefactor, Daniel, dies too. The minister who befriended Jessica in the first book does not escape the carnage: he suffers a stroke which prevents him from continuing his ministry. Only Jessica herself survives unscathed, "a smile struggling through her tears". Like so many sequels, *Jessica's Mother* is a pale shadow of the book which preceded it, and the character of Jessica is now almost indistinguishable from the many simpering children who populate evangelical stories of the time.

Mrs. O.F. Walton's notorious *Little Dot* (1873) is a later imitation of Jessica but the story embodies all the unhealthy aspects of the genre that Hesba Stretton took care to avoid. Mrs. Walton's story is set entirely in a cemetery and is concerned with a small girl's conversion by a gravedigger, her curious devotion to the grave of a recently buried child, and her unhealthy preoccupation with her own death, which takes place none too soon. Hesba Stretton's books are rarely morbid, and one must admire the restraint that prevented her from concluding *Jessica's First Prayer* with the death of its heroine. Many writers of evangelical stories employed nauseous lisping heroines but few are as tiresome as little Dot:

> "Mr. Solemn," she said one day, "don't you wish you were just like a bird?"
> "No," said the old man, "no, Dot, I'd rather be digging my graves."
> "But, Mr. Solemn, they've got two wings," she went on.
> "And what would you do with two wings, my little dear?" said the gravedigger.
> "I'd go right up into the sky and look for my little girl," said Dot.

Amy Le Feuvre was another writer who liked angelic infants but the dialogue she wrote for them was, at times, unfortunate. Milly, in *Probable Sons* (1895), says at one point: "I was just waving to God, Uncle Edward. I thought I saw him looking down at me from the sky." Hesba Stretton did employ a ration of little Gips, Dollys and Dots in her own work but they never have the exaggerated innocence of Mrs. Walton's Dot or Amy Le Feuvre's abominable Milly.

Few of Hesba Stretton's contemporaries could rival her skill at constructing sensational plots. *A Thorny Path* (1879) opens with a woman deserting her blind father and small daughter at night in Kensington Gardens. *Little Meg's Children* (1868) concerns the efforts of a small girl to care for her brother and a baby in a garret and describes the death of the baby as a result of an injudicious dose of gin. *No Place Like Home* (1881) is about the imprisonment of a small boy wrongfully accused of attempting to steal pheasant eggs. *The Lord's Purse-Bearers* (1882), perhaps her most disturbing book, describes the appalling situation of children who were starved and kept in total darkness so that they would look particularly piteous when taken out to beg. Even Mrs. Moss, the harridan who rents these children by the day to older beggars, has to admit that one of her charges is in a deplorable condition. "You'd better take little Lucky," she tells a prospective customer. "Fidge is sech a object, too harrowin' for the West End, if you're going there. He does very well round about here [the East End] where folks is used to objects, and wants somethink out o' the common."

It is easy to see in scenes like these the qualities which Dickens admired in Hesba Stretton's writing. Her books may have been designed to inspire sympathy for the deprived, but she always enlivened this intention with vivid characters and dialogue. In *A Thorny Path* the deserted blind man and the child are given shelter by Mrs. Clack, a dealer in old clothes and a character with distinct Dickensian qualities:

Mrs. Clack felt herself very much put about and embarrassed by the presence of a man in her house. ... True, he was an old man and blind; but he was as strange and almost as dreaded a creature to her as if Don had brought one of the savage wild beasts from the Zoological Gardens to find a shelter in her quiet little home. She knew almost nothing of man and his ways. Though she called herself Mrs. Clack on her business cards, she had no actual claim to the title, for she was a single woman. She had been reared and trained in a small orphanage in the country, where sixteen orphan girls were brought up in strict seclusion, never seeing any man nearer than the aged clergyman, who preached to them with the rest of his small congregation from the pulpit of the village church. . . . Mrs. Clack was a quiet, small, timid person, who seldom spoke above a faint undertone, as if all she had to say partook of the nature of a secret. Even in her own house she seemed to make herself as small as possible, and to take up as little room as she could. To have a man there who spoke in a loud and deep voice, and who stretched his legs right across her narrow hearth, blocking up the way to the fire, was the heaviest trial that could have befallen her. She said to herself she would rather have been laid low in sickness. "It is a cross, a heavy cross!" she murmured between her teeth.

Mrs. Clack's cross is soon lifted: the old man dies of smallpox contracted from infected clothes in her shop.

"There are multitudes . . . of these street Arab tales, most of them written from fancy," wrote Charlotte Yonge.[7] But Hesba Stretton never wrote from fancy. Her books were based on a first-hand knowledge of urban slums and written from a dedicated desire to expose these conditions and to encourage active effort to eradicate them. Miss Yonge complained that some of her books were "written for special purposes" and this was, of course, true. Other writers, though, were content to express their special purposes openly in the text. "Brenda", the author of *Froggy's Little Brother*, liked to interrupt her stories with impassioned appeals for money, old clothes or Christmas dinners. Hesba Stretton was too skilled a writer to make such explicit appeals in her books; in these matters she preferred action to words.

The condition of the poor and, in particular, homeless children was her especial concern. It was not shared, though, by a large majority of the middle and upper classes, who condemned such philanthropy and claimed that the appalling conditions of the poor in the cities of Victorian England were merely a part of the natural order. Charles Harper wrote in 1894:

Philanthropy, of sorts, we have always with us, and the undeserving need never lack shelter and support in a disgraceful idleness while the tender-hearted or the hysterical amateur relieving-officers are permitted to make fools of themselves, and rogues and vagabonds of the lazy wastrels who will never do an honest day's work so long as a subsistence is to be got by begging . . . [The] appeal to the charitable and pitiful folks of England . . . [has] captured many thousands of pounds wherewith to succour the unfit, the criminal, the unwashed; the very scum and dregs of the race whom merciless nature, cruel to be kind, had doomed to early extinction. But mouthing and tearful sentimentality has interfered with beneficent natural processes, and the depraved and ineffectual are helped to a longer term of existence, that they may transmit their bodily and mental diseases to another generation and so foul the blood and stunt the growth of the nation in years to come.[8]

Hesba Stretton had a ready reply to opinions such as these:

There are philosophers among us who teach that it is unwise to stretch out a helping hand to those who are struggling for existence; that nature selects the strongest and fittest for survival; and if we interfere with her we do so at the cost of perpetuating an enfeebled and deteriorated race. But these boys and girls ... are the very individuals whom nature has selected for existence, who prove their selection by having outlived the innumerable perils of their hard life. A few amongst them might have perished in the end if left out in the cold of the streets, but the majority have lived long enough to live and grow up.[9]

Other members of the privileged classes considered "the scum and dregs of the race" to be a decorative addition to the London scene. The fashionable artist Dorothy Tennant declared in the introduction to a volume of her vapid drawings of homeless children that the pictures she had previously seen of the poor appeared to be false and unauthentic:

They were all so deplorably piteous – pale whining children with sunken eyes, holding up bunches of violets to heedless passers-by; dying matchgirls, sorrowful water-cress girls, emaciated mothers clasping weeping babes. How was it, I asked myself, that the other side is so seldom represented? The merry, reckless, happy-go-lucky urchin; the tomboy girl; the plump untidy mother dancing and tossing her ragged baby; who had given this side of London life?[10]

She goes on to offer intending artists some useful advice on obtaining convincing street Arab models:

If you have no rags to start with, and shrink from keeping them by you, the best way is to find an average boy, win his confidence, give him sixpence, and promise him another sixpence if he will bring you a boy more ragged than himself. This second boy must be invited to do the same, and urged to bring one yet more "raggety". You can in this way get down to a very fine specimen.

Hesba Stretton was not content to confine her philanthropy to the printed page. She became associated with Benjamin Waugh in the *Sunday Magazine,* and, in consultation with him, she published a letter in *The Times* in 1884:

Few people have any idea of the extent of active cruelty, and still more of cruel neglect, towards children among our degraded and criminal classes. Some years ago the rector of Spitalfields stated ... that hundreds of children were systematically ill-treated and starved for begging purposes. Cases of flagrant and excessive cruelty are constantly being brought before the magistrates, but hundreds of others a little less malevolent never come to the light of public courts. In Liverpool, a "Society for the Prevention of Cruelty to Children" has been started.... The need for a national society of this kind is very great.... I trust that some of your philanthropic and influential readers who possess the gift of organization may plan out and set on foot such a society, and deliver us as a nation from the curse and crime, the shame and sin, of neglected and oppressed childhood.[11]

A lengthy correspondence ensued, and Hesba Stretton returned to the fray more than once: "The inarticulate cry of London children ought to be listened to, and will be listened to sooner or later. Only while we linger they perish."[12]

Her appeals were successful. On 8 July 1884, a public meeting held at the Mansion House resulted in the formation of the London Society for the Prevention of Cruelty to Children. Speakers at the meeting included Lord Shaftesbury, Dr. Barnardo and Angela Burdett-Coutts, and Hesba Stetton remained an active member of the executive committee until her resignation in 1894.

The "special purposes" of her books were therefore realized in practice. Yet she was always aware of the dangers of unwise charity:

There is one serious danger to be guarded against arising from our sympathy with street-children. Nothing is worse for them, neglect itself is far better, than the easy method of gratifying our emotional pity, and pacifying our conscience, by simply taking money out of our purse and dropping it into their outstretched little hands. Better to drop a live coal upon the quivering palm! ... Whatever the pretext may be, however plausible the reason for begging, it is always a cruel wrong to the child when we suffer it to succeed.[9]

The exploitation of children for begging purposes was one of her particular concerns: "I look upon giving to a beggar as a crime similar to giving strong drink to one already drunken: giving to a child who is begging is but tying a millstone about his neck and drowning him in the depths of a sea of misery." In the preface to the second edition of *The Lord's Purse-Bearers* she wrote:

Since ... the following story was written, the condition of children in England has been greatly improved by the passing of beneficent laws, and by increased diligence on the part of the public and the police in putting them into action. This has been done chiefly by the National Society for the Prevention of Cruelty to Children. In cities and towns these laws have made a marked difference to the children.

Hesba Stretton did not limit her philanthropic concern to the poor of the cities. She examined rural conditions in England in *No Place Like Home* (1881) and the persecution of Russian Protestants in *The Highway of Sorrow* (1894) and *In the Hollow of His Hand* (1897). *Max Krömer* (1871) was written as a result of her observations of the plight of child refugees in the Franco-Prussian war. In *Alone in London* (1869) she drew attention to the lack of hospitals for children.

Despite her tireless efforts to achieve social reform and the steady stream of books which she wrote between 1866 and 1906, Hesba Stretton constantly avoided publicity. She never married, and her sister Elizabeth, who also assumed the surname Stretton, remained her constant companion:

A very rare and beautiful friendship existed between these two, who for over seventy-eight years were never separated. In birth they were but two years apart; in death only eight months.... Nothing was ever done by one without the knowledge, advice, and consent of the other. Each always used the plural pronoun when speaking of her projects, opinions and possessions.... The most devoted companionship of husband and wife was, in duration and completeness, not to be compared with the actually life-long attachment and comradeship which existed between the sisters.[13]

Elizabeth died in February 1911 and her sister in October of the same year. They lie buried in the same grave in the churchyard at Ham Common in Surrey.

Although E. Nesbit approved of the "pathetic simplicity" of Hesba Stretton's writings, her books are little remembered today. Yet she avoided the morbidity and intense sentimentality which marred the work of other evangelical writers, and pathetic descriptions of degradation and poverty were, to her, of less importance than the exposure of cruelty, injustice and neglect. Unlike her contemporaries, Hesba Stretton was not content merely to appeal for sympathy in her books. Her contribution to the reform of the laws concerning the care of children and her efforts to establish a national society for the prevention of their neglect are significant, and have been recognized as such. We may laugh now at *Jessica's First Prayer* but the influence of this short book on the reading public and the social attitudes of Victorian England qualifies both the story and its author for special consideration in the study of literature for children.

REFERENCES

1. From a letter to Ada Breakell, quoted by Doris Langley Moore in *E. Nesbit: a Biography* (Benn, 1967).

2. *Seed Time and Harvest*, December 1911.

3. "Hesba Stretton: a Memoir", *Sunday at Home*, December 1911.

4. Gillian Avery, *Nineteenth Century Children: Heroes and Heroines in English Children's Stories 1780–1900* (Hodder and Stoughton, 1965).

5. Quoted by Brian Alderson in "Tracts, Rewards and Fairies", *Essays in the History of Publishing*, edited by Asa Briggs (Longman, 1974).

6. Eliza Keary, *Memoir of Annie Keary* (Macmillan, 1883).

7. Charlotte M. Yonge, *What Books to Lend and What to Give* (National Society's Depository, 1887).

8. Charles G. Harper, *Revolted Woman: Past, Present and to Come* (Elkin Mathews, 1894).

9. Introduction by Hesba Stretton to *Children Reclaimed for Life: the Story of Dr Barnardo's Work in London*, by Godfrey Holden Pike (Hodder and Stoughton, 1875).

10. Mrs. H. M. Stanley, *London Street Arabs* (Cassell, 1890).

11. *The Times*, 8 January 1884.

12. *The Times*, 26 May 1884.

13. Hesba D. Webb, "Hesba Stretton: a Personal Note", *Sunday at Home*, December 1911.

SIGNAL QUOTE

Mary Rayner in "Some Thoughts on Animals in Children's Books"
(*Signal 29, May 1979*)

How animals are treated in children's fiction and in information books raises very wide questions, questions not only of literary technique and traditions but, more deeply, of truth and morality. We are all quite happy to tell the story or sing the ballad about a family of foxes and how the father fox brings home the goose, but most of us are not exactly over-eager to describe factory farming and the processes which have brought the oven-ready chicken

From *Mr. and Mrs. Pig's Evening Out*
written and illustrated by Mary Rayner

as far as the table. "Once upon a time there was a broiler house full of chickens." Almost inconceivable, isn't it? For of course in the latter case it is we who are the cunning foxes, and it is our little ones who crunch on the bones-o. Except that we have so organized it that most of the time we can ignore the processes of fattening and slaughter; the chicken is presented in the supermarket without head or feet, little different from a cabbage or a loaf of bread, in order that no one need feel that frisson of guilt or revulsion. No longer does the grey goose cry out quack, quack, quack, with his legs hanging dangling down-o....

... Even in the most accurate, the most objective of wildlife fiction writing there has to be a certain amount of falsification, of humanization, in order to engage the reader's interest and make him identify with the protagonists. This is true even if the animals are endowed with only a few basic qualities such as courage or physical endurance. You cannot actually be said to have courage unless you have a concept of death, or at least of pain....

... If you are a writer, the younger the child you are trying to reach the harder your task. All fiction works through association and echo, through the emotional charge carried by scenes and images. With young children the range of experience, of images which you can assume to be common knowledge, is very narrow. And you have not got available to you what is available to the writer of fiction for older readers: you cannot build up a rounded character through lengthy description, incident and dialogue. Therefore you use animal characters.

The Seventies
in British Children's Books

ELAINE MOSS

Elaine Moss is one of England's foremost commentators on children's books. Writer, reviewer, broadcaster, she also keeps in direct touch with children in her work as a part-time librarian in a London primary school. *Children's Books of the Year* (Hamish Hamilton and National Book League) was her annual review of the previous year's publishing, and served as a catalogue for the National Book League's touring exhibition 1970–79. In 1977 the Children's Book Circle gave her its Eleanor Farjeon Award for outstanding services to children's books. Elaine Moss has contributed to almost every issue of SIGNAL: personal articles about authors, artists, issues, occasions. Regular readers of the magazine will be disappointed that one of these was not chosen to represent her here. But no one else could have written the article which follows, an over-view of the children's book world during the past ten years, especially prepared for this collection.

My morning post (19 June 1979) has just arrived. I find in it a letter asking me to address a meeting of the Educational Publishers Council and the Children's Book Group of the Publishers Association, a sign that school books and leisure reading are drawing closer together; there are copies of two new children's book magazines: *Children's Book Bulletin* "for news of progressive moves in children's literature", and *Dragon's Teeth*, Bulletin of the National Committee on Racism; and a parcel full of Oxford University Press novels reprinted on paper that this publisher would not have used as stuffing for packages a decade ago.

My mail on any particular day cannot justifiably be said to reflect anything. Nevertheless, ten years ago, when I was embarking on the *Children's Books of the Year* venture, I am fairly sure that none of the social or economic interests mirrored in the random mail I received this morning would have been manifest.

Looking back on a decade of children's book publishing when the decade isn't over is like asking oneself whether yesterday was well spent. Only tomorrow will tell; which is good in a way because one has the opportunity to hazard guesses, to put forward hopes, to give early warnings – and to be proved wrong.

Before I began to consider the children's books of the 1970s objectively – as a development from the 1960s and as a precursor to the 1980s – I had not realized how distinctive decades, which one thinks of as arbitrary notches on the calendar, can be.

To write about children's books and authors in the sixties it would have been sufficient to be a responsive literary person, with an eye capable of seeing picture books as works of art: the decade that brought us Brian Wildsmith's *ABC* and Raymond Briggs's *Mother Goose Treasury* (two landmarks in the history of illustration) brought us also Alan Garner's development from *The Weirdstone of Brisingamen* (1960) to *The Owl Service* (1967), Philippa Pearce's *A Dog So Small*, Helen Cresswell's *The Piemakers*. It was a quality decade in children's books in which the only consumer considered by reviewers was the child who could absorb the literary story, the painterly picture book: these were published in profusion.

But in Morna Stuart's *Marassa and Midnight* (a story about Negro twin slaves, one in San Domingo and one in Revolutionary France), Nina Bawden's *On the Run* (a multi-cultural inner-city adventure), Goscinny and Uderzo's *Asterix the Gaul* cartoon stories, Wezel's *The Good Bird Nepomuk* (a wordless picture book from Czechoslovakia), K. M. Peyton's *Flambards* trilogy for teenagers who enjoyed reading and Pan Macmillan's Topliners for the uncommitted reader we had (but did we realize this in 1969?) the seeds of the many developments that were to become conscious issues in the seventies.

The broadening of the scene in the 1970s has scattered the viewpoints from which commentators analyse it. The literary reviewer of children's novels, the art critic as picture-book buff, survive. Like

dinosaurs in a noisy modern zoo they are respected as the proto-
types from which trendier animals, in response to a changed
climate, have evolved.

Sociological Concerns of the Seventies

By the beginning of 1970 the atmosphere surrounding children's
books was altering perceptibly. The blossoming of the genre in the
sixties had earned children's books a respectability never before
contemplated, let alone demanded. Space in national newspapers
was given to them, and specialist journals were devoted to them.
The best of both worlds was thought to be worth striving for: children's books were different (requiring separate treatment and
specialist reviewers) but the same (in the mainstream of national
literature and entitled to serious critical study on that level). The
assumption that only the literary book was worth consideration,
the neglect of the needs of the learning, perhaps non-literary, child,
sowed the seeds of the polarity – pure criticism versus child-oriented
comment – that has been a mark of the seventies.

The 1970s were child-centred in the realms of education; they
were years in which Britain was coming to terms with its post-
Imperial role as a multi-cultural nation; they were feminist (rather
different from non-sexist) years. All these factors had their bearing
on the content of the books children were offered.

In education the decade began with the setting up of the Bullock
Committee (1972) to examine language across the curriculum. In
1975 *A Language for Life*, its report, was published. Thorough in
its examination of the status quo and far-reaching in its recommendations for increasing children's awareness of books through
changing attitudes and approaches in teaching, the Report has had
some impact. Though most of its recommendations have not been
implemented, it has significantly strengthened the hands of those
who believe in books as being part of the life of all children all
the time.

As satellites to the Bullock Report, though unconnected with it
in any direct sense, Penguin Education published many books on

language in education, notably Patrick Creber's *Lost for Words* and Connie Rosen's *The Language of Primary Schoolchildren*. Longman's Breakthroughs, a series pioneered by David Mackay and based on speech patterns of young children, were one of the first results of the concentration of educationists on language as a key to learning, to reach the five-year-old direct. With their unstilted prose and their illustrations by artists who looked at urban life and interpreted it in a lively manner, Breakthroughs, along with Leila Berg's Nippers (Macmillan), brought the real book closer to the classroom. The erosion of the barrier between books children read for pleasure and school textbooks, between "net" and "non-net" books as the trade calls them, had begun.

The Exeter Conference, initiated in 1969 by the late Sidney Robbins as a way to bring teachers into direct contact with the authors of children's books, was a good seventies-type idea which had some positive spin-off (such as the journal *Children's Literature in Education*) but was in part counter-productive. There were authors who felt quite properly that it was no concern of theirs how teachers and children responded to their books: a novel for children is, or can be, a work of art with a right to live regardless of its potential consumer. And there were teachers who, while interested to listen to and meet the children's book establishment, recognized that their own experience, of large mixed-ability classes and little time, was so far away from the solitary life of the author (particularly the author who claimed he was "writing for himself") that debate could only end in acrimony. The bridge across this divide has begun to be built. The Arts Council Writers in Schools project has forged links among authors, teachers and school students, releasing and channelling creative energy, often with dramatic results.

The Schools Council Project *Children's Reading Interests* reported in mid-decade, with few surprises but some interesting individual studies of child readers' preferences. Aidan Chambers's *Introducing Books to Children* was published in 1973 to support teachers in their difficult task of mediating books (output of publishers up, up, up in the seventies) to the young. For *The Cool Web* Margaret Meek and her colleagues at the University of London Institute of Education collected academic papers and journalistic pieces that, in unison and well organized, make a strong thrust

John said,
"It is fun
to have a picnic
under a tree."

Rover was at the picnic.
Kitty too was at the picnic
under the tree.
22

Kitty said,
"It is fun
to have a picnic
in the tree.

See, see, see,
I am in the tree.
Rover can not catch me, me."
23

The Beacon Reader, Book One Stage, *Old Friends*, first published in 1928 with illustrations by Marcia Lane Foster, was just one of the many reprinted reading schemes still flooding the classrooms in the 1970s. That learning to read could not only be fun but also be related to most children's own experience was Leila Berg's message in the Nipper series. Below, a double page from *When Dad Felt Bad* (Little Nipper) by Charles Causley with illustrations by Richard Rose, 1975.

Dad said,
I bet
it's what I ate.

Too much to drink,
said Mum,
I think.

from both banks – the educationist's and the author's. And it is not without significance that among the new authors for children in the seventies there are, as we shall see later, several teachers.

But the architects of the bridge must take care. There is dynamite around, in the shape of activists who are less concerned with standards of literacy and bookless homes and schools than they are with what they consider to be inaccurate reflections of our society in the children's books most young people will never read. We do not live in a society with equal opportunities for the sexes: if our children's novels and picture books uniformly represented such a society, the image would be false. But we do live in a multi-ethnic nation, and children's books have been tardy in their adjustment to the post-war changes. Among the media, children's books are a soft option for attack, and attackers have tended to concentrate on surface blemishes while ignoring the literary quality, emotional content (so often the ingredient that children identify with) and philosophical messages *as a whole*. At the beginning of the decade anyone deeply concerned with children's books and desperately trying to reach children with all that was available was apt to find his/her path strewn with red herrings.

Rosie's Walk, Pat Hutchins's wryly humorous picture book about a hen who walks calmly through the farmyard oblivious (or *was* she?) of the fox's constantly hampered efforts to catch her, was described as anti-feminist by commentators who had missed the whole point of the story because they had stood too close to it. About *Little Black Sambo* there was much real cause for concern; a stereotyped black hero called Sambo would have died the natural death that Janet Hill, in a wise article in the *Times Literary Supplement*, said was his due in the 1970s, had it not been for the fact that Helen Bannerman (in 1899) had hit on a classic picture-book formula. *Little Black Sambo* was not banned in Britain; he was allowed to live on under a heavy, much-publicized cloud.

Banning is censorship. Censorship deprives people of the experience of making their own judgements and leads towards the imposed standards of a totalitarian society. In Britain, where even a core curriculum in schools is viewed with deep mistrust, healthy scepticism may do battle with and defeat the attempt that appears, as 1984 looms, to be threatening the source material of children's publishing. The first issue of the "progressive" *Children's Book Bulletin* (which, as you may remember, arrived the morning I started writing this survey) has in it a code of practice called "Guidelines to be used in the Production of Anti-Racist Non-Sexist Books". One need scarcely pause to consider the effect on fiction (information books and reading schemes are altogether different) of using "guidelines", since all of us have seen series which, for one purpose or another, have been written within prescribed limits. Rosemary Stones and Andrew Mann, the editors of the new magazine, have done a great deal through the Children's Rights Workshop and the Other Award to show how relevant existing material can be brought to more children who need it but whose teachers or parents may not know about it. So far, so good. But the first number of their *Children's Book Bulletin*, while carrying some thought-provoking reviews, goes a great way further along the road American activists have taken towards censorship at source. If we do not want to follow this road in Britain in the 1980s we must quickly awake to the significance of its direction.

Certainly the foundations of this highway to pre-fab politikidlit have been laid, eccentrically sometimes and without much sense of history or perspective, in the seventies. Bob Dixon's *Catching them Young*, for instance, or the Writers and Readers Co-operative's *Sexism in Children's Books: Facts, Figures and Guidelines* (guidelines again!) can only make their mark with those who are interested in the sociological content of literature but unmindful of its peculiar essence, part of which is the beauty of a language they seek to put in splints. More far-reaching and much more entertaining in the sex-equality stakes is Cadogan and Craig's study of stories for girls, *You're a Brick, Angela!*, which is subtle and persuasive instead of strident and hectoring.

The publication in 1979 of Martin Jeffcoate's *Positive Image* is the most encouraging sign that a central path through the minefield of race relations can be trod if the British of all colours are made aware that there is indeed a way forward in the 1980s. Mr. Jeffcoate's wide experience in schools in Kenya and Britain, his passion for books, his willingness to describe experiments that backfired as well as those that worked, make his book a beacon of hope for the future.

Economics of Publishing

Educational thinking and political thrusts were not alone in exerting influence on children's books in the 1970s. The economic state of Britain affected every business enterprise in the country, and publishing for children reflected the strains and constraints, the initiatives and the curtailments that survival in this climate was to demand.

The Introductions to the nine volumes of *Children's Books of the Year* (the tenth is still in the making) record, amongst gloomy forebodings, many significant changes dictated by economic pressure. "We shall be witnessing the far-reaching effect of the industrial and economic situation on children's books" (1970). 1973 might go down "as a year in which publishers made the most of boom conditions that still prevailed" (a 25% rise in production that was to prove an unhealthy trend later in the decade) "feeling in their bones that an enforced restructuring of the whole children's book scene was round the corner". The Introduction to the 1974 volume is prefaced by Mel Calman's cartoon "Spare a penny to help publish a book" and is spattered with economic references: 2,618 new children's books published despite the many pushed forward into 1975 by the knock-on effect of the Heath three-day week; an acute paper shortage; the beginning of publishers' headaches over keeping backlist books in print, because of warehouse costs and printing costs rising simultaneously. How would a declining backlist (in children's publishing the profit on backlist books had, up till now, been the wealth that could be invested in new ventures) affect the children's book editor's view of the future? Would safety become the only method of survival? And was safety to be found in international editions of picture books printed abroad, in international packages of glossy non-fiction, in hardback publishers starting their own paperback lists, in smaller books (at a relatively high price) or in larger books that looked worth £3 or more?

Children's book publishing depends heavily on the institutional market of libraries and schools; 1976 was the Local Authority crisis year, with headlines in newspapers such as *Bookless in Bucks* indicating the slashing of library services. To the layman it would have seemed sensible for publishers, faced with a contracting home market, to have reduced their numbers of new titles; but economics is a discipline with its own mystique, of which butter mountains in Europe are a symbol. Economics dictated that more and more new titles should be published to meet the reduced demand for books generally; the reason for this was the shortage of cash and the desperate need for quick return on investment. New titles sell faster than backlist books. Cash can be re-invested in more new titles. But the new titles had to be published in short print runs to avoid the cost of warehousing. So in 1976 25% more children's titles were published than in 1971 but in very short print runs, a dangerous and sad practice which meant that new books could go out of print for ever after perhaps two years of life. "Buy now!" one said to anyone lucky enough to have a book fund. And to editors, between the devil (the computer printout supplied by the sales director) and the deep blue sea (a contracting institutional market and rising costs): "Back your own judgement." For, one could fairly ask, which sales director, what computer, would have predicted the phenomenal success in market terms of an immensely long novel (with Greek quotations at the head of each chapter) about displaced rabbits on Watership Down?

Libraries and schools, as the decade advanced, were faced with the choice of buying multiple copies of a book in paperback or a single hard-covered edition. Libraries that had never bought paperbacks began to do so. Publishers of hardbacks started to experiment with simultaneous hard and paperbound editions of the same book: Kestrel/Puffin, Collins/Fontana Lions, Abelard Schuman/Grasshoppers, and the Usborne books faced both ways at once. Faber sold off some of its paperback rights to Puffin, but is currently investing in a stiff paperbound hybrid in an attempt to keep libraries supplied with backlist titles. Oxford University Press began a paperback list early in the decade, then axed it; but in order to keep some of its better-known titles in print it has resorted to the practice of using excessively cheap paper and illustrated board bindings – the princes disguised as paupers that were part of my morning mail on June 19th. A splendidly produced series of information books from Pan Piccolo (the Explorers series) is also available in hard covers from Ward Lock, whereas certain paperback Dinosaurs appear in hardback, now, on the Evans list. So to some extent the pattern of original hardback publishing followed by a paperback edition of the book perhaps two years later (the norm in 1970) has been reversed, hardback publishers now occasionally buying rights from originating paperback houses. This profusion of practices mirrors the economic complexity of the decade.

1979 is still with us. During the decade we have seen a 50% increase in the number of new children's titles published annually (from just under 2,000 to just over 3,000); we have seen the price of a hardback children's novel rise from about £1 to an average of £3.50; we have seen the paperback price go up from 20 pence, or thereabouts, to 60 pence, and there are murmurs about very steep increases in price to come – if the market will bear it.

Looking back, one can see that children's book publishing has become the victim of its own success. Booming into a profitability that in several instances spawned separate children's book companies within general publishing firms, it suddenly had to face up to the strains recession and inflation were imposing on industry as a whole. Companies that have been bought as part of large business empires' diversification plans are under severe pressure of a kind that is foreign to and inimical to good children's publishing. In the past the popular, and predictably fast-selling, title was considered to be the foundation from which a promising new author could be launched at an initial loss. In the brave new world of decisions led by sales forecasts, however, every book is supposed to pay its way, and editors who lack crusading zeal can find their wings not just clipped but pinned firmly to their sides. As we enter the eighties, the battle between the editor-with-flair and the sales-department-with-figures appears to be shaking some of the edifices of good children's book publishing, both hardback and paperback. It seems doubtful, in this economic climate, that we shall see many publishers embarking on small select lists with an individual flavour such as Julia MacRae Books (1979), as a division of Franklin Watts Ltd., hopes to establish.

Fiction in the Seventies

But what of the books themselves, and of the authors and artists whose work for children was so prolifically published in the turbulent seventies? It is impossible to look back on the decade in its final year and predict which of its books, if any, will become "classics", for children's classics must have that enduring child appeal which cannot be judged by adults standing up close to books not written for them anyway. All one can usefully do is try to identify those that are examples of trends we have seen developing.

So, Alan Garner's *Stone Book* quartet? Richard Adams's *Watership Down*? The *Stone Book* quartet seems likely to survive as a literary peak; one can imagine observers of the future remarking that Alan Garner's work was a symphony rousing the intellectual young reader of the seventies to an awareness of the dying crafts that once gave man his dignity, and the local dialects that used to distinguish him from his fellow countrymen. In the year 2001 the historical researcher may handle the first editions of the Garner quartet printed (well, photo-lithographed) on fine cream paper and illustrated with etchings by Michael Foreman, and marvel at the skill with which author, artist, publisher and printer could inter-weave their crafts and make the medium – a finely produced book – reflect the author's message.

Watership Down, on the other hand, must surely be the supreme example of a freak success that resulted in self-perpetuating sales stimulated partly by the non-book media, so much a feature of the scene in the latter half of the twentieth century. An ugly, expensive, unillustrated hard-cover book with a cheap black-line jacket design printed on buff-coloured paper (probably soon to be worth a fortune on the antiquarian market, for it was a small first edition) then became a children's paperback, a deluxe hard-cover book illustrated (in matching slipcase) by John Lawrence, a paperback for adults, an animated cartoon film (with a book of the film); and, from the film's musical score, came a hit single in the "Top Twenty".

But was either of these phenomena really a children's book? What *is* a children's book was the question being asked throughout the seventies when adults were gradually discovering that the genre so described could be the repository of fine writing as well as of the coarser bran that is part of the stuff of children's reading. Is there a line to be drawn between children's novels and adults'? If so, where does it come?

The needs of the reading adolescent became a preoccupation of

"*Watership Down* must surely be the supreme example of a freak success that resulted in self-perpetuating sales stimulated partly by the non-book media." (See p. 58.) (1) Hazel Underwood's jacket for the first edition published by Rex Collings. (2) and (3) Pauline Baynes's covers for the Penguin and Puffin editions. (4) The Penguin edition rejacketed with a still from the film, that also featured on (6) the CBS record and (7) the CBS cassette and on (8) the Penguin "Film Picture Book" edition. (5) John Lawrence's case and jacket for the Penguin/Kestrel Illustrated Edition the seventies – as a counterbalance, perhaps, to the alarmist press reports on illiteracy among school leavers (which led to the Adult Literacy campaign). But could the teenage reader who had read literary children's books avidly, jump into modern adult fiction with its avant garde themes and experimental techniques? A century ago the progress from *Alice's Adventures in Wonderland* to Dickens, the Brontës and Thackeray was natural and gentle. But nowadays the jump from the best in children's fiction – *Tom's Midnight Garden*, say – to a Booker Award winner such as John Berger's *G* was a veritable moonshot into uncharted territory. Some kind of bridge literature was thought to be necessary.

It is commonly said, and wrongly, that the narrative art is dead in adult fiction. The thrillers of Frederick Forsyth, the fantasies of Ian Fleming, the romances of Barbara Cartland (to name but a few British bestsellers) to be found on every station and airport bookstall are visible proof that the narrative art is alive in popular adult fiction and is big business. Teenagers read adult bestsellers, of course; they also read magazines and the various series that are published by educational departments of publishing houses for direct sale to schools (see Margaret Marshall's *Libraries and Literature for Teenagers*, Deutsch, 1975). What is missing in their leisure reading is, it has been felt, the literary novel with an adolescent hero or heroine seen coming to terms with the world and self. Both Salinger's *Catcher in the Rye* and Golding's *Lord of the Flies*, published on adult lists, had attracted a huge following among adolescents because each was a literary masterpiece born out of the author's personal obsession with the flowering of personality, with youth in dilemma. Such books stood out. Was there not therefore a place within the widening area of so-called children's publishing for literary books, perhaps technically unconventional, with a strong adolescent theme?

William Mayne's *A Game of Dark*, John Gordon's *The House on the Brink*, Jane Gardam's *Bilgewater*, Ivan Southall's *Josh* and William Corlett's *Gate of Eden* were published, with jackets carefully designed to invite the intended readership, on children's lists. So were Alan Garner's complex and challenging *Red Shift* and Jan Mark's haunting fantasy of the future, *The Ennead*. Even Gollancz, with its outstanding list of American teenage novels (including Hinton's *That Was Then, This Is Now* and Cormier's *I Am the Cheese* – good examples of, respectively, realism and new fictional techniques used with startling brilliance), does not have a separate series for its adolescent fiction. Only The Bodley Head, with its New Adult label, has chosen to identify those books whose form and content remove them from the sphere of interest of under-twelves.* Launched with Paul Zindel's seminal book in the field, *The Pigman* (first published in America), it has gone on to publish novels from Scandinavia by Gunnel Beckman, from Australia by J. M. Couper, and home-grown – by Emma Smith, Peggy Woodford, Aidan Chambers. The teenage novel, given impetus by the New Adult label of The Bodley Head, now finds its way into adult libraries and on to special shelves in youth libraries, whereas before, because it fell between two spheres of interest, it had tended to be ignored.

Jackets are a front-line sales force in a visually oriented society. Publishing for teenagers demands first-rate book covers. In the seventies the move was towards realism, often photographic (4). All these jackets (2, 3 and 4 are for special teenage lists) successfully convey the mood and contents of the books. Collectively they suggest the wide spectrum of teenage fiction interests.

* The "Oxford Novels" with their fine printing and line illustrations are an entirely sixties concept.

In bookshops, however, where to put these hybrid creatures (too advanced in literary construction or subject matter for children yet not sufficiently fully explored to give satisfaction to the mature adult reader) has been a major headache. Because the problem has not been resolved, paperback teenage fiction has not had the outlet it deserves through bookshops, which cater for children and for adults but generally speaking do not recognize the bridge. This was defined for me by Jill Paton Walsh when she said that, had *Goldengrove* and *Unleaving* been intended for adults, she would have approached the writing quite differently; yet no one could describe them as children's books.

Is the teenage novel towards which many children's authors have gravitated because of the good critical reception accorded to it on children's book pages (where it does not properly belong) and the recognition that follows, a real art form? In the sixties the novels of Rosemary Sutcliff, Barbara Willard, Henry Treece and K. M. Peyton could mingle pleasantly with children's books or with adult historical novels. But the teenage novel set in the seventies has the aggression and the character of its intended readership, and is therefore an awkward phenomenon uneasily accommodated. Is it a bridge to adult fiction – if such a bridge is necessary? Or is it, as some authors who have written well-received novels in the genre tend to fear, a literary cul-de-sac? Finite answers to these questions will not be forthcoming until the current wave of concentration on the adolescent recedes.

Our researcher in the year 2001 (who took a look at the *Stone Book* quartet, you will remember) might decide to study the change in the background to and characters in children's fiction in the process of examining what was happening in the world around him when he, in his thirties in 2001, was a child in the 1970s. The popularity of science fiction in the period when the Man *on* the Moon joined hands with the Man *in* the Moon as a fantasy figure (there is no boundary between the real and the imaginary when the real experience is vicarious) will be evident. Teenagers were offered hundreds of SF titles, often by authors for adults, while the younger child's heroes tended to be by-products of American or British T.V. series, the *Star Trek* books or *Dr. Who* stories.

The researcher would discover that the children's novel was only slowly beginning to reflect the multi-cultural nation that he remembered from his own schooldays. He would observe that, though the British tradition in fantasy literature was being maintained by authors like Penelope Lively and Diana Wynne Jones, children's fiction was being stretched to envelop contemporary situations that cut across class and colour. And if he is sharp, he will notice the efforts that were being made to retain literary standards while accommodating valid fresh demands from those who recognized the importance, at a certain stage of development in a person's life, of identification with fictional situations in practical as well as emotional terms.

The authors most likely to interest him will be Jean MacGibbon and Alison Prince, Bernard Ashley, Jan Mark and Gene Kemp, who between them resuscitated the defunct school story (three of them are teachers), and wrote not about *The Fifth Form at St. Dominic's* or *The School at the Chalet*, but about the local comprehensive (in *Hal* and *The Doubting Kind*) or primary (in *Terry on the Fence*, *Thunder and Lightnings* and *The Turbulent Term of Tyke Tiler*). Jan Needle tackled the problems faced by an immigrant Pakistani family in Bradford in a novel called *My Mate Shofiq*, a book that offended some white liberal guidelines-addicts because abusive epithets were not edited out of the dialogue: we were being asked, it seems, to present a realistic picture of Pakistani experience in Bradford without showing the hero's subjection to the unsavoury nicknames that were part of the reality. Farrukh Dhondy, an Indian teacher and a gifted author, described the book as "funny, violent and authentic. Its positive strength," he added, "is that it doesn't see Asians as victims. *Shofiq* is probably the first book written in Britain which tackles race and refuses to fall into community relations bathos" (*Children's Book Bulletin* No. 1, June 1979). Farrukh Dhondy himself won the Collins prize for a group of multi-ethnic short stories with *Come to Mecca*, a compassionate, sad, funny, even-handed collection (for teenagers) of great power and persuasion; this book more than any other may emerge as the reliable barometer of seventies' aspiration.

Collins' initiative in launching this prize was a sign of the dearth of multi-ethnic material, as well as an earnest of the goodwill awaiting it when time was ripe for it to emerge. But during the 1970s the need for novels of good quality centring on non-white heroes or heroines was filled to a large extent by the publication in Britain of novels that originated in the United States – by authors such as Rosa Guy, Virginia Hamilton and Louise Fitzhugh.

Race relations, though far and away the most important socio-logical concern to emerge in children's fiction, was not the only contender for a place in front of the mirror. The politics of Ulster found their reflection in the series of non-sectarian novels by Joan Lingard (beginning with *The Twelfth Day of July*), in Sam McBrat-ney's *Mark Time*, in Peter Carter's *Under Goliath*. Life at the bottom (of a pile of cans in the supermarket when shelf-filling, for instance) was illuminated by the work of Susan Price in *Sticks and Stones* and other novels; Winifred Cawley and Gwen Grant wrote with cheerful gusto about their own working-class childhoods, and Stanley Watts was acclaimed as a young person's D. H. Lawrence when *The Breaking of Arnold* was published in 1971.

Anti-sexism took many forms; Marjorie Darke in *A Question of Courage* looked back to suffragette struggles; Gene Kemp in *The Turbulent Term of Tyke Tiler* painted an unforgettable picture of a unisex eleven-year-old immersed in the everyday politics of home and primary school (the surprise ending of this book causes an uproar when it is read aloud to mixed groups of Tyke's age); Michael Foreman in *All the King's Horses*, a tongue-in-cheek picture book about an Amazonian princess who wrestles her suitors out of the ring, succeeded in getting across the message that girls can be other than blue-eyed fair creatures whose fathers pick hus-bands for them, far better than the so-called "non-sexist" picture books imported from Italy by the Writers and Readers Publishing Co-operative: these were aggressively anti-male.

Picture Books and Verse

Michael Foreman emerges as just one of the many picture-book artists in the seventies who began to use the medium to express ideas beyond the comprehension of the under-sevens, the tradi-tional picture-book age. Although under-sevens look at and enjoy picture books by Charles Keeping, Quentin Blake, Graham Oakley,

Anthony Browne, Colin McNaughton and Michael Foreman himself, the social and political satire is appreciated only by the more mature reader, from the age of nine upwards. As 1979 draws to a close, many of those who use books with children are a long way from recognizing the readership for this new art form, despite the glare of publicity for it attracted by the publication of Raymond Briggs's *Fungus the Bogeyman*, an evocation of a murky sub-world (the Alternative Society?) spun in gloom-green watercolour and a vocabulary of punning virtuosity.

Along with this upward trend in interest in picture books there developed a compensatory swing towards simplicity. John Burningham's *Mr. Gumpy's Outing* and his Little Books series, Helen Oxenbury's *ABC of Things*, Ray and Catriona Smith's *The Long Slide*, Allan and Janet Ahlberg's *Each Peach Pear Plum*, Robert Crowther's *Most Amazing Hide-and-Seek Alphabet Book*, Mary Rayner's *Mr. and Mrs. Pig's Evening Out* and Pascale Allamand's *The Camel Who Left the Zoo* were among the outstanding picture books for the very young to emerge in the decade; while Nicola Bayley, launched by Jonathan Cape with her minutely detailed, jewel-like illustrations for *Nicola Bayley's Book of Nursery Rhymes*, had a double appeal to patient child and perceptive adult.

Dan Jones, an East London painter of the Lowry school, provided an inner-city, 1970s, political gloss on many an old nursery rhyme in *Mother Goose Comes to Cable Street*, one of the few effortlessly multi-cultural picture books to emerge in the decade. (Other artists in this field were Errol Lloyd and Ossie Murray, who illustrated Petronella Breinburg's *Sean* and *Sally-Ann* books.) *Mother Goose Comes to Cable Street* has a vogue among older children who enjoy the fun of the fresh interpretation of rhymes they already know. The verse of poets like Mike Rosen in *Mind Your Own Business* and Roger McGough in *In the Glassroom* is in the same catch-life-and-look-at-it spirit. Colloquial and sharply humorous, their work (they are joint authors of *You Tell Me*) has direct appeal in an age when creative writing by schoolchildren, encouraged by the Arts Council's Writers in Schools project, has been flourishing.

Perhaps this is the place to record the mushroom growth of community publishing which, sparked off by Centerprise in Hackney,

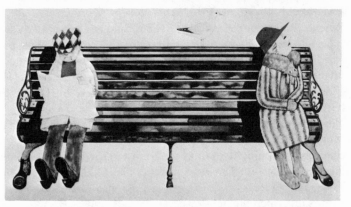

The revolt against authority, the futility of the daily round, the alternative society and the gap between the social classes, as seen in some outstanding picture books for older children in the seventies: respectively, Quentin Blake's illustration from *How Tom Beat Captain Najork and His Hired Sportsmen* by Russell Hoban; Colin McNaughton's *The Rat Race*; Raymond Briggs's *Fungus the Bogeyman* and Anthony Browne's *A Walk in the Park*.

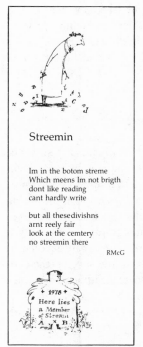

Streemin

Im in the botom streme
Which meens Im not brigth
dont like reading
cant hardly write

but all thesedivishns
arnt reely fair
look at the cemtery
no streemin there

          RMcG

✝ 1978 ✝
Here lies
a Member
of Streamin
A   B

Then it sank down in a heap
And it promptly fell asleep.
O its fearful snores astounded one and all!

(Though the music had no title
It was like a loud recital
On the organ at the Royal Albert Hall.)

One of the shortest poems of the 1970s, Roger McGough's "Streemin" from *You Tell Me* by Roger McGough and Michael Rosen – and certainly the longest poem for children written in the 1970s, Charles Causley's *The Tail of the Trinosaur*, a story in "24 shakes". The 120 pages are deftly linked by Jill Gardiner's illustrations.

encourages embryonic talent by giving it local exposure in booklet, or indeed book, form. As technology develops and word processors descend from the realm of wishful possession into common practical use, outlets will increase. Maybe in the year 2001 a child (paraphrasing the title of a popular seventies picture book) may ask "Why are there more writers than readers, Grand-dad?" But that is a question we do not have to answer in 1979. What we do know is that, here and now, the writing of authors published by community publishers is reaching a readership that was non-existent at the beginning of the decade. Whether there will develop from this a new readership for the books published by mainstream publishers, whether the work of authors for community projects will cross-fertilize with that of authors published nationally, it is too early to tell. But it would be sad if the two rivers did not find their way into a common sea.

Information Books

The technological revolution has already had an immense influence on the information books of the seventies. The possibility of packaging series for the international market seized upon by Octopus, Hamlyn, Macdonald, Usborne and many others brought into being the corporate authorship of many flavourless books by committees of experts. The glossy bland colour photography (dug up by a researcher from a photo library), the two-page spread devoted to each aspect (whether important or minor) of the subject, the captions, the potted, often meaningless, text became unbearably familiar – though Usborne's Know How series struck sparks from their readers by inviting them to share in the fun of experimenting with science, conjuring, detection.

Spurned as dehydrated food by the critics, these "packages" were welcomed and bought by teachers for many reasons, of which total accuracy could not have been one. (Margery Fisher's *Matters of Fact*, published in 1972, had interesting things to say on the subject of accuracy and the dangers of blind belief in the printed word.) Where else, teachers asked with some reason, could you find pictures and basic information that might be offered to a child of perhaps thirteen with a reading age of seven or eight? And for children *of* seven or eight, with an average to high reading age, the Macdonald type book was a first step to discovering for themselves how fishes live, what games Romans played, how their own grandparents travelled about. With so much project-based learning in primary schools, resulting in the decline in the use of the history or geography textbooks that had been sold in sets by non-net publishers, the rise of Macdonald style information books was inevitable. This does not mean that there is not plenty of scope for improvement in these series which, though designed for school use, are individually sold as "net" books. Their success highlights the need for the committed zoologist, archaeologist, botanist, sportsman, historian to write stimulating personal books about their own fields of interest for the young disciple.

Canute-like, and in this spirit, the *Times Educational Supplement* set up its Information Book Awards to encourage publishers to improve their standards in this area, giving its prize in the second year to David Hay's *Human Populations*, part of Penguin Education's ill-fated schools project, a brilliantly conceived, far-sighted series that, despite being ahead of its time, should somehow have survived. As the years went by, two publishers became conspicuously successful in winning *T.E.S.* awards: Kestrel with books on single subjects (*Window into a Nest*, *Street Flowers*, *Tournaments*) and The Bodley Head, with books that are part of their Archaeology and New Biology series. Each book was a shining example of what can be done by specialists working for children, and richly deserved the limelight thrown on it by the *T.E.S.* Odd, therefore, that the winner in the senior section in 1977 should have been the volume called *Man and Machines* in Mitchell Beazley's Joy of Knowledge encyclopaedia, for this is an advanced example of the authorship-by-committee, design-by-convenience, multinational-edition publication that has been such a widespread feature of information book publishing in the decade.

Television is one medium that is often made the scapegoat for "falling standards" in education; yet, looking at the seventies, one can see that in the field of information it has made an enormous contribution, even leaving aside the programmes specially tailored for school use. As one example, David Attenborough's *Life on Earth* was watched by children of all ages who then clamoured for the B.B.C. book based on the series. Its complex text is enlivened by captioned colour photographs of the highest quality that illustrate Mr. Attenborough's quest (children love quests) to discover the roots and growth of life on this planet. In response to pressure from some less literate children (in the nine- to ten-year-old group) I decided to buy this single volume, which cost around £8 and was published for the adult market, for the primary school library in which I work. It has received greater attention, attracted deeper and more far-reaching discussion than Macdonald's *The Life of*

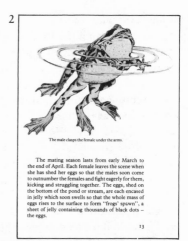

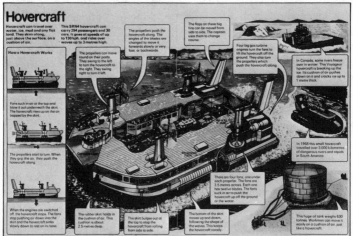

Two that won *Times Educational Supplement* Awards and one that did not. The award winners (1) Richard Mabey and Sarah Kensington's *Street Flowers* and (2) *Frogs, Toads and Newts* by F. D. Ommanney, illustrated by Deborah Fulford, have captioned watercolour pictures and a running text. But they are less typical of information book publishing in the 1970s than (3) Usborne's *How Machines Work* in which each double spread gives visual stimulation, supplemented by cut-away sections and bubble captioning. Packaging for the international market influenced this development in presentation.

Fishes, The Life of Birds, The Life of Plants, which together cost more, cover less and lack the personal touch, that magic spark which sets light to creative thinking.

Nature photography of a high calibre such as the Oxford Scientific Film Unit has produced (for Flanagan and Morris's *Window into a Nest*, for example, and the Whizzard/Deutsch Nature's Way series) invites the child in to observe nature's secrets, slowly unfolding. For other documentary-type books, too, the camera, which is generally believed to be a truthful recorder, has proved useful. A. & C. Black's series called Strands, showing the daily life, religious practices, eating habits, occupations of the many ethnic groups that make up modern British society, is one outstanding example; Kestrel's monotone-photograph series on people at work (*Newspaperworker, Railwayworker*, etc.) is another.

Books and other media are mutually supportive on the whole, but it is also true that the provision of books in schools has been threatened to some extent in the 1970s by audio-visual equipment.

The camera is generally believed to be a truthful recorder. These two photographic picture books, Sean Lyle's *Pavan is a Sikh* and *Berron's Tooth* by Joan Solomon and Richard Harvey, focused on different aspects of the multicultural society.

I cannot regard books as a "medium for information retrieval" (though they are one, of course); but I have no difficulty whatsoever in applying that awkward term to "hardware" and its accompanying "software". The place of audio-visual aids as part of education is only my concern in so far as it affects the provision of books. The relatively high cost of other media equipment must in some measure be responsible for the state of affairs described by the Books for Schools working party in the National Book League pamphlet *Books in Schools*. The purchase of "software" (film, slides, tapes) for "hardware" (cameras, projectors, cassette players) that is not fully operational cannot make financial sense in a period of economic crisis. Books may fall apart from use but they do not go out of order.

Reviewing and Promotion

So what has been the dominant theme of the seventies in children's books? We have seen social forces at work: educational thinking, sex-politics and race relations have entered the field strongly, not in opposition to the literary book but as centrifugal forces which will spread the pattern of content and the points of physical identification across sex, class and colour.

Centrifugalism was evident too in the business of publishing, where international editions of picture books and series of information books "packaged" for sale throughout the world have become the lynchpins of many a list. With this emphasis on diffusion, it is not surprising to discover that in reviewing, promotion and bookselling, decentralization has also become the keyword.

In criticism, the growth of a strong literary establishment view of children's books early in the decade gave rise to factional opposition later. *The Times*, the *Sunday Times*, the *T.L.S.*, the *Guardian*, the two *Telegraphs*, the *Observer*, and Margery Fisher's *Growing Point* became the bastions of general children's book reviewing; while the *T.E.S.*, Woodfield and Stanley's *Junior Bookshelf* and the School Library Association's *School Librarian* catered for librarians and teachers. Many 1970s projects swept through the breach that Anne Wood's *Books for Your Children* (and the activities of the Federation of Children's Book Groups) had, in the sixties, made in the establishment wall, and thrust out in all directions.

Looking back, in the summer of '79 when the *Sunday Times*, *The Times* and all its supplements had been off the streets for seven months due to an industrial dispute over new technology (another force that influenced the course of publishing in the seventies was trade union activity, one result of which was a decision by the Society of Authors to affiliate with the Trades Union Congress), these thrusts seem to have been fortuitous. Everywhere the voices of teachers, librarians, parents (combined with those of children in Hertfordshire's carefully blended *Material Matters*) are being heard on the subject of children's books. The proliferation of book review sheets and small journals published by various schools library services, local education authorities, and colleges of education is heartening: these in no way replace the need for national press coverage but they are evidence of a welcome upsurge in do-it-yourself comment, a parallel to the community publishing already mentioned. Indeed those two new magazines that arrived in my mail on 19 June 1979 were both offshoots of community groups.

But let us return to the year 1970, which saw the birth of two journals: SIGNAL, whose decade of life, independent of publisher support by way of advertising and untied by its open-door policy to any particular aspect of children's books, is celebrated in this volume, which reflects the journal's eclecticism; and *Children's Literature in Education*, originally intended to be the vehicle for carrying the words of wisdom spoken at the Exeter Conference to the world outside (but now a rather less happy American/British mix of classroom-oriented articles, published in the U.S.A.). Neither of these journals is a medium for straight reviewing: *Children's Book Review*, which began publication in 1971, was just that, but its life proved short.

The decade saw a flood of books on children's literature, however; some originated in America, others here. By and large the contributions worth noting were original works rather than the compilation of reprints of articles roughly sewn together by editors and pushed through presses. The shining exception to this generalization is *The Cool Web* which, because of Margaret Meek's gift for editing, shaping and writing fresh linking commentary, for bringing articles together in order to throw questions into the arena, involves the reader in her argument.

Among the original books on children's literature published during the decade there was *The Thorny Paradise*, for which compilation Edward Blishen invited well-known children's authors to write articles on why and how they write for children; and there was John Rowe Townsend's *A Sense of Story*, which concentrated on the narrative art of major writers, both British and American.

Though not strictly within my terms of reference, since it is American in origin, Bruno Bettelheim's *The Uses of Enchantment* made such a vital contribution to the thinking of the decade that to omit it would be absurd. Subtitled "The Meaning and Importance of Fairy Tales", it is a most significant statement on the life-enriching force of story in childhood. Since folk and fairy tale are universal and for all time, this book, born of disciplines related to but other than our own, reinforces from outside our conviction that the *emotional* content of traditional tales speaks more directly to all children (from single-parent families, immigrant communities, residential homes) than the surface *physical* similarities that agitators for pre-fab politikidlit urge publishers to produce.

Gillian Avery helped us to see modern movements in perspective with *Childhood's Pattern*, in which she demonstrated clearly that society has always sought its own reflection and the reflection of its moral standards in the heroes and heroines it offers young readers. Margery Fisher in *Who's Who in Children's Books* puts all those characters into their own settings, a mammoth task which, incidentally, has proved popular with children as well as invaluable to workers in the field. Dorothy Butler's *Cushla and Her Books* is an exploration of the part picture books can play in infancy, based (1970s style) on the experience of using them with one severely handicapped child. This book, along with Brian Alderson's academic and idiosyncratic catalogue for the National Book League's *Looking at Picture Books* exhibition, may point towards more critical interest in that expanding field in the 1980s.

For *After "Alice"*, an exhibition of "children's reading" to celebrate the centenary of the Library Association in 1977, Christine

Kloet selected books and comics that children, left to themselves, have chosen as favourites (Biggles, Blyton, Borrowers, Beano, Basil Brush) as well as the literary landmarks of the century. The catalogue for this exhibition was notable for its superb production as well as for its author's sense of perspective.

Exhibitions were just one of the promotional channels that typified the centrifugal forces at work in the seventies. The National Book League Touring Exhibitions – of which my own *Children's Books of the Year*, which began its life in 1970, is one – spread and developed into a network that covered the British Isles, while the catalogues to the exhibitions found their way all over the world. Other organizations such as the Youth Libraries Group and the School Library Association were making booklists too, to help teachers and parents cope with the huge number of children's books in print. SIGNAL entered the field with Alan Tucker's *Poetry Books for Children*, Lance Salway's *Humorous Books for Children* and Jill Bennett's *Learning to Read with Picture Books*, all of which were used as bases for N.B.L. Touring Exhibitions, as indeed were the four *Reading for Enjoyment* booklists originally published in 1970 by Children's Booknews Ltd., a subsidiary of the Children's Book Centre.

The Children's Book Centre itself, the biggest children's bookshop in Britain (the world?), which sold children's books far and wide, moved into grand new premises in the latter part of the decade – and into a financial situation that resulted in control of the enterprise being taken over by Jim Slater (of Slater Walker repute) from Eric Baker, a committed children's bookman. That this was a sign of the (bad) times one glance at the windows of Children's Book Centre today (crammed with adult bestsellers and mammoth stuffed toys) will demonstrate.

But all was by no means gloomy on the bookselling front in the 1970s. Several new children's bookshops appeared; Heffers of Cambridge in 1979 transformed its children's bookshop into a model of what children's bookselling can be; the Book Boat was launched on the Thames (next to the *Cutty Sark*); Centerprise of Hackney became the first of a long line of community booksellers, most of which have support either from the local authority or from an Arts Association, to open a children's department. By far the most exciting and imaginative development, however, was the foundation of the School Bookshop Association (in 1976) as the centre for information about the setting up of bookshops in schools. There were already bookshops in some schools, due to the initiative of Penguin. But until the Bullock Report declared that it "becomes increasingly the responsibility of the school to make it possible for children and parents together to see and select books which can be bought and taken home", a full-scale open thrust into schools was impossible. Peter Kennerley was the initiator of the movement and edited its magazine, *School Bookshop News*.

School bookshops enabled parents and children to "see and select"; there were also, in the 1970s, several mail order book clubs (Scholastic, Bookworm, Puffin School Book Club) in operation. These paperback ventures appear to be highly successful, but there is some evidence that the selling of hard-cover children's books by mail order through book clubs is less so.

Taking all these developments into account and adding to them the nationwide activities of the Federation of Children's Book Groups (which celebrated its tenth anniversary in mid decade) one can see that the sale of books directly to the children who will be tomorrow's adult readers increased substantially in an era when the economic trends threatened the supplies of books available for borrowing through school and public libraries.

But publishers must still promote their books if anyone with funds to spend is to buy them. Giant promotion schemes like the Publishers' Association Children's Book Show, a prominent feature of the London children's book calendar in the sixties, also went through a stage of decentralization (Leeds 1971, London and Bristol 1972, Manchester 1973, Glasgow 1974) as a preliminary to giving way to a much less ambitious and costly two-day event, the Blooms-bury Conference and Trade Fair in 1975. In 1976 the Conference subject was, significantly, "Are we publishing the right children's books?" and the voice of every sphere of interest covered in this survey was heard. In 1977 the Book Fair itself was dropped, which means that there is now no major children's book show or fair in Britain, though many small shows take place with publisher support. National Children's Book Week, which has now come to rest in October, has the advantage of attracting publicity from the media; but cramming hundreds of events into a single week means that publishers, authors and artists are in impossibly heavy demand over a short seven-day stretch, whereas many would prefer to spread their support for events throughout the year.

A number of prizes for children's books are announced in or around National Children's Book Week, including the Library Association's medals. In 1970 there were only three established prizes for children's books: the Library Association's Carnegie and Kate Greenaway Medals, and the *Guardian* Award. In 1979 there are eight, with others pending. Again the centrifugal force is in operation, for there is now the Other Award (which concentrates on content of a multi-cultural, anti-sexist or working-class nature), the occasional inclusion of a children's book award among the Whitbread Prizes, the Mother Goose Award for new illustrators, the *T.E.S.* Awards (see above) and the Signal Poetry Award; and there is talk of two fresh awards, from the Arts Council and the Society of Authors, coming in the eighties. If the spread of awards comes to mean the highlighting of different kinds of books (according to the terms of reference for each prize), that must be healthy; but the tendency for award givers to reflect one another's leanings, manifest at the present moment, is rather disturbing.

The only award given annually in the children's book field for work that is not authorship or illustration is the Eleanor Farjeon Award "for distinguished services to children's books". If any quick pointer were to be sought to dominant trends of children's book activity in the 1970s, the list of winners of this award would provide it. By and large the recipients have been people actively engaged, through teacher training, storytelling in parks, book clubs, exhibitions and the establishment of a study centre outside Melbourne in Australia, in the spread of knowledge about children's books to the people who are in a position to reach out with those books to children. Television has helped all of us to reach the child at home: by the serialization of children's novels, with programmes like *Playschool* and *Jackanory*, and Yorkshire T.V.'s new series of programmes about children's books called *Book Tower*. That the last Eleanor Farjeon Award announced in the seventies (in 1979 for the year 1978) was to Joy Whitby, who was responsible for the initiation of all these programmes, was symbolic of a decade in which it was recognized that if books were to be published for children, the children who were the potential readers were an important consideration. This may sound like a truism, but in some quarters it is still anathema.

In the 1970s the emphasis shifted from the adults who wrote, illustrated, published and criticized children's books to the channels through which these books could be brought into the hands of the child. For whatever the child's race, sex, circumstance, stories are the medium through which he can come to terms with his existence and become that supreme being, his own person. Because the seventies were the period during which these movements gained impetus, years in which the needs of children were recognized and considered, years in which the child was seen as an integral part of the book he read, this survey of the decade was entitled not *British Children's Books in the Seventies* but, a subtle difference, *The Seventies in British Children's Books*. For the spirit of the age has deeply affected our view of what we are doing. For better or worse? We do not know.

PUBLISHERS OF CHILDREN'S BOOKS MENTIONED

Richard Adams: *Watership Down* (Rex Collings, 1972). Allan and Janet Ahlberg: *Each Peach Pear Plum* (Kestrel, 1978). Pascale Allamand: *The Camel Who Left the Zoo* (Cape, 1976). Bernard Ashley: *Terry on the Fence* (Oxford University Press, 1975). Helen Bannerman: *Little Black Sambo* (Chatto & Windus, 1899). Richard Barber: *Tournaments* (Kestrel, 1978). Nina Bawden: *On the Run* (Gollancz, 1964). Ñicola Bayley: *Nicola Bayley's Book of Nursery Rhymes* (Cape, 1975). Petronella Breinburg: *My Brother Sean* (Bodley Head, 1973). Raymond Briggs: *Fungus the Bogeyman* (Hamish Hamilton, 1977). Raymond Briggs: *The Mother Goose Treasury* (Hamish Hamilton, 1966). John Burningham: *Mr. Gumpy's Outing* (Cape, 1970). Peter Carter: *Under Goliath* (Oxford University Press, 1977). Winifred Cawley: *Gran at Coalgate* (Oxford University Press, 1974). William Corlett: *The Gate of Eden* (Hamish Hamilton, 1974). Robert Cormier: *I Am the Cheese* (Gollancz, 1977). Helen Cresswell: *The Piemakers* (Faber, 1967). Robert Crowther: *The Most Amazing Hide-and-Seek Alphabet Book* (Kestrel, 1978). Marjorie Darke: *A Question of Courage* (Kestrel, 1975). Farrukh Dhondy: *Come to Mecca* (Collins, 1978). Geraldine Lux Flanagan and Sean Morris: *Window into a Nest* (Kestrel, 1975). Michael Foreman: *All the King's Horses* (Hamish Hamilton, 1976). Jane Gardam: *Bilgewater* (Hamish Hamilton, 1976). Alan Garner: *The Owl Service* (Collins, 1967). Alan Garner: *Red Shift* (Collins, 1973). Alan Garner: The *Stone Book* Quartet, published by Collins: *The Stone Book* (1976); *Granny Reardun* and *Tom Fobble's Day* (1977); *The Aimer Gate* (1978). Alan Garner: *The Weirdstone of Brisingamen* (Collins, 1960). John Gordon: *The House on the Brink* (Hutchinson, 1970). Goscinny and Uderzo: *Asterix the Gaul* (Brockhampton, 1969). Gwen Grant: *Private – Keep Out* (Heinemann, 1978). David Hay: *Human Populations* (Penguin Education, 1972). S. E. Hinton: *That Was Then, This Is Now* (Gollancz, 1971). Pat Hutchins: *Rosie's Walk* (Bodley Head, 1968). Dan Jones: *Mother Goose Comes to Cable Street* by Rosemary Stones and Andrew Mann (Kestrel, 1978). Gene Kemp: *The Turbulent Term of Tyke Tiler* (Faber, 1977). Joan Lingard: *The Twelfth Day of July* (Hamish Hamilton, 1970). Richard Mabey: *Street Flowers* (Kestrel, 1976). Sam McBratney: *Mark Time* (Abelard, 1976). Jean MacGibbon: *Hal* (Heinemann, 1974). Roger McGough: *In the Glassroom* (Cape, 1976). Roger McGough and Michael Rosen: *You Tell Me* (Kestrel, 1979). Jan Mark: *The Ennead* (Kestrel, 1978). Jan Mark: *Thunder and Lightnings* (Kestrel, 1976). William Mayne: *A Game of Dark* (Hamish Hamilton, 1971). Jan Needle: *My Mate Shofiq* (Deutsch, 1978). Helen Oxenbury: *ABC of Things* (Heinemann, 1971). Philippa Pearce: *A Dog So Small* (Kestrel [when Constable], 1962). K. M. Peyton: The *Flambards* Trilogy, published by Oxford University Press: *Flambards* (1967), *The Edge of the Cloud* and *Flambards in Summer* (1969). Susan Price: *Sticks and Stones* (Faber, 1976). Alison Prince: *The Doubting Kind* (Methuen, 1975). Mary Rayner: *Mr. and Mrs. Pig's Evening Out* (Macmillan, 1976). Michael Rosen: *Mind Your Own Business* (Deutsch, 1974). Ray and Catriona Smith: *The Long Slide* (Cape, 1977). Ivan Southall: *Josh* (Angus and Robertson, 1971). Morna Stuart: *Marassa and Midnight* (Heinemann, 1966). Jill Paton Walsh: *Goldengrove* (Macmillan, 1972). Jill Paton Walsh: *Unleaving* (Macmillan, 1976). Stanley Watts: *The Breaking of Arnold* (Kestrel, 1971). Peter Wezel: *The Good Bird Nepomuk* (Wheaton, 1967). Brian Wildsmith: *ABC* (Oxford University Press, 1962). Paul Zindel: *The Pigman* (Bodley Head, 1969).

PUBLISHERS OF SPECIALIST BOOKS MENTIONED

Brian Alderson: *Looking at Picture Books* (National Book League, 1973). Gillian Avery: *Childhood's Pattern* (Brockhampton, 1975). Bruno Bettelheim: *The Uses of Enchantment: The Meaning and Importance of Fairy Tales* (Thames & Hudson, 1976). *Books in Schools* (National Book League, 1979).

Edward Blishen: *The Thorny Paradise: Writers on Writing for Children* (Kestrel, 1975). Dorothy Butler: *Cushla and Her Books* (Hodder, 1979). Bullock Committee: *A Language for Life* (H.M.S.O., 1975). Mary Cadogan and Patricia Craig: *You're a Brick, Angela!: A New Look at Girls' Fiction from 1839–1975* (Gollancz, 1976). Aidan Chambers: *Introducing Books to Children* (Heinemann, 1973). Bob Dixon: *Catching Them Young* (Pluto Press, 1977). Margery Fisher: *Matters of Fact: Aspects of Non-Fiction for Children* (Brockhampton, 1972). Margery Fisher: *Who's Who in Children's Books: A Treasury of the Familiar Characters of Childhood* (Weidenfeld & Nicolson, 1975). Martin Jeffcoate: *Positive Image* (Writers and Readers Publishing Co-operative, 1979). Christine Kloet: *After "Alice"* (Library Association, 1977). Margaret Marshall: *Libraries and Literature for Teenagers* (Deutsch, 1975). Margaret Meek *et al.*: *The Cool Web: The Pattern of Children's Reading* (Bodley Head, 1977). John Rowe Townsend: *A Sense of Story* (Kestrel, 1971). John Rowe Townsend: *Written for Children* (Kestrel, rev. ed., 1974). *Sexism in Children's Books: Facts, Figures & Guidelines* (Writers and Readers Publishing Co-operative, 1976). Frank Whitehead et al.: *Children's Reading Interests* (Methuen Education/Evans, 1974).

From *Rosie's Walk* written and illustrated by Pat Hutchins

SIGNAL QUOTE

Ursula Le Guin in "Dreams Must Explain Themselves"
(Signal 19, January 1976)

Most of my letters about Earthsea books from American readers are from people between sixteen and twenty-five. The English who write me tend to be, as well as I can guess, over thirty, and more predominantly male. (Several of them are Anglican clergymen. As a congenital non-Christian I find this a little startling; but the letters are terrific.) One might interpret this age-difference to mean that the English are more childish than the Americans, but I see it the other way. The English readers are grown-up enough not to be defensive about being grown-up.

The most childish thing about *A Wizard of Earthsea*, I expect, is its subject: coming of age.

Coming of age is a process that took me many years; I finished it, so far as ever I will, at about age thirty-one; and so I feel rather deeply about it. So do most adolescents. It's their main occupation, in fact.

The subject of *The Tombs of Atuan* is, if I had to put it in one word, sex. There's a lot of symbolism in the book, most of which I did not, of course, analyse consciously while writing; the symbols can all be read as sexual. More exactly, you could call it a feminine coming of age. Birth, rebirth, destruction, freedom are the themes.

The Farthest Shore is about death. That's why it is a less well-built, less sound and complete book than the others. They were all about things I had already lived through and survived. *The Farthest Shore* is about the thing you do not live through and survive. It seemed an absolutely suitable subject to me for young readers, since in a way one can say that the hour when a child realizes, not that death exists – children are intensely aware of death – but that he/she, personally, is mortal, will die, is the hour when childhood ends, and the new life begins. Coming of age again, but in a larger context.

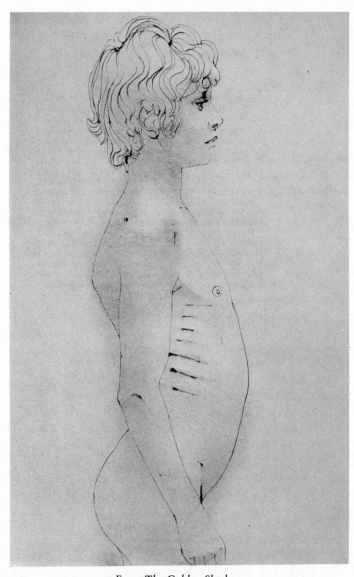

From *The Golden Shadow*
written by Leon Garfield and Edward Blishen
and illustrated by Charles Keeping

82

On the Elvish Craft

JANE CURRY

Jane Curry is an American writer of children's books who spends
as much time as she can in England. She has also lectured on children's books at the University of California at Los Angeles. This
article is adapted from a talk given at the University of California
at Berkeley two years before its publication in the May 1970
SIGNAL.

Once upon a time "fantasy" was two words. Both came – through
Old French and Latin – from the Greek φαντασία, which means,
literally, "a making visible". Certainly all fantasy is that, whether
it is a shape and substance given to things not actually present, to
the stuff of secret dreams, or to things which never were or could
be. And certainly, for writers and readers – adult or child – who
are concerned with the *art* of fantasy, the word is still as broad
as all imagination. But this very breadth makes for difficulties, particularly when we begin to talk about "excellence in fantasy for
children" or "the function and nature of fantasy". The definitions
presented by this writer or that, one reviewer or another, tend to
exclude from serious consideration many books whose excellence
lies outside that definition. It is for this reason that I think it worth
recovering a distinction we lost perhaps forty or fifty years ago.
It would be pedantic and impractical to go the whole way and pro-
pose that the one sort of fantasy should be spelt *fantasy* and the
other *phantasy*, but though we may be past reviving the *ph* spelling,
the distinction itself is particularly useful and illuminating when
we look at modern fantasy for children; for of that lost *ph* the
Oxford English Dictionary said in 1901 that "... *fantasy* and *phantasy*, in spite of their identity in sound and in ultimate etymology,
tend to be apprehended as separate words, the predominant sense

of the former being 'caprice, whim, fanciful invention', while that of the latter is 'imagination, visionary notion'".

Children's fantasy is, of course, no more amenable to categorizing than any other sort of literature, for few books will fit snugly into pigeonholes unless they have first been forced – if ever so slightly – out of shape. However, our favourites do seem to incline either towards "caprice, whim, fanciful invention" at one end of a continuum or towards "imagination, visionary notion" at the other. The inclination may be slight, it may be extreme; and a single definition that has to reconcile P. L. Travers's *Mary Poppins* with George MacDonald's *The Golden Key* will probably end by leaving one out in the critical cold (probably poor *Mary Poppins*, who has not been the same since Hollywood sat on her). MacDonald partisan though I am, I should hate to think that a concern for the difficult emotional realities of recognizing death and loving life must make me think the less of that other great delight – having tea with Mary Poppins's Uncle, Mr. Wigg, at a table floating in mid-air. It is increasingly fashionable to insist upon "relevance" or "emotional validity" as criteria of excellence in fantasy, and these are demands we *must* make of the *ph* sort of fantasy. But not of Mary Poppins, or many others. There are excellences and excellences. I would suggest, always with qualifications and reservations in mind, that the two broad types of fantasy differ in focus, in tone, technique, and quality of insight in much the same way that fairy tale differs from myth. In the one our attention is focused primarily on the story or action itself; in the other it is the feeling, the emotional dimension, that holds us.

Rat and Mole, Toad, Mary Poppins, Arrietty and her family, the young Bilbo Baggins, and the Reluctant Dragon – though they make an odd assortment – stand together in their relationship to us. We feel affection for them, and sometimes it may be a very special affection indeed, growing deep into the roots of our childhood. And yet it is those other fantasies – the ones we might spell with *ph* – which intrigue me. They are not "dear" to us. It may be nearer the truth to say that they have a power *over* us. If we care for Lucy Boston's Green Knowe books, William Mayne's *Earthfasts*, C. S. Lewis's chronicles of Narnia, Tolkien's *Lord of the Rings*, George MacDonald's Curdie books, Alan Garner's

Elidor and *The Owl Service*, or Phillippa Pearce's *Tom's Midnight Garden*, our feeling for them is of quite a different quality.

Of course, I know that many children who delight in Pooh and later in the Borrowers may never feel a comparable involvement in the worlds of Garner or Mayne, and I think that is their loss; but at the same time I know that is *my* involvement speaking. Most of us will incline one way or the other – to the familiar or to the visionary – even though we may enjoy both. Our emotional response to the differences in the landscapes of the created worlds is probably more revealing than we imagine. Each of these worlds – in its own terms – is rational, consistent, and obedient to its own logic if it is good fantasy; but they may be rational in different ways, and we respond to them according to our own emotional and intellectual natures ("we" being children and adults alike).

Fantasy "with an *f*" moves in a real, an "actual" world. It may not be our own world or our world as we know it, but it is a sharp, clear, definite world, very substantial, quite tangible. Magic, when it is invoked, is presented as the most natural thing imaginable. This straightforwardness gives the fairy tale its conviction, and in those stories ostensibly set in our own world, it can be wonderfully funny. Joan Aiken's Armitage family lives in a comfortable suburban world where sea monsters off the Sussex coast and unicorns in the garden are immensely interesting but not in the least astonishing; and in Edith Nesbit's *The Story of the Amulet*, Robert and Anthea show the Queen of Babylon around the British Museum in one of the more irresistibly comical scenes of a beautifully worked-out tale of time travel. In these stories the characters simply *are*, and we believe in them. The incredible can seem incredibly simple and quite clear, thank you. But then, the question these stories pose is "What happens?" not "Why?" or "How?"

The fantasy of the lost *ph* does not move in this well-lit world where stories develop in a straight line from one adventure to the next. Its characters are not static in their given natures, but learning, growing. It is more a world of Becoming than of Being. In it there is more concern for potentiality than for actuality; for what we could be rather than what we are. Much is elusive, intangible, shadowed – moving in a landscape of chiaroscuro rather than one of hard edges and primary colours – for the world of inner feeling *is* more elusive than the external world of action.

In a sense the same distinction runs broadly through all of literature: there is narrative, at its "purest" an impersonal form involved with physical action within time; and the lyric, personal, and timeless. I have suggested that in the first sort of fantasy plot is most important, and the action proceeds in a linear fashion from one adventure or encounter to another, but by this I do not mean to imply any judgement of value. Butter Crashey and the Twelves (in Pauline Clarke's *The Twelve and the Genii*) in their heroic journey to the Brontë Museum at Haworth face direct conflicts and clearly defined dangers, as do Bilbo and the dwarves in their quest for Smaug's treasure. This is excellent stuff, the best sort of traditional original fantasy; but because of my own inclinations, it is that other sort of fantasy I am interested in exploring briefly here: its nature and the source of that fascination which goes beyond delight.

For the lack of a better term and because we *have* abandoned the distinction through spelling, I will call the more "visionary" fantasy simply "contemporary" fantasy.* As a term, "contemporary" provides a useful contrast to "traditional", and is particularly fitting when we think of contemporary literature's concern with character and time and place rather than with plot in any classic, linear sense. Certainly there is action in "contemporary" fantasy, but it is rarely, if ever, simply a picaresque series of adventures like bright Venetian beads on a string. More often – if it approaches real excellence – it is shaped as a single pearl is shaped: a whole built up around a theme, or person, or place, or relationship.

---

*1979 Reconsidering, nine years after the original appearance of this article, I find myself uncomfortably aware of the inadequacy of my proposed alternatives of "contemporary" and "traditional" fantasy for the old distinction between *ph*antasy and *f*antasy. The modern fantasies of magical worlds that are in one way or another descendants of medieval romance are, if anything, more traditional than any latter-day invention in the predominantly comic tradition of these past hundred years. "High fantasy", as a term, may be an apt description of those tales at the farther end of the spectrum for the purely comic, but what of the Nameless Lands between? Such critical complications of dealing with fantasy as a genre fascinate me, but their sorting-out would require an article quite different from and longer far than this, and so, for now, I must confine myself to registering unease with my original choice of terms. More than ever I regret that lost *ph*. J.C.

Alan Garner has suggested (in the *Times Literary Supplement*, 6 June 1968) that this sort of storytelling at its best, aware of the many levels of experience it relates, gives us books like onions: "An onion can be peeled down through its layers, but it is always, at every layer, an onion, whole in itself." Pearls were once called "onions" for just this reason, the root of the word being in the Latin *unio*, unionis: unity, singleness. I think I prefer Garner's onion image to the pearl because it also suggests a pungency, a sense of being rooted in the good earth, which is a characteristic of much "contemporary" original fantasy. A story may, like *The Children of Green Knowe*, stand quite still in a lovingly realized landscape and grow, sending down roots into the why and how of things. Magic, when it is invoked – as it is in *Elidor* – can be as obscure and awesome as nature itself; for after all it is seen as a power derived from nature.

When this contemporary fantasy does move, often it moves in quite a different fashion. The "plots" of *Tom's Midnight Garden*, or *The Children of Green Knowe*, or even *The Voyage of the "Dawn Treader"*, if reduced to the old-fashioned book-report type of summary, might sound either static or confused; yet much of their strength is *in* their movement. Much as Susanne Langer says of poetry, their "... argumentation is the semblance of the thought process, and the strain, hesitation, frustration, or the swift subtlety of mental windings, or a sense of sudden revelation, are more important elements in it than the conclusion" (*Feeling and Form*, Routledge & Kegan Paul). In other words, such tales move – in however fantastic a world – much more as our own lives do: defying attempts to pigeonhole our days, presenting difficult moral and ethical choices, offering no easy or final answers, and involving us deeply and immediately. They are tales that can more precisely be said to have grown rather than to have been constructed or made.

This organic wholeness is directly related to their very personal quality. They are (I think) more suited for reading all in one swoop (or two or three) off in a corner by oneself than for reading aloud in classroom or bedtime instalments, and this personal quality is equally evident in the way many of them are written. A traditional original fantasy may well have its genesis in that wonderful flash-of-a-question "What if ...?" "What if there were an amulet that allowed you to travel where and whenever in time you wished?" "What if mice could work effectively in the world of men?" or "What if there were one dragon who didn't want to go around wreaking havoc?" From there on adventures can abound. But the basic premises of contemporary fantasy are not so easily stated; and though the process of writing *may* not be any more time-consuming or painstaking, it is usually more complex, erratic – a more deep-down experience, and a process more intuitive than deductive. Alan Garner's description in the *T.L.S.* of the growth of *The Owl Service* reveals a process of conception and development in which the first ideas, subsequent research, and images and fragments from books, film, and conversation all are brought together in what Coleridge called the "well of unconscious cerebration", and only later consciously shaped. Detail comes as the story is told, and this spontaneity itself helps "to give the whole an organic development".

Organic development. It is not an easy thing to achieve. Many writers of children's fantasy begin with more or less traditional structures and in successive works grope toward this more organic unity. Alan Garner's own first books are more episodic, and for E. Nesbit the process of discovery was even longer. She had been writing for a number of years before she achieved the wonderful traditional fantasy of *The Phoenix and the Carpet*, *Five Children and It*, and *The Story of the Amulet*, and she went on to something more in *The Enchanted Castle*.

Now, *The Enchanted Castle* is not the favourite of adults who did not meet E. Nesbit in their childhood. Its movement is strange to them. The Ugly-Wuglies are too horrific, they say; and the living statues are fine only until you come to the monster lizard; and then there is the American gentleman who shoots at ghosts, and the adults coming along with their "love interest", or one of them being laid low by a vicious blow from an Ugly-Wugly.... Worst of all, you cannot tell whether the magic is magic or mysticism or make-believe. Poor adult readers! As in so many things, they would like to be secure, to know; not simply to believe. Children know they do not *know*; but that delicious balance Miss Nesbit strikes, *not* allowing us to be sure, is the stuff belief and fascination grow from. The story begins with Gerald and Jimmy and Kathleen discovering a castle, a maze, and a sleeping princess with a magic ring. But the castle and maze are really only hidden in the grounds of Lord Yalding's estate, and the princess is Mabel, the housekeeper's niece. The ring? To Mabel's dismay, it *is* magic, but a magic whose strange and shifting logic the children never quite master. The ambiguity, the enchantment touches everything: time, place, people, things, and feelings. The mood shifts continually. It is never far from laughter even in terror, and deepens at last to a vision the children and the lovers share of the oneness of time and the universe.

I met *The Enchanted Castle* on a school-library bookshelf in Kittanning, Pennsylvania, when I was ten years old. It was just at eye level, and the title caught me. I had never heard of E. Nesbit, but I liked H. R. Millar's drawings and, borrowing the book, read it straight through. I haven't been quite the same since (a statement that sounds more drastic than it is, for we can say the same of many things). When at last the book was overdue, I took it back to the library, but omitted to write down the author's name and so in time forgot it. When shortly afterward we moved to Johnstown, Pennsylvania, neither my new school nor the public library had any enchanted castles. But it stayed with me. Twenty years later I ran across it quite by accident in Foyle's and bought it in a state of excitement I find impossible to describe. I think I must have run all the way to the Reading Room of the British Museum, where I sat down to read it through. And it was not the same book. Because, of course, I was not the same. I read it as a postgraduate student of English literature reads: affecting some (however slight) critical detachment. But when I put my two readings side by side, the remembered one was still too fresh and vital to be killed by the adult, informed, critical enjoyment; and seeing that, I puzzled over the loss until I halfway understood it, and *The Enchanted Castle* could come back in almost all of its magic and power. When I read it now, twenty-seven years blow away with the wind.

Why should a book of fantasy gain such a power over the imagination? In *Tree and Leaf* J. R. R. Tolkien says of Faërie that its magic "... is not an end in itself, its virtue is in its operations: among these are the satisfaction of certain primordial human desires. One of these desires is to survey the depths of space and

time. Another is ... to hold communion with other living things."
I would add – remembering *The Enchanted Castle* – "and to be
aware that even things inanimate have, in some sense, life and
power".

The fascination with time in contemporary fantasy is, if possible,
even more striking than the richly conveyed landscapes in which
they are played out. There is great force in the recognition that
today holds yesterday and tomorrow within it: that "past",
"present", and "future" are not labels to put on isolated pigeonholes (fantasy being in many things a great antidote to pigeon-
holing). "I don't understand," says Gerald in *The Enchanted Castle*,
alone in his third-class carriage, "how railway trains and magic
can go on at the same time." But the same moment *does* contain
the mundane and the marvellous. Physical time and psychological
time may run together, keeping apace, and still be experienced as
differing widely in duration. In *The Cuckoo Clock* Mrs. Molesworth wrote, " 'And what is slow, and what is quick?' said the
cuckoo. '*All* a matter of fancy! If everything that's been done since
the world was made till now, was done over again in five minutes,
you'd never know the difference.' "
These are riddles that fascinate children – who can, incidentally,
be far more knowledgeable than many others on the theories of
time advanced by space-travel theoreticians. The children in *The
Story of the Amulet* are fascinated too:

> "I don't know," said Cyril.... "This about time being only a thingummy
> of thought is very confusing. If everything happens at the same time —"
> "It *can't!*" said Anthea stoutly, "the present's the present and the past's
> the past."
> "Not always," said Cyril.
> "When we were in the Past the present was the future. Now then!" he
> added triumphantly.

But time's appeal is deeper than the fascination of puzzle and
speculation. In some stories the awareness of the past in both children and adults can become so vivid, its relationship to their own
present so clear, that the distinction between memory and dream
is lost, as in *Tom's Midnight Garden* or *The Children of Green*

Knowe. In the latter, Tolly sees his friends from the past, Alexander and Linnet and Toby, in church. At the sight of Linnet's dog,

... Tolly gave a little squeak of laughter, but it was luckily drowned in the peal of bells that broke out.

Mrs. Oldknow said: "Wake up, Tolly. A Happy Christmas to you! We are going back in my friend's car, so you will soon be in bed. Did you have nice dreams?"

Tolly looked quite bewildered. "Yes, Granny," he said. "Were you asleep too?"

"Perhaps," she said. "I hardly know."

Even if it were a dream, the touch of the past is alive. TIME NO LONGER says the grandfather clock in *Tom's Midnight Garden.*

People from other times touch the present in part because for Lucy Boston, Philippa Pearce, William Mayne, and Alan Garner, places hold their pasts within them. In *Tom's Midnight Garden* the old manor house garden reappears each midnight behind the house where Tom's aunt and uncle have a flat, and where there are "really" only the paved backyards and dustbins of a crowded suburb. Beyond his accidental relationship with the girl Hatty, it is not chance that Tom should share the private world of her garden, for his own garden at home is the private world he and his brother share: a little town garden with an apple tree. And yet it too is a rich and exciting place. Mrs. Oldknow's love for Green Knowe and its past grows out of Mrs. Boston's love for the long past of her own Manor House at Hemingford Grey; William Mayne's hills and standing stones are all solidity and mystery together, all strength and tenacity, like the people who live among them. The Welsh valley of Alan Garner's *The Owl Service* sees a tale played over and over again, today's children caught in the tragic pattern of an ancient myth whose origin is in that valley, a myth that tells us truth about jealousy and betrayal, and the danger of asking someone to be what she is not. Places become characters; and these tales touch on experiences which are the rhythms of life, endlessly complex.

Traditional and contemporary original fantasy: at one extreme Product; at the other, Process. At these extremes one offers resolution, a world of tidy reassuring endings; the other can offer a deeper hope, for all its ambiguity. The one works through comedy, puzzle, and suspense in a world that is ultimately knowable. The other may present us with *real* mysteries in the philosophical or theological sense of the word; for it can deal with emotions, origins, higher powers, and things transcendent. Writing on fantasy in the August 1965 *Horn Book* Loren Eiseley has quoted Coleridge's explanation that as a boy he had no difficulty in comprehending his father's attempt to convey the wonders of astronomy:

[For] from my early reading of fairy tales and genii etc. etc., my mind had been habituated *to the Vast*, and I never regarded *my senses* in any way as the criteria of my belief. I regulated all my creeds by my conceptions, not by my *sight*. . . . I know all that has been said against it [fantasy]; but . . . I know no other way of giving the mind a love of the Great and the Whole. Those who have been led to the same truths step by step, through the constant testimony of their senses, seem to me to want a sense which I possess. They contemplate nothing but *parts*, and all *parts* are necessarily little. And the universe to them is but a mass of *little things*.

Beyond this, fantasy offers on the one hand entertainment, re-assurance, and – yes – escape; on the other, involvement, provocative ideas and insights, consolation, and the intensification of feeling. Tolkien says, "To the elvish craft, Enchantment, Fantasy aspires, and when it is successful of all forms of human art most nearly approaches." Whimsical fantasy may give us deep delight, but visionary fantasy can give us joy. And here again I would like to emphasize that, though I seem to have been talking in categories, the image of the continuum is nearer truth. Few books would fit any category without having a branch or two lopped, and most painfully. *The Wind in the Willows* is, of course, traditional origi-nal fantasy (or beast fable, if you wish); but when Rat and Mole go at dawn in search of little Portly Otter, they are given a vision of the deep beneficence of Nature itself in the great god Pan – and they feel joy in all its awfulness. Joy is a surprise every time we live it; and if joy remembered is not the same thing at all, still each time we do feel it, our capacity for feeling is deepened.

But then, I like to think that the adventures and trials of fantasy stretch our imaginative capacities in many ways. When in *The Enchanted Castle* poor Mabel is stretched to a thin, elongated twelve feet tall, the problem is so real that we are almost beyond laughter; and despite our concern, we are beyond alarm:

"Well, to look at her as she is now," said Gerald, "why, it would send anyone off their chump – except us."

"We're different," said Jimmy; "our chumps have had to jolly well get used to things. It would take a lot to upset us now."

With Gerald and Jimmy we know that there is nothing to do but to *act*.

Dreamers would not survive in fantasy.

Amateur Joys

JULIA MacRAE

Julia MacRae is a publisher of children's books in Britain. Before setting up her own list, Julia MacRae Books in association with Franklin Watts Ltd., she was children's book editor at Collins and then managing director of Hamish Hamilton Children's Books. Her support of the infant SIGNAL was immediate, and we were encouraged to receive this light-hearted piece for our second issue, May 1970.

An amateur according to the O.E.D. is "... one who is fond of; one who cultivates a thing as a pastime". It is a comfortable definition and it is a comfortable status to have. The amateur can relax without having to carry upon his shoulders the weight of too much erudition, and he is often freer to enjoy his "pastime" than the dedicated professional. I am an amateur book collector. I have no specialist knowledge, no fierce collector's passion, but a response is awakened in me when I see certain books and have that I-can't-live-without-it feeling. There is no logic in my collecting, nor any frenzy. In a haphazard way a small collection of books I am "fond of" is growing apace, and all sorts of random reflections occur as I look at them. As a publisher, many of my thoughts about books of the past are, inevitably, linked with parallel thoughts about books of the present.

The reasons why some books appeal more strongly than others may be obscure. The feel, the look, the smell of a book can often exercise a powerful influence. All these things compelled me to buy an inexpensive 1891 edition of *Robinson Crusoe*, published by Cassell & Company. The typography is daunting: what appears to be an 8-point type set in 43 lines on a page size $9'' \times 6\frac{1}{4}''$, 432 pages in all, tipping my bathroom scales at 6 lb. I have a suspicion I should not be impressed by such physical details, but one of the joys of being an amateur is that one can quite unashamedly be impressed by all the wrong things. The chief glory of my *Robinson Crusoe* is its one hundred and twenty illustrations by Walter Paget; and, thanks to the fact that each illustration has a generous caption, it is possible to read one's way through the illustrations without having to tackle the 43 lines in 8-point. The illustrations are photographically faithful to the text and marvellously vivid. The savages are noble, Crusoe is the very epitome of Victorian manhood, and all the right moments are illustrated: one black-bordered full-page illustration bears the caption *I stood like one thunderstruck*, and there indeed stands Crusoe, plainly thunderstruck, but losing none of his Victorian cool as he assumes the classic pose, hand shading his eyes, gazing at The Footprint. Furthermore, the illustrator was not one to spare the sensibilities; gore is drawn in meticulous detail. Crusoe's first encounter with Friday is graphically depicted: rippling with muscles Friday stands, holding in one hand Crusoe's sword and in the other hand the head of a cannibal he has just decapitated.

If the captions are not in themselves sufficiently explicit, the running heads provide a further excuse for never having to go so far as to read the text. In the endearing manner of the times, each right-hand running head is a summary of the page beneath: *My happy deliverance* is immediately followed by *My pots and wickerware* and *My paddock for the goats*. The reader is at once reassured that Crusoe has been spared and has set himself up very cosily; that he is, in fact, enjoying considerable domestic comfort, since the running heads continue with *My new clothes* and *My country seat*. It is hard to feel sorry for the castaway in such circumstances; but the idyll is short-lived, for the stark running head on the next page simply reads *Terror!*

This handsome, pompous edition is *the* Robinson Crusoe for me, and I look with awe and envy at those one hundred and twenty illustrations in all their Victorian splendour. What, I wonder, will collectors in a hundred years' time make of today's novels for children? Satisfying to read they might be, and are, but surely not so satisfying to look at or to handle? With few exceptions, novels for older children are no longer illustrated. It is claimed that children like to make their own pictures in the mind's eye, but it would be more honest to admit that illustrations have largely been done away with as a cost economy. Faced with the daily headache of spiralling printing costs, the publisher acknowledges that fiction is hard enough to sell at the best of times, and that adding the extra cost of illustration might well price it out of the market. A sad reflection – and a sad situation for the artist who needs the discipline of drawing well in line before he can adequately master the technique necessary for the full-colour picture book.

I have another book that makes me envy the days when binding and illustration could be lavish and extravagant: *Robin Hood: a Collection of Poems, Songs and Ballads Relative to that Celebrated English Outlaw*, edited by Joseph Ritson and published in 1884 by George Routledge. The binding is a design in gold, green and red, with butterflies (though why *butterflies* for Robin Hood?), and the indescribably awful lettering clearly reads Bobin Hood. This edition has thirty-two black-and-white illustrations by Gordon Browne – it was quite usual for Victorian title pages to state the exact number of illustrations, and I like to think of reinstating this practice: "... with 17 drawings by Margery Gill", and so on. There are also a number of crudely coloured plates, and a handsome decorated border in red surrounds each page of type. The book is pure delight for the Robin Hood-ophile, although I could wish that the illustrator had chosen to make the characters less like drooping pre-Raphaelite gentlemen and more like flesh-and-blood outlaws. This, however, is part of the book's charm, as is the glossary for readers understandably bemused by such expressions as *marry gep with a wenion* or *ferre and friend bestad*.

Another feature of book production which has largely been abandoned is the inclusion of advertising. I will admit that it is not an aesthetically attractive feature, but it makes for hilarious reading, and immortalizing a publisher's blurb by binding it in with the book provides the social historian with a useful guide to the books of the times which have long since been forgotten. I was first attracted to *The Calendar of Nature*, published in 1834, by an enchanting advertisement quite blatantly facing the title page:

THE
TWELVE ORIGINAL DESIGNS
MADE FOR THIS WORK
BY MR. CATTERMOLE
ARE TO BE DISPOSED OF;
AND MAY BE SEEN AT
MESSRS. COLNAGHI AND CO'S.
PALL-MALL, EAST

What a way for a publisher to avoid storage headaches! If only we could announce with such sublime confidence that the original art work for our books was to be "disposed of", private view and all. But nowadays we need the art work for all sorts of reasons: foreign sales, paperback editions, exhibitions in schools and libraries, reproduction in journals, all the subsidiary activities that are the daily business of the successful modern publisher.

I wonder if Mr. Cattermole's original designs still exist somewhere? They are very appealing – a series of twelve engravings to illustrate each of the months of the year, set as half-titles to introduce the subsequent prose section about the month. The book is distinguished for me by the linguistic contortions the author, identified only as M, performs to describe the simplest things; thus his definition of Spring is the month of April, which "with its warm gleams of sunshine and gentle showers has the most powerful effect in hastening the universal *springing* of the vegetable tribes, whence the season derives its appellation". The key word is italicized just in case the reader happens to miss the point, and the whole thing conjures up an alarming vision of the "vegetable tribes" leaping about with Triffid-like ferocity.

But not all the vanished aspects of the book need to be regretted. From America comes *The New England Primer, an Easy and Pleasant Guide to the Art of Reading*, published in Boston for the Congregational Church. My edition has the date 1877 handwritten inside the binding, but the tone and style of the book reflect its earlier origins. Easy and pleasant! This little book is unremittingly pious and doom-laden. I had always known of the didacticism and moral fervour of many early children's books, but reading *The New England Primer* brought this unlovable characteristic home to me with a wallop. Pity the poor child whose ABC gives for U: *Upon the wicked God will rain a horrible tempest*, and for L: *Liars will have their part in the lake which burns with fire and brimstone.* Death is everywhere: one of the woodcuts shows a woman heavily draped in widow's weeds brooding with her child beside a monumental tombstone. The poem beneath this singularly depressing picture is equally crushing:

UNCERTAINTY OF LIFE

I in the burying place may see
  Graves shorter there than I;
From death's arrest no age is free;
  Young children, too, may die.

My God, may such an awful sight
  Awakening be to me!
O that by earthly grace I might
  For death prepared be!

Death was a subject of great concern to the Victorians, too. It is perhaps easy to overlook the virtues of Victorian books for children when we condemn their vices. Sometimes painful subjects were treated with a degree of honesty relatively rare in fiction writing today, so cautious have we become about the supposedly delicate sensibilities of the child. *Seven Little Australians* by Ethel Turner is the Antipodean *Little Women,* and I was given recently an edition of 1896, the sixth. The book includes a death scene that reduces me to helpless tears whenever I read it; and yet, like the death of Beth, it is an emotional release because it is fundamentally honest in its presentation, not hesitating to state that death happens to us all, and need not be feared. The compassion of the writer puts death into its proper perspective, unlike the poem I quoted, which is too much concerned with the fear of God. How many writers today would dare to describe a tragic and harrowing death as uncompromisingly as Ethel Turner? Judy, the gay and spirited heroine of the story, has been struck by a falling tree while saving the life of a baby, and is now most graphically and reluctantly dying:

The child was crying now. "Oh, Meg, I want to be alive! How'd you like to die when you're only thirteen? Think how lonely I'll be without you all."

The tears streamed down her cheeks, her chest rose and fell. "Oh, say something, Meg! – hymns! – anything!"

Half the book of *Hymns Ancient and Modern* danced across Meg's brain. Which one could she think of that would bring quiet into those feverish eyes that were fastened on her face with such a frightened, imploring look? Then she opened her lips:

> "Come unto Me, ye weary,
> And I will give you rest.
> Oh, b⊢——"

"I'm not weary, I don't want to rest," Judy said in a fretful tone.

These are real children reacting to a terribly real situation, but there is nothing about this scene to disturb the average sensitive child, because the child will respond to the honesty of the treatment. It will make little girls cry, no doubt, but they will be crying for all the right reasons as Judy dies, game to the last, surrounded by the love of her stricken family. We ask our writers today to give children more realism. I believe it is emotional, not just environmental, realism which is needed.

If the reading of *Seven Little Australians* makes me reflect on fiction writing today, looking at the books of the French artist Boutet de Monvel sets me wondering about the modern picture book. Boutet de Monvel must be ranked as one of the greatest picture-book artists of all time, and the two books I have of his tempt me to abandon my amateur status and seriously pursue the collecting of *all* his books. I have an undated edition of his *Jeanne d'Arc* (but the introduction by Boutet de Monvel himself bears the date April 1896). *Jeanne d'Arc* is a collector's item, a rare book, and looking at it I can see why, for not many people would part with such a book once they had it. Even in his own time Boutet de Monvel was acknowledged to be a master artist, and proofs of his pictures were printed on special paper and sold in a portfolio. In his studio in New York Maurice Sendak showed me a set of such proofs, which he had been lucky enough to find, and I thought how right it was that one of today's supreme artists should so respect and value one of the supreme artists of yesterday.

What strikes with such force about Boutet de Monvel is how wonderfully well he *draws* – a faculty too often missing in modern picture books where lavish colour can disguise a basic clumsiness in the draughtsmanship. Boutet de Monvel's use of colour is subtle and delicate, and the detail in his pictures is miraculous: a double-page spread of Joan confronting her accusers at her trial is as dramatic as any picture I have seen; there are thirty-eight other characters in the scene, and each one of them is instantly alive, the faces drawn with such skill that one knows exactly what each is feeling – fear, curiosity, hatred, suspicion, pride. The crowd scenes in this picture book are unforgettable: the coronation of the Dauphin, the battles, the processions, all precisely detailed but imbued with a compassionate imagination which makes this, for me, one of the truly classic picture books. Boutet de Monvel had a story to tell and he drew it well – surely the two basic ingredients of a good picture book? This fine artist had a marvellous sense of the absurd, too. The second book I have of his, *Vieilles Chansons et Rondes pour les Petits Enfants*, is full of deliciously witty decorations surrounding the music setting on each page. I admire our great trio of Crane–Caldecott–Greenaway as much as anybody, but for wit, delicacy, high drama and absolute sureness of touch I give Boutet de Monvel the edge, although I think Randolph Caldecott comes very close to him.

These are the books I love most; there are others – some older, some very recent, and some in the process of being published now – which mean a great deal to me, and maybe will give pleasure equally to a collector in the future. The interesting thing for me is that I view these books not as a "collection" but as part of a chain, part of the ever changing, ever fascinating and always unpredictable pattern of publishing.

Dark Rainbow:
Reflections on Ted Hughes

JOHN ADAMS

At the time this article was published in the May 1971 SIGNAL, John Adams was a lecturer in English at St. Paul's College, Cheltenham. He is now working in local-radio development in Scotland. A postscript bringing his ideas about Hughes up to date appears at the end of Brian Morse's article (page 121).

The publication last autumn of Ted Hughes's latest book of poetry, *Crow*, prompted me to look back over the work Hughes has done and ask what kind of influence he has been on children and teachers during the last ten years. For this poet, I suggest, has had more influence on children through his own writing and his selection of material for B.B.C. schools programmes than any other living poet. His poetry, especially the animal poems of *The Hawk in the Rain* and *Lupercal*, have an immediate and sensational vitality that appeals as much to the eight-year-old as to the adolescent; there is a freshness and a precision in his language which sharpens the reader's perception of certain animals; and since he writes (or used to) mostly about animals it was natural that his poetry should often be the starting point of a child's experience of poetic realism. His work, too, fitted with the mood of encouraging a child's intuitive response to things, an emphasis on strong feeling in opposition to the mechanistic formalism of society. As a stimulant to creative writing, his poetry is very successful; and in his talk, "Capturing Animals", Hughes has helped to increase a child's awareness of how someone begins to write poetry. I find myself asking, however, what in the long term Hughes has to offer in his poetry beyond the "bounce and stab" of "a ravening second".

In his lecture at the Exeter Conference (published as "Myth and Education" in *Children's Literature in Education*, March 1970), Ted Hughes attacked the scientific attitude to life that was being taught in our schools as an ideal which he characterized as "a completely passive attitude of apathy in the face of material facts". By this he means in part qualities of detachment and objectivity, but he adds to them the phrase "inwardly inert" and justifies this by citing the man who coolly photographed a woman being mauled to death by a tiger as the epitome of this idealized objectivity, and presumably the society that upholds the ideal. I mention this because Hughes has often been accused of celebrating violence, especially animal violence, though it would be more accurate to say that it is not violence for itself that Hughes admires, but the unimpeded efficiency and directness of the predatory instincts. Nevertheless, he observes animals in the act of killing and being killed, and humans in the moment of dying: what *is* his attitude?

You'll have noticed how all the animals get killed off at the end of most poems. Each one is living the redeemed life of joy. They're continually in a state of energy which men only have when they've gone mad. This strength arises from their complete unity with whatever divinity they have.... These spirits or powers won't be messed up by artificiality or arrangements. This is what *The Otter* is about and *The Bull* is what the observer sees when he looks into his own head. Mostly these powers are just waiting while life just goes by and only find an outlet in moments of purity and crisis because they won't enter the ordinary pace and constitution of life very easily.... People are energetic animals and there's no outlet in this tame corner of civilization. Maybe if I didn't live in England I wouldn't be driven to extremes to writing about animals. My poems are not about violence but vitality. (Interview with John Horder in the *Guardian*, 23 March 1965)

The energy he senses in animals is akin to human frenzy, and though he here calls it vitality, it is clearly destructive. Energy must expend itself; and progressively in his poetry the language of energy has more sharply defined associations – from the "bang of blood in the brain" of the first "Jaguar" to the "second glance" in "Wodwo" "Like a thick Aztec disemboweller". Unlike Lawrence (whose sense of the instinctive life in animals Hughes has narrowed) Hughes is almost always an observer or admirer – detached. Where Lawrence opens himself to a meeting with animals, Hughes watches and captures them, an act that precludes involvement. I find this not very different, in effect, from the state of paralysis induced by the scientific attitude he condemns. And if you look at *Crow* as the latest stage in his development, the sensational vitality (as he calls it) has been completely taken over by sensational destructiveness. Crow is a persona that allows the poet complete detachment:

> a black rainbow
> Bent in emptiness
> over emptiness
> But flying

Flying, it is true, but only to feed on the carrion. The blackness, the visceral violence, the repetitive screeching, the crudeness: it is not enough to state, as Hughes does in a recent interview with Egbert Faas (*London Magazine*, January 1971), that the violence that produces a sordid nightmare murder for T.V. could in another way produce great moments in Beethoven, and expect that to justify these poems. It is not force in itself that I or the rational sceptic is afraid of: it is the relentless, hopeless numbness of the Crow utterances, without range and without the possibility of renewal. Consider "A Grin":

> There was this hidden grin.
> It wanted a permanent home. It tried faces
> In their forgetful moments, the face for instance
> Of a woman pushing a baby out between her legs
> But that didn't last long the face
> Of a man so preoccupied
> With the flying steel in the instant
> Of the car-crash he left his face
> To itself that was even shorter, the face
> Of a machine-gunner a long burst not long enough and
> The face of the steeplejack the second
> Before he hit the paving, the faces
> Of two lovers in the seconds
> They got so far into each other they forgot
> Each other completely that was O.K.
> But none of it lasted.

Here the cynical preoccupation with the momentary agony, the purely physical sensation of birth, death and copulation (in many ways indistinguishable here), is like the photographer using shock tactics to show us "the truth" about the human condition. Inwardly he is inert. The poet of "A Grin" is also the poet of "Pike", perfect killers with "the aged malevolent grin".

"Pike" is a poem much used by teachers to stimulate children into using their imagination. As a precursor to *Crow*, look again at the poem: Hughes invites us to admire their "delicacy and horror", their dancing and their stillness, but above all the perfection of the killer's weapon and "life subdued to its instrument". The anecdotal section puts the instrument into practice:

> Finally one
> With a sag belly and the grin it was born with.
> And indeed they spare nobody
> . . . . . .
> One jammed past its gills down the other's gullet.

Good description and the elusive dream darkness at the end, we say, but apart from the iron staring eye of the dead pike, there is nothing more than a mere assertion in this poem. The earlier stanzas depend upon ellipsis for their terseness; there's no truly poetic concentration here. The final stanzas are evocative but only of a creepy atmosphere, not a precise experience: in this respect there is something of Dylan Thomas about the poem.

Assertion is not the energy of poetry: realism is not a substitute for the image. The observation of "Pike" is in much the same category as the new picture book by the van Lawick-Goodalls, *Innocent Killers* (Collins), sensational kills by wild dogs, hyenas and jackals – a vicarious delight in killing. "Hawk Roosting", another one of the most popular poems with teachers, evinces the complacency of the perfected predator, unevasive, direct "through the bones of the living", killing where he pleases. It is a very simple piece of verse in bold but unevocative language. Children get a strong thrill reading it – "My manners are tearing off heads" (fear and delight). Of this poem Hughes has said:

... what I had in mind was that in this hawk Nature is thinking. Simply Nature. It's not so simple maybe because Nature is no longer simple. I intended some Creator like the Jehovah in Job but more feminine. When Christianity kicked the devil out of Job what they actually kicked out was

Nature ... and Nature became the devil. He doesn't sound like Isis, mother of the gods, which he is. He sounds more like Hitler's familiar spirit. There is a line in the poem almost verbatim from Job. (*London Magazine*, January 1971)

The poem as a poem is not invested with the weight that Hughes suggests is there, because like much of his poetry it is assertive rather than associative; it has the qualities of good prose, which is another reason why teachers use it and children read it.

Ted Hughes is against falsity, especially false writing. In *Poetry in the Making* he condemns the practice of asking children to copy Keats or Milton in their own writing:

All falsities in writing – and the consequent dry-rot that spreads into the whole fabric – come from the notion that there is a stylistic ideal which exists in the abstract, like a special language, to which all men might attain.

He offers new models instead. In the chapter "Writing about people" he recommends Keith Douglas's "Behaviour of Fish in an Egyptian Tea-Garden", a stylish performance with clever metaphor but not profound, and primarily exhibiting detachment; Philip Larkin's "Mr. Bleaney", flat and homiletic; and Hughes's own chip serenade, "Her Husband". Against these uninspiring pieces (and they are presumably meant to inspire or stimulate children to write) Hughes does recommend "You're" by Sylvia Plath and "Elegy" by Theodore Roethke, which both have some warmth and vitality (in the accepted sense) of people writing as they want to about others in a sympathetic way.

Cutting children off from the literary tradition of England may free them from certain stylistic inhibitions, as Hughes intends, but it also leaves them severed from the accumulation of poetry that is distinctively English in terms of cultural growth. This is a falsity, because Hughes, while acknowledging his own debt to Shakespeare, Lawrence, Blake and others, would make available to children mainly modern poets drawn from a wide sweep across Europe and America, in an attempt to keep them free from "the terrible suffocating, maternal octopus of ancient English poetic tradition". He believes in the internationality of poetry – "a universal language of understanding" – but unlike Pound he seems to have no historical view.

In his anthology of modern English poets *Here Today*, he claims that what matters in poetry "is that we hear the dance and song in the words. The dance and song engage the deepest roots of our minds and carry the poet's words down into our depths." And yet among the poets in this selection the only one with a memorable song and dance is Charles Causley; the "music" of "Au Jardin des Plantes" is borrowed from Lawrence and weakened; R. S. Thomas, John Arden, Adrian Mitchell and James Michie have a distinctive tone to them; but the rest are either songless and danceless or modish bits of doggerel such as Kingsley Amis's "Autobiographical Fragment":

> When I lived down in Devonshire
> The callers at my cottage
> Were Constant Angst, the art critic,
> And old Major Courage

or empty verses like "Disturbances" by Anthony Thwaite:

> After the darkness has come
> And the distant planes catch fire
> In the dusk, coming home ...

Listen to the records which accompany the book, and I think the weaknesses are clear enough. To what extent Hughes himself was responsible for the selection is a matter for conjecture, but from his introduction, it is clear that he has totally misjudged the quality of this anthology of modernity, while at the same time lending it the support of his name.

So far I have been concerned with the poetry of Hughes that has been used with children and the selections Hughes has made for educational purposes from the works of others. The poetry he has written for children is in a distinctive style of fantasy and surrealism. *Meet My Folks!* is the nearest he has come to writing about people close to him, and although he has acknowledged the difficulty of writing about certain close relationships – in his case, his mother – one has to admit that the results are a curious mixture of lolloping rhymes. They are too particularized to have any universality, and yet there's hardly a hint of feeling towards the characters he writes about. These are, he says in *Poetry in the Making*, not his real relatives but invented ones. In one way Hughes is suggesting that children (and he himself) should disguise their family pen-portraits to minimize embarrassment; in another way he is implying that you can be more honest under a veneer of invention. So "My Sister Jane" is a portrait of a crow:

> At meals whatever she sees she'll stab it –
> Because she's a crow and that's a crow habit.

There is something harsh in these lines both in sound and sense, that is at variance with the jokey style of semi-nonsense. "All these poems are a sort of joke," he says; "... The best jokes are about real things and real people: one does not have to be fantastic." It would seem that Hughes does need to be fantastic to cope with real people, but the results are not a success. It is true that children enjoy the momentary meeting with these poems, but they are not likely to return to them as they are to Lear or Old Possum because there is virtually no sympathetic power in them. In *The Earth-Owl and Other Moon-People* Hughes explores a surrealist landscape inhabited by the creepy and the deeply disturbing fears at the bottom of dreams: the phantasmagoric ambience has a dream reality that every child knows, but the preoccupation or obsession with animal energy and its corollary of human weakness stands out crudely and with a strangely didactic note, not really as good as Swift. On this moon, earthly order is inverted: in the "Moon Man-hunt" when foxes have the upper hand, man writhes in fear:

The sweat jumps on his brow freezingly and the hair stands on his thighs.
His lips writhe, his tongue fluffs dry as a duster, tears pour from his eyes.
His bowels twist like a strong snake, and for some seconds he sways there
    useless with terrified surprise.

As a piece of verse, whether for children or adults, this is obsessionally narrow and heavy-handed, and in a way sadistic.

The paradox of Ted Hughes is that on one side he has been promoting creativity in children's writing and emphasizing the vitality of his own verse, while on the other he shows little sympathy for humanity and tends towards a narrower and blacker view of life to the point of chaos. Here, I think, is the nature of Hughes's influence: momentarily it is for a burst of creativity, without any sustaining power; there is no development or growth of his poetry, but a fierce burning-out.

The references for titles mentioned in this article are incorporated with those for Brian Morse's article and appear on page 125.

Poetry, Children and Ted Hughes

BRIAN MORSE

Brian Morse had recently received an Eric Gregory Poetry Award when he wrote this response to John Adams's article for the September 1971 SIGNAL. He is now a primary school teacher in the West Midlands and has just published his first full-length children's novel.

A guiding myth of our time is that art – "good art" – humanizes, the case that it *should* being linked to the unproven hypothesis that it *can* or *does*. The impassioned work of men like George Steiner would seem to have gone much of the way towards exploding this concept. Art makes us aware, opens up possibilities of behaviour and attitude, gives us insight into our own lives and others': it may make us better lovers or philanthropists or citizens; as likely it will make us better murderers or torturers or thieves. The same set of circumstances may debase one man or enlighten another.

Horrifying as it may seem, that is precisely what Steiner's historical research suggests, and in face of such a conclusion the artist cannot be held responsible for the deficiencies or limitations of his fellow citizens. Even the clearest writers can be misread – and have been, and will be. The most obvious case of a connection between a corrupt society and its artists (Steiner's case, in fact) is Nazi Germany, the Germany not only of Nietzsche and Wagner but of Beethoven, Goethe, and Schiller. The more noble the vision, the farther the fall: which suggests that, in the area of literature vis-à-vis its public, there is no certainty of cause and effect, particularly if we are going to talk about the moral validity of its message. All a writer can do is be as unambivalent as possible, and then *hope* he is read properly. This is as likely to operate on the level of the individual – child or adult – as on the level of whole societies, for the reading of, say, a poem involves much more than the mere fact of the poem.

To mention the name of Ted Hughes in this context may seem, on the face of it, ridiculous, except that the judgements John Adams made in his article in the last SIGNAL, "Dark Rainbow: Reflections on Ted Hughes", were based directly on the assumptions Steiner so devastatingly questions. Mr. Adams contended that the vitality of Hughes's poetry is spurious and exhibits a cynical and negative view of life such as denies man his full humanity. He locates the evidence for this aberration in Hughes's latest book, *Crow*, inferring it to be a natural development from the earlier books, *The Hawk in the Rain* and *Lupercal*, which are widely used in teaching children. Not content with saying that, due to the view of life Hughes propounds, his poetry is bad for children, Mr. Adams also used the same grounds of attitude to experience (the alleged cynicism) to condemn the poems as bad literature and to claim that in some way they are a betrayal (particularly with regard to their affinity to certain East European poets) of "The Tradition". Apart from the question whether Mr. Adams's reading of Hughes is correct, the article did not seem to me to have considered whether the danger would, in any case, really lie in the attitude expressed rather than in the *way* it is expressed, and led me inescapably to question the grounds upon which we choose or censor poetry for children.

If art has any purpose, it is to supply a ritual need for the imaginative exploration of our surroundings and emotions and to enhance the quality of the exploration. Though nothing, of course, guarantees the use to which such a liberation of the mind is put, the better the literature the better this function is performed. And since art always operates in the context of a life history, a classroom, a contemporary culture, and since all that it can truthfully be said to do is strengthen our awareness of this context, it seems to me that when we question whether or not a piece of art is "good" for children, goodness ought to lie in the specifically literary merits: quality of imagination, sense of language, rhythm, choice of imagery, clarity and control of thought. These, more than the subject, are the hallucinatory, the beguiling elements in a work of literature: these are what shape the mind and it is here we should be looking for our positives.

Apart from the obviously traumatic or incomprehensible, what, above all, we should *not* be giving children is the boring, the second-rate, the confused, the outworn, the shrill – anything that will kill an interest in literature or muddy one's reactions to it. These, like our popular trash art, are more corrupting to the imaginative life than violence intelligently placed and articulated. Regardless even of difficulty, a clearly controlled work of art will, on any level, always lay bare more for our inspection than its opposite.

Boring, second-rate, confused: these things Hughes's poems are not; and, as it happens, they do not seem to me to be cynical either. There does indeed lie beneath the realistic surface of the poems in *The Hawk in the Rain* and *Lupercal* a thought-out and deeply felt attitude to experience that is perhaps harsh, perhaps pessimistic, perhaps in the face of an immovable object even cynical – but not one that cancels out the poems' immediacy and word-vitality. His latest volume, *Crow*, deals with certain kinds of suffering and despair which, for certain people, cannot be subsumed by adopting the traditional stance of benevolent scepticism, and before which it is not possible to remain perpetually ironic and reasonable. I would argue that Hughes's estimate of human nature is not warped, but very much more sane and realistic than Mr. Adams would have us believe; and that precisely because, with great skill, he gives the "grand ideals" a straight look in these later poems, his poetry is interesting and, in the context of a wider view of ourselves, important. I would also argue that Hughes's poetry prompts us to look at our idea of The Tradition, particularly with regard to children, in the light of what it has meant to British poetry in the last thirty years.

This might be the place to point out that, in any case, poetry is a highly controlled way of communicating intuitive truths, not a moral regulator. Rarely does "the good writer" – or "the good man" – operate by a moral logic. Health and sickness, in these terms, sometimes waver uncertainly in the writing of Shakespeare, Pope, Swift, Lawrence, Eliot, Pound, to name but a few. Some seem to regard art as a superior form of reality; first and foremost it is *another person's* idea of reality.

*

In the matter of poetry for children we too often pay a back-handed compliment to its "powerful magic" by accepting a sort of lowest common denominator verse, thereby giving the idea that poetry really is boring, twee, sissy, the kind of ethereal thing you need an ethereal, unworldly spirit to get anything out of. Objectively, the gap between the kind of literary experience the child is probably being dished up at school and what in real life he's already experienced, or knows about at second-hand (not just sex, but the whole gamut of human behaviour), is likely to be great. So by being too careful, we gut literature and remove its immediacy and distinctiveness; and if you put a child off "good literature", he will fill the imaginative vacuum with television or comics. Or rather, most children are doing that anyway. It's a matter of bringing them back.

The least role literature can perform in the classroom is to be the place where a child meets the harder facts of reality (pleasant and unpleasant) – ideally better than the television parlour of adman's fantasy where he has no means of reacting beyond the age's tendency to present life and history as a kind of sensationalized package holiday. But having decided that it can fulfil this function in education, what literature is going to answer the need?

It is dangerous to assume too quickly: "The Tradition". Today we have something of the difficulty (though of a different kind) in reading the classics of English literature that we have in reading a dead language. Not that The Tradition *is* dead, but we are far away from its themes, its ideals, its proprieties, even – and especially – its language. Otherwise we wouldn't continually be listing up its qualities on our fingers. The sheer fact that we have not produced a great *English* writer since Lawrence implies that what our relationship to The Tradition *might be* needs some serious thinking. It is not sufficiently realized how much we have to learn to read, say, Shakespeare or Keats – not for exam purposes, which is comparatively easy, but in order to reach any significant rapport with the play or poem. How difficult, then, for a child of this age, without the Bible, the classics, without any particular belief in the good or just society, to get a clear, distinctive experience from his reading. What we need is a way into literature; providing it is of quality, it ought, then, to be contemporary in language and contemporary in spirit. Is the essential question to ask, as John Adams does, where it comes from?

We live in a society that, apparently, is concerned only with its external trappings (although it has a tendency to talk about spiritual values), post-Christian, space-age. We inhabit what McLuhan calls a global village: as much as the adult the child will be aware of carnage in Vietnam, civil war in Ulster, mental illness. He is probably living in some awful town or city. He is assailed by the images of the consumer society.

What I am arguing is that the literature he reads ought to be giving him an experience equally distinctive and be articulating at least a part of what he feels and knows about. Not literature that shocks, but literature that takes its place with vividness beside the headlines. By no means is this kind of literature necessarily about war, violence and corruption: it will need to be known by virtue of its language, imagination, emotional intensity, clarity of thought, immediacy of theme. If the subject is contemporary, it need not be so in the obvious way. Hughes's poetry is a good example: though about nature, it has the feel of the present, of being written in history. Like another poet's, Rimbaud's, Hughes's poems often share the sharp perception and intensity of childhood, flooded with energy, occasionally without discrimination, but reflecting a man who does not run away from his deepest experiences.

Art goes dead when it is cut off from the real sources of the poet's awareness, what he feels and suffers most strongly, and this is surely true, too, of the reader who in confusion retreats into escapism. Something of the sort has happened to British poetry in recent years: it has fallen back on being literary, or self-deprecatory, or on mimicking other times and places. (It was sad that, in criticizing Hughes, Mr. Adams could offer no substitute for Hughes's educational role.) Our poetry is no longer confident to risk the large gestures, the large themes. The appeal of the Liverpool Scene poets was not only their boyishness and youthful seriousness, but the sheer fact of talking – or seeming to talk – straight from the heart.

Hughes himself has something to say on the subject. In his

introduction to the poems of the Yugoslavian, Vasko Popa, he wrote:

Their poetry [Popa's, Herbert's, Holub's] seems closer to the common reality, in which we have to survive, than to those other realities in which we can holiday, or into which we decay when our bodily survival is comfortably taken care of, and which art, particularly contemporary art, is forever trying to impose on us as some sort of superior dimension. I think it was Milosz, the Polish poet, who when he lay in the doorway and watched the bullets lifting the cobbles out of the street beside him realized that most poetry is not equipped for life in a world where people actually do die. But some is.

It would be misleading to think that the poets Hughes admires are exclusively concerned with war, concentration camps, and the evils of the totalitarian state. Without embarrassment or artifice their real themes are those that elude English art at the moment: love, death, courage, honesty, beauty.

Mr. Adams quoted Hughes as saying about himself, "Maybe if I didn't live in England I wouldn't be driven to extremes to writing about animals." It is this contradiction between our complacent institutions and civilized assumptions, and the energy inside us that erupts at times in subtle or not so subtle violence (because essential man never comes quite to terms with the world he creates) that Hughes feels more strongly than most. Hughes went on to say about these East European poets:

They have had to live out, in actuality, a vision which for artists elsewhere is a prevailing shape of things but only brokenly glimpsed through the clutter of our civilized liberal confusion.

In attempting *his* escape from our "civilized liberal confusion" Hughes has, however, not lapsed into chaos, as Mr. Adams asserted. Instead, in an age where atrocity and outrage are presented with the same bland intensity as an advert for baked beans, he substitutes a suitably stripped-down version of man, the man of *Wodwo*, the man of *Crow*. When all the glitter is stripped away, this is the version we live with and which history teaches us to live with; but it does not strand us high and dry with the stench of corruption and cynicism: it makes love, faith, compassion, bravery more meaningful – even if unexpected. Children are as emotionally aware of these things as adults and want to meet them articulated.

So it is futile to discuss literature for children except in the context of "the present situation".

It would be futile to deny that there is a great deal of violence in Hughes's poetry, or that the poems draw much of their immediacy from the "vitality" (sheer violence in Mr. Adams's reading) of the animals. Yet the point is that Hughes writes about it in clear, simple language – language the children can understand – and his attitude is not so simple as pure admiration. He draws a meaningful distinction between beast and man which shows that man is more likely to be shocked and revealed by the animal than to be helplessly paralysed by its "efficiency". For the progression from *The Hawk in the Rain* to *Crow* is not a gratuitous one: Hughes has always been moving towards a direct vision of man, pessimistic but not warped.

In the title poem of *Wodwo* Hughes writes about a man who is hardly yet other than an animal, but human in the crucial sense of possessing self-consciousness and intellect. Probably, in this inverted hero, we will scarcely recognize ourselves. But all the same, it is an honest description. We are used to meeting ourselves mirrored in "those other realities in which we can holiday". It would be a mistake to mix this up with simple cynicism, the attempt "to do the dirty on life". It is rather a realism open to all possibilities, not closed to uncomfortable facts. *Crow*, which follows *Wodwo*, is a direct development along these lines. The wodwo's distinctive quality was to "go on": "Very queer but I'll go on looking" – not only the physical search but the intellectual questing. For the wodwo is carrying out the most primitive of philosophical investigations: "What am I?" It is struck with surprise that it can control its own actions, that it is not controlled *by* them:

> Do these weeds
> know me and name me to each other have they
> seen me before, do I fit in their world? I seem
> separate from the ground and not rooted but dropped
> out of nothing casually I've no threads
> fastening me to anything I can go anywhere
> I seem to have been given the freedom
> of this place what am I then?

It has an amazed delight in its freedom – "I've no threads / fastening me to anything I can go anywhere" – and while one has the sense that it really is going to rush off and answer all these big questions ("I suppose I am the exact centre": echoes of "Hawk Roosting"?), one also realizes that it is acting out a peculiarly universal and tragic drama: as well as wodwo it is also, potentially, Oedipus or Lear or modern man trapped by the uncertain gifts of his intellect. One is reminded of Hughes's adaptation of Seneca's *Oedipus*: "'I will find the answer' is that an answer?" Or its opposite, the trapped rat of "Song of a Rat", which

> ... pants

> And cannot think
> "This has no face, it must be God" or

> "No answer is also an answer"

The wodwo, which has barely crossed the borderline between animal and man, is clearly distinguished by its desire to "go on looking". On the other hand, the animals with their "vitality" are unconscious and volitionless. They live in a moral vacuum. Hughes is quoted as saying: "The animals are continually in a state of energy which men only have when they've gone mad. This strength arises from their complete unity with whatever divinity they have."

The poem "Thrushes" from *Lupercal* clearly brings out the distinction. The thrush is "more coiled steel than living", it has "bullet and automatic purpose". It has an

> efficiency which
> Strikes too streamlined for any doubt to pluck at it
> Or obstruction deflect.

While the animal is only responsible to its automatic behaviour patterns (as the shark in the quest for blood will even devour itself), in the same poem man's characteristic is his self-consciousness and its perils: his acts are pitched against the background of heaven and hell, aware of it at the same time that he is aware that deep in him he is linked with the animal.

This link is not violence in any simple aspect, for man has been utterly changed by his knowledge. The animal's vitality in man is the disturbing repressed energy in his make-up which at opposite extremes can fuel art or war, love or murder. For man is inevitably out of touch with nature. When he is not messing about with or preying on it, he is discomposed or shocked by his vision of the beast. In "The Bull Moses" the man perched on the barn door takes

> ... a sudden shut-eyed look
> Backward into the head.

As his eyes become accustomed to the darkness inside, he sees emerging as though out of the depths of space and history

> Something come up there onto the brink of the gulf,
> Hadn't heard of the world, too deep in itself
> to be called to,
> Stood in sleep.

But far from being aggressive the stud bull has been tamed

> ... as if he knew nothing
> Of the ages and continents of his fathers,

and Hughes's response to this is a vision of great sadness for the animal's loss:

> He would raise
> His streaming muzzle and look out over the meadows,
> But the grasses whispered nothing awake, the fetch
> Of the distance drew nothing to momentum
> In the locked black of his powers.

Though the bull has not shown a glimmer of recognition of his presence, for the man there is symbolically only one conclusion when the animal is led back in by the farmer:

> I kept the door wide,
> Closed it after him and pushed the bolt.

– shutting in not only the bull but his own half-articulated fears, as if he and not the bull were the repository of some sacred knowledge.

From a different point of view, in the last poem from *Five Autumn Songs for Children's Voices*, we have an emblematic vision of man's petty destructive forces encroaching upon the animal world. It is raining, and while on the road the farmers cause a traffic jam and inside the cars

... the kids inside cried and daubed their chocolate and fought
And mothers and aunts and grandmothers
Were a tangle of undoing sandwiches and screwed-round gossiping heads
Steaming up the windows,

the stag that is being hunted runs through his "private forest". The sodden huntsmen feel "rather foolish" until suddenly the hounds catch the stag's scent and the world becomes strange for the animal.

> The blue horsemen on the bank opposite
> Pulled aside the camouflage of their terrible planet.

Significantly the poem does not describe the actual kill, but ends with the crowd, whose representatives are the apocalyptic "blue horsemen". They

> got back into their cars
> Wet-through and disappointed,

because presumably they have missed seeing their vicarious thrill.

This is a point of contact between human and animal that Hughes concentrates on, not man's envy of their violence. As he has said in *Poetry in the Making*: "About fifteen my life grew more complicated and my attitude to animals changed. I accused myself of disturbing their lives. I began to look at them from their own point of view." So, in "An Otter", the animal

> Yanked above hounds, reverts to nothing at all,
> To this long pelt over the back of a chair.

It is a consistent attitude of reproach, for Hughes's animals, as he presents them, are neither pets nor hunting trophies nor zoo animals, but the genuine wild beast and thriving on their wildness. They are described with the loving care of the nature-lover conveying the fascination of something that has a life and beauty of its own: and which, shut up in a matchbox or a jam jar or a stall – or indeed in a poem – to make a pet of, is destroyed. On the other hand it is not a sentimental vision: it does not tell you that animals are better than men, but places them for what they are. If the animal violence is not presented in conjunction with moral outrage, the reason is that the animal is volitionless and cannot measure its actions; not because Hughes has been paralysed by it. The "blue horsemen" and "their terrible planet" are inside *us*.

"Wodwo", the poem, dealt with a creature who has just become man, and *Wodwo*, the volume, represents a period in Hughes's poetry when the focus of attention is changing from the animal to man. For only gradually has Hughes begun to talk about man with the vigour and lucidity of the animal poems. As if unable to gain sufficient distance from his subject, he had an early tendency to lecture and hector: take away the object to be *seen* – the animal – and he was too often left with an abstract conception to embody and the result was programmatic assertion, a failure and boredom of language. With *Wodwo* this began to change, and it must be emphasized the *Wodwo* (less known in the classroom than the previous books) is probably his finest collection so far. Many of the poems have the genuine kind of difficulty that increases our appreciation with every additional reading, sharing the vividness but little of the simplicity of the earlier poems. The language has a sensuous apprehension of reality with a nearer counterpart in Keats than the rich but undirected texture of Dylan Thomas (Mr. Adams's suggestion), more resonant and full of associations than the occasional prose flatness of *The Hawk in the Rain* and *Lupercal*. There is a large conception of form, a freed sense of rhythm with some of the flexibility of Biblical prose or Middle English alliterative verse – a more complete escape from the iambic pentameter than English derivations of recent American experimentation. The vivid imagery, richer rhythms, concrete detail and drama of the situation, relying more on the image to do the work than the bare statement, bring him to a point where he seems able to think through his verse, rather than talking straight at us and seeming obvious and awkward in the process.

Although the manner is very different, *Crow* continued the process *Wodwo* began, the change of emphasis from beast to human kind. *Crow* is Hughes's attempt to draw together in an epic folk tale the two strands of his poetry, human and animal, in what is, in effect, an alternative and non-Christian interpretation of history, a reworking of the Biblical stories and other mythical moments of

human crisis. The crow protagonist undergoes all the suffering –
and more – that Hughes usually associates with human existence,
and as a symbol, or just as an experiencer, has all the advantages
of being mythical and unreal and therefore flexible. Occasionally
the crow is an irritating hook on which to hang the theology –
in the better poems one may find oneself ignoring its presence; but
it is a symbol and a way of giving the narrative direction rather
than, as Mr. Adams suggests, allowing the poet "complete
detachment", and therefore complete freedom to indulge his cynicism and repudiate the richness of life. If the method is to shock
by a surrealist accumulation of detail and a rougher technique than
in *Wodwo*, the intention, again, is not so simple as to degrade.

Crow lies a little aside from the debate about poetry for children,
being an illustration of poems which have too much emotional
complexity to be readily appreciated. Since, however, it is closely
connected with the conception of man in the earlier books, I would
like to look at a few examples where, from Mr. Adams's reading,
one would expect him to be most cynical. For what is really unusual
about *Crow* is that the facts of birth, life and death are not encapsu-
lated in the normal relieving vision of hope and abstract affirmation.
Hope, love and faith are facts too.

See these lines on the dying Christ from "The Smile":

> And the crowd, shoving to get a glimpse of a man's soul
> Stripped to its last shame,
> Met this smile
> That rose through his torn roots
> Touching his lips, altering his eyes
> And for a moment
> Mending everything
>
> Before it swept out and away across the earth.

Or these, from "Notes for a Little Play", a poem about nuclear
war: two survivors, mutations,

> ... sniff towards each other in the emptiness.
>
> They fasten together. They seem to be eating each other.
>
> But they are not eating each other.

They do not know what else to do.

They have begun to dance a strange dance.

And this is the marriage of these simple creatures –
Celebrated here, in the darkness of the sun,

Without guest or God.

The detachment in the following lines, from "Crow's Account of the Battle", allows the "facts" to speak for themselves. In the context, moralizing would be self-indulgent, and in any case the texture of the verse makes it unnecessary.

The bullets pursued their courses
Through clods of stone, earth and skin,
Through intestines, pocket-books, brains, hair, teeth
According to Universal laws.
And mouths cried "Mamma"
From sudden traps of calculus,
Theorems wrenched men in two,
Shock-severed eyes watched blood
Squandering as from a drain-pipe
Into the blanks between stars.

Presumably because of the poem's visionary, myth-making aspects, many of the reviewers compared the author of *Crow* to Blake. Despite their sophistication and knowingness, the people of Hughes's poems do have a kind of innocence, the innocence of

very queer but I'll go on looking.

This is a poetry without dogma; and – because of that – the kind of poetry we want for children.

John Adams's postscript in 1979: There are, I admit, some indestructible things about Ted Hughes's poetry. For one, his subject is indestructible, matters of life and death, the kind of basics that don't date and don't change. For another, his language and his images, which have that hard-nosed, specific, concrete quality, don't get easily destroyed by time or use either. And for another – the thing I find most surprising and reassuring – the fact that he is still writing poetry at all. Ten years ago I thought he was at the point of burning himself out, but since then in what he has written and what he is writing now there are some fascinating changes of direction and assumption even though the best and distinctive qualities of Hughes's work remain unchanged.

And what a range of work he has done in that time: just look at it. There is his version of Seneca's *Oedipus*, his experiments with Peter Brook into practical dramatic use of primitive and universal language (Orghast); there's his (as he called it) "alchemical cave drama" *Cave Birds* in collaboration with artist Leonard Baskin, a book of poetry, originally intended for children, *Season Songs*; there's *Gaudete*, a sequence which, we're told, was originally designed as a film scenario about a changeling clergyman although it could easily be read as a radio drama; there's *Moon-Bells and Other Poems* in the Chatto Poets for the Young series and winner of the first Signal Poetry Award; *Remains of Elmet*, a sequence about the Pennines in collaboration with photographer Fay Godwin, and in the autumn of 1979 *Moortown*, a verse journal on his experience of farming in Devon. Add to that his selection of Shakespeare's verse, another of Emily Dickinson's, his own selection, 1957–67, and his work for the Arvon foundation on creative writing and you are faced with the fact that Ted Hughes continues to be a strong and inescapable presence in poetry in Britain.

It would be unrealistic at this point to try to gauge what kind of influence he has proved to be but what is clear is that some of his earlier work for children, like *Meet My Folks!*, is enjoyed for its fun and vitality far more than I once thought likely – as its reissue in 1977 as a Puffin paperback testifies along with the response of some children I know who don't usually enjoy poems (they say) but find this book "very good". And *The Iron Man* has established itself as part of the storehouse of children's storytelling, a bit of myth-creation that has really worked. The success of *How the Whale Became*, however, is perhaps best evidenced by the experience of teachers in a part of our country where religion is still a destructive force: its use in a primary class is enough to damn a teacher as unfit to educate young minds.

But apart from those teachers who are trading their God-fearing careers against the revelation, through Hughes, of the mysteries of evolution to nine-year-olds, what are we exposing children to in Hughes's more recent work? Since the zero-point of *Crow*, that "black rainbow", I think there has been a shift, broadly speaking, in the relation of the poet to his subject so that his perceptions of life and death no longer have that objective concentration upon the momentary and the sensational which leads to annihilation. Instead I think there's a much more affective role that the poet gives himself in his own poetry, and this is particularly evident in his work for children. In *Season Songs*, for instance, there is a piece called "December River", in which he looks for salmon.

> ... So, day in day out, this whole summer
> I offered all I had for a touch of their wealth –
> I found only endlessly empty water.
>
> But I go now, in near-darkness,
> Frost, and close to Christmas, and am admitted
> To glance down and see, right at my heel,
> A foot under, where backwater mills rubbish,
> Like a bleached hag laid out – the hooked gape
> And gargoyle lobster-claw grab
>
> Of a dead salmon, and its white shirt-button eye.
>
> That grimace
> Of getting right through to the end and beyond it –
> That helm
> So marvellously engineered
>
> Discarded, an empty stencil.
> A negative, pale
> In the dreggy swirlings
> Of earth's already beginning mastication ...

The dramatic moment of this poem readily brings to mind "Pike", and although the mythology that surrounds each fish is quite different, there is an attention to similar detail – the grin grimace, the eye, the gape: what is markedly different is the poet's interpretation of these things within the poem – "That grimace / Of getting right through to the end and beyond it"; and later,

> As I lifted its child-heavy rubbery bulk
> Marbled crimson like an old woman's fire-baked thigh.

These are images and associations of a familiar and family world that we can share. I find it reassuring to realize that Hughes, after all, does belong to a tradition of English poetry, which in part includes Wordsworth and Coleridge, and to see him recognizing that tradition implicitly in his work. Poems like "Mackerel Song" and "The Harvest Moon" show another development of Hughes, a new sense of humour, not a black humour but in the first a nice sense of self-parody and in the latter a kind of friendly surrealism. The *Moon-Bells* collection, too, contains similar work, emphasizing the witty lunatic theme and better, I think, than the earlier *Earth-Owl and other Moon-People*. I am also aware that the very elements that I find humanizing and strengthening in Hughes's work can, when done less successfully, make the poetry slip into sentimentality. Now I've been educated to think that sentimentality is a Bad Thing and to be avoided at all costs. The cost I find is too high: the merely human are necessarily sentimental at times and when Hughes's poetry, as in "Tigress", slides into the sentimental in the last couple of lines –

> I look into her almond eyes. She frowns
> Them shut, the fur moving down on her brows.

I can take it; but when it lurches into the pious, as it does in "The Golden Boy" (from *Season Songs*) I can't.

Remains of Elmet, the most recently available work at the time of writing, I find in many ways the most interesting. It's a very bold thing for a poet to do, to share a book with a photographer, because photographs, particularly the sharply dramatic black and white photos by Fay Godwin, tend to have a more immediate appeal than poems, even sharply dramatic poems like Ted Hughes's. But I think it's a success because both poems and photos bear the imprint of people working and living in a particular place during a particular period. The book, which records a society in an historical dimension, is a long way forward from the trap of a Yorkshire childhood which, to some extent, imprisoned Hughes's earlier thinking about his past. It's one of the less useful parts of the Romantic tradition, I think, that it overvalues the individual experience of childhood at the expense of the wider, and more significant, social experience. In many of these poems Hughes uses his childhood memories but goes beyond them. The industrial experience, and relics, in a predominantly rural context is the experience of a significant part of Britain's population, and Hughes reminds us in his introduction that the Calder Valley, his principal subject, was the "cradle for the Industrial Revolution in textiles", and became "the hardest-worked river in England". His poems, and the photos, highlight the decay and impotence of a once vigorous industrial community.

John Wain, in his citation on Hughes's winning of the Signal Poetry Award (S I G N A L, May 1979), describes the life that the poet "confronts through his rural imagery" as "raw and unmistakable, life as it might be lived on the factory floor or in the roaring traffic canyons of a city". It seems to me that the life Hughes is confronting in *Remains of Elmet* is not part of this greenfield versus factory floor approach (*life as it might be lived*): it belongs, I suggest, to a more realistic tradition of looking at one's origins, here a Pennine industrial valley, and recognizing the forces that have shaped the people who live and work there:

> Something that was fingers and
> Slavery and religious, reflects sky.

This, I think, could be a useful direction for Hughes's work to take, a direction that will be helpful to both children and adults.

Books by Ted Hughes referred to and/or quoted from in the articles by John Adams and Brian Morse; Faber and Faber and Viking Penguin: *Cave Birds* (1972), *The Earth-Owl and Other Moon-People* (1963) [USA *Moon Whales and Other Moon Poems* (1976)], *Season Songs* (1976); Faber and Faber and Harper and Row: *Crow* (1971, 1972), *Gaudete* (1977), *The Hawk in the Rain* (1957), *Lupercal* (1960), *The Iron Man* (1968) (USA *The Iron Giant*), *Moortown* (1979), *Remains of Elmet* (1979), *Wodwo* (1967); Faber and Faber and Atheneum Publishers: *How the Whale Became* (1963); Faber and Faber and Doubleday & Company: *Poetry in the Making* (1967), *Seneca's Oedipus* (1969); Faber and Faber and Bobbs-Merrill: *Meet My Folks!* (1961); Chatto and Windus: *Moon-Bells and Other Poems* (1978). Ted Hughes's talk "Capturing Animals", originally broadcast on the BBC's Listening and Writing series, appears in *Poetry in the Making*. Hutchinson Educational: *Here Today* (1963).

SIGNAL QUOTES

Alan Tucker in "On Poetry and Children"
(Signal 1, January 1970)

It is fashionable to consider the universe a huge game in which all the pieces are illusions. Everything is conditional on everything else and only exists insofar as it can be compared with what it isn't. Language is the most effective way of making sense of such ideas, and poetry, with its multiple meanings and the clarity of its subtlety, is the most complex form of language. Poetry is a game that is too difficult for us, so we play it instinctively. It's time we took to studying its rules with full conscious attention. Instead we mislead children into thinking it's a lot of crap about fairies....

... It is said that the foetus lives through all the stages of evolution in its nine months of development. Since the external world "exists" only in our minds, we build awareness of it organically, as a process of growth. The child's appreciation of poetry will echo the historical growth of man's awareness of his environment. The earliest poems known are about men and society: the Epic of Gilgamesh, Homer, the biblical stories and myths. Nursery rhymes are similarly packed with heroes and hero legends: Jack Horner, Little Miss Muffet, the Queen of Hearts, and Lazy Nan. For a young child *people* demand first attention; they move against a misty background from which solid objects only intermittently loom. As children grow more perceptive, their attention is taken by animals, then by moving inanimate things: clouds, the wind, the sea, rain, trees and flowers. Parallel with the development of observation is the growth of language, and insofar as this relates to children and books, it is admirably described in Kornei Chukovsky's *From Two to Five* (University of California Press; C.U.P.). Children who have just begun to talk in phrases – and the phrase is the basic unit of language, not the word – use rhyme, assonance, repetition, to help them: "night-night" instead of "good-night"; "bye-bye" instead of "good-bye", and so on. Object/word, event/

phrase are learned together. This is a vast game, a confidence trick in which we have complete confidence. We laugh at inconsistencies in the system: when is a door not a door? When it's o-pun. Humour deals with double meanings, and seems to be a gift. Poetry deals with multiple meanings (and seems to be a rare gift). We have no absolutes. We learn to distinguish everything around us by painstaking comparison, an obvious process for the early years but one which the poet believes continues throughout life. Science compares by weighing and staring and prodding. The poet compares by describing: My love is like, My love is. The two methods spring from the same urge: to know; and both are essential. We cannot weigh an abstraction, but it exists, and we need poetry to get at its intangible reality....

...I believe children should never be offered anything that is either denatured or tarted up. A love of poetry comes effortlessly and naturally to all of us as part of the experience of language, of the very way we think. But this will be killed if we are misled at an impressionable age into thinking verse a matter of rhetoric, prettiness, and artificiality. When today's children move on to adult literature, few of them will be religious, even fewer capable of bringing the necessary scholarship and aptitude of mind to pure philosophy. The only useful contact they will have with great minds – or any mind at all – will be through literature. All the listening to music and looking at paintings of a lifetime cannot *make sense* with the explicitness of literature (and it is that final explicitness which is so difficult and essential to grasp). Everyday life does little to expand the mind, a fact that has also become true of travel on a globe where every city is metropolis. In its blundering, coy, silly-self-conscious way, poetry is the one form of literature that isn't written "to sell – and sell quickly" as Pound puts it. We should give our minds to it.

Griselda Greaves in "The Key of the Kingdom"
(Signal 30, September 1979)

The true poet lives through a chaos that most adults have chosen to shun. He sees connections within the chaos, which he translates into a form that is recognizable and bearable.... The small child is living through a continuous chaos, similar to that of the artist, and an emotional order is essential for his proper growth. This order is inherent in good poetry and, sensitively selected, is accessible to the small child. I am not advocating an unrelieved diet of metaphysics. I am suggesting that adults should not be frightened of reading to small children poems that may be considered "difficult". The child may well understand them better than the adult does.

From *Cakes and Custard*, Children's Rhymes
compiled by Brian Alderson and illustrated by Helen Oxenbury

Translator's Notebook

ANTHEA BELL

Anthea Bell is an award-winning translator specializing in French and German books for children and young people, with over sixty translations to her credit. Her one contribution to SIGNAL so far came in the January 1979 issue with a review article; the present article was written especially for this book.

"Corsica." We're confronting Goscinny and Uderzo's *Astérix en Corse*, my colleague Derek Hockridge and myself. "What would you say is the sum total of English general knowledge about Corsica?"

"Napoleon."

"And?"

"Napoleon, full stop."

Whereas the French have all sorts of inside knowledge and staple jokes about Corsica: wild pigs and chestnuts and ferociously smelly cheese; proud, aloof women jealously guarded by their menfolk; complicated family relationships and the vendetta. And then there's Tino Rossi, popular Corsican singer, mention of whose works permeates this book.

"What on earth are we going to do about Tino Rossi?"

Shelving Tino Rossi for the moment, we start tentatively playing with words. "We'll have to go nap on Napoleon." "And all things bony."

The differing degree of French and English general knowledge about the island is one reason why this title in the *Astérix* saga, published in 1973 in France, has waited until now for an English version. The translation of something which depends as much as *Astérix* on wordplay and puns has, in any event, to be very free, often more of an adaptation, if anything like the same humorous effect is to be produced in English. And if the material òn which the jokes are based is unfamiliar itself to the young English reader, there are extra problems. About half Asterix's fixtures against the Romans are played at home, so to speak, and half away. When it comes to the away matches, the French and English share a number of cherished notions about Daft Foreigners. Spain means bullfighting, flamenco, the tourist trade. Switzerland means numbered bank accounts, yodelling, fondue. But when the people of the little Armorican village which persists in defying Julius Caesar take him on nearer home, in other parts of Gaul – or here, in Corsica – the English reader is less likely to share the stock assumptions of the original.

There's another and related reason why this title has waited some time for a translation: the story features a grand reunion of the Gauls' friends from previous books, both foreigners from Britain, Spain, etc., and allies from other parts of Gaul who speak in French regional accents. Since the saga is firmly set in Gaul, with a map of France at the beginning of every book, we could hardly substitute English regional speech without destroying the precarious illusion upon which all translation is based. Give a man from Marseilles, say, a Mummerset accent, and we'd have readers stopping to wonder why. So some different type of joke must be found, since we're determined not to admit defeat and simply translate straight, losing the verbal byplay which, in every *Astérix* book, reinforces the basic humour of the story line. This has sometimes involved the rewriting of whole frames – in one case, of an entire page where the French jokes depended on an Auvergnat accent. (All done, needless to say, with the author's approval.) It was not until we had translated the titles where this problem arose, notably *Le Bouclier Arverne* (*Asterix and the Chieftain's Shield*) and *Le Tour de Gaule* (*Asterix and the Banquet*) that we could have characters from these books making a guest appearance in *Asterix in Corsica*.

"We'll have to substitute for those accents again, when they turn up for the party." The party in question is held to celebrate the anniversary of the famous Gaulish victory of Gergovia. We glance at the pages involved. "At least we have the Ancient British idiom fixed." To the French, of course, we too are Daft Foreigners, who drop everything for afternoon tea (*le five o'clock*), and tend to translate English phrases literally into French in our dreadful accent. We remember discussing with the late and sadly missed René Goscinny the way to try transferring this effect back into English, for *Asterix in Britain*. A fluent English speaker himself, and the most helpful and approachable of authors, he listened to and approved our suggestion that the only feasible solution was to adopt an exaggeratedly upper-crust, dated, Wodehousian style. "Jolly good show, old boy, eh what, old fruit...." "Ah!" said Goscinny suddenly. "Old fruit – that's nice, I wish I'd thought of that ... *vieux fruit*," he murmured happily. We treasure this as a golden memory: golden as the pear grown inside the bottle of pear brandy with which he was hospitably regaling us in his Paris flat.

"At least the great mint sauce joke doesn't come up again in this book." For naturally, we English consume mint sauce with everything. Mention mint sauce to the French and they fall about laughing. We muse now, briefly, on the great mint sauce joke. "Wonder where the French get it from?"

"Same place as we get the notion that they subsist on snails and frogs' legs, I suppose."

"You know something? They're selling lamb-and-mint-sauce flavoured crisps in the supermarket." We digest this, figuratively speaking. Perhaps we *are* Daft Foreigners, and the French aren't so wide of the mark....

Back to the problems of *Corsica*. Besides the French original, we have what might be called our translating kit around us. There's a folder labelled "Asterix – Names, Jokes, Oddments, Etc.", full of things that might come in useful some day. There are reference books. It's amazing how often people say, "But you're a translator; surely you don't need dictionaries?" Translators need the biggest, best dictionaries going. Translators wear out their dictionaries. Among our old faithfuls are *Walker's Rhyming Dictionary*, the *Oxford Dictionary of Quotations*, *Roget's Thesaurus*, and a new faithful, the new *Concise Oxford Dictionary*, easily the best of the Oxford English Dictionary range for this purpose, being the most up-to-date and colloq., as the entries put it. Any of these may set the mind jumping from word or phrase A in the original French, to a related subject, to word or phrase B which will provide a comparable bit of wordplay in English.

Invisible, but also with us, we have our basic principles for translating *Astérix*. If we stop to work them out, they're something like this:

a) The idea is to render, as faithfully as possible, the *feel* of the original.

b) With humour of this intensely verbal nature, the translation must follow the spirit rather than the letter of the original; we must therefore often find jokes which are different, though we hope along the same lines as the French jokes.

c) They must, of course, suit Albert Uderzo's wittily detailed drawings, in particular they must fit the expressions on the speakers' faces.

d) From the purely technical point of view, they must be about the same length as the original wording, or we shall create difficulties for the letterer trying to get the English text into the speech-bubbles.

e) Very important: we will try for the same kind of mixture of jokes as in the French, where Asterix appeals on a number of different levels. There's the story-line itself with its ever-attractive theme of the clever little fellow outwitting the hulking great brute; there is simple knockabout humour, both verbal and visual, which goes down well with quite young children; there are puns and passages of wordplay for older children; and there is some distinctly sophisticated humour, depending on literary or artistic allusion, for the adult or near-adult mind.

f) We will also have the same number of jokes as in the French. If we just can't get one in at the same point as in the original, we'll make up for it somewhere else. And we won't drag English jokes in by the hair of their heads, but if there is an obvious gift we'll use it, even if there was no counterpart in the French. (This, again, was done with the author's approval; up to the last two translations, with his personal go-ahead on the typescript of each English version.) Such a gift has been the fact that while the conventional French means of representing a hiccup is "Hips!" its English equivalent is "Hic!", so that drunken Roman legionaries can be allowed to hiccup in Latin: "Hic, haec, hoc." We are grateful to Gibbon, too, since in appropriate places the Romans may be seen declining and falling all over the place.

We were visited, once, by a young man earnestly studying our translations of *Astérix* for a mini-thesis, as part of his work at Nanterre University. He had assigned our versions of every single frame to one of four categories: *un gain, une perte, une équivalence, une compensation.* "You see," said he, "I am treating this like Shakespeare." He was, too; it was rather unnerving. But he certainly had the general idea.

"A lot of names here in *Corsica*." As with the jokes, the ingeniously spoof Gaulish and Roman names of Goscinny's characters, formed as they are of real French words and phrases, usually need rethinking in English. A few, like Stratocumulus, are all right in both languages, but most of the others have to be replaced. Our folder of oddments contains a list of Names Already Used, which we bring up to date after every title, for fear of repeating ourselves: a necessary precaution, as the list now runs to some two hundred and twenty names. By the time we're through with *Corsica* there will be about another thirty on it. We also have odd lists, made from time to time, of possible names *not* yet used. In the current story, Asterix and Obelix are off to help the Corsicans, whose names also end in -ix. Kind little boys write to us with suggestions for Gaulish names; in fact we're usually searching for more *Roman* names, since the basic Gaulish characters go on from book to book, but require a new set of Roman opponents to be polished off each time.

"Not so many Romans as usual in this book, actually. There's this centurion, Gazpachoandalus, early on." We are pleased when, like Goscinny, we can make a whole phrase into a Roman name (Sendervictorius and Appianglorius, a couple of Roman soldiers), but owing to the difference between the normal word order of noun and adjective in English and French, it is generally much harder to make up such compounds in English. We do, however, have quantities of English adjectives ending -ous, which can sometimes be used on their own to make a name approximating to its bearer's character (Insalubrius), or combined with a noun to give a Roman two names (Odius Asparagus). "He's a minor character, the centurion." We glance at Names Not Yet Used. "You know, we've never yet called anyone Hippopotamus; he's a big hefty fellow, and it would be a simple one; quite small children might like it." He becomes Hippopotamus.

"What about the mad keen recruit, though?" He's Sciencinfus in French, he volunteered to come to Corsica, hoping for good promotion prospects, unaware that the rest of the garrison are anxious only to steer very clear of the stalwart Corsican resistance fighters. He's a more important character. We can't, offhand, think of a good name, and set him aside for the time being. "And then there's the corrupt Governor of Corsica – the *very* corrupt Governor. We've already used Spurius, haven't we?"

We don't even have to check our list for this (he was half the name of another beefy soldier, Spurius Brontosaurus), because we remember our delight at the time in recalling that Spurius is an absolutely genuine Roman name, belonging to the gentleman who helped Horatius keep the bridge in the brave days of old. However, it turns out we've never called anyone Perfidius, and perfidious this Governor most certainly is, cheating all and sundry in the most devious ways.... Devius? No, we go for Perfidius in the end.

"Most of the names are Corsican, though. A few can stay, like Salamix and Carferrix, but the others will need changing."

"Especially the chieftain. Oh, *bother* Tino Rossi!" For the name of the Corsican chieftain who turns up near the Gaulish village, a hostage of the Romans, is Ocatarinetabellatchitchix, from one of Rossi's songs. Not nearly enough English people have heard of the singer, let alone the song; we can't possibly retain it. "It *would* be nice to have a song, because of the bard's comment – 'Funny, that man's name inspires me; I've got an idea for a song.'"

"And later on, that conversation between the Governor and the keen recruit." The keen recruit can't get his tongue around the Corsican's name, and twice adds the wrong refrain: Ocatarinetabella-ploumploum ... Ocatarinetabellasoinsoin. In both instances the Governor, horrified to learn that this dangerous character is back in Corsica, corrects him: "TCHITCHIX?"

"Boney was a warrior, way ay ah, Boney was a warrior, John François."

"Is it still well enough known?"

We canvass the opinion of our families and friends. It seems to be. (To my surprise, even my French sister-in-law strikes it up. In French.) So our Corsican chief becomes Boneywasawarriorwayayix, and the bard's reference to a song stands. We add, "Maybe a shanty." Going on to the refrain joke, we pick and choose among the English possibilities on offer, ending up with Boneywasawarriorpomtiddlypom ... Boneywasawarriorheynon-nyno. And then there's this other place, where Obelix, on being introduced, gets the name wrong, as well he might. *"Eh bien, Omarinella –"* And the Corsican corrects him. *"Catarineta."*

"Either Nelson or Wellington, don't you think?"

We settle for the latter. "Wellingtonwasa –" Correction: "Boneywasa."

Our Corsican joins the big party on the anniversary of Gergovia. Along come the guests, with their foreign or regional accents. The lady from Lyons is easy enough; naturally she enjoys being lionized. But there are frames and sequences where the joke depends entirely on mutual misunderstanding of accents. For instance, a man from Marseilles talking to an Auvergnat: *"Vé! C'est un peu bieng organisé, cette fâite!" "Chette quoi?"* And so on. To make up for the loss of all this, we try the possibilities of the word "punch". Chief Vitalstatistix wants to offer his guests a special treat, *une bagarre*, a go at thumping the Romans. We work out a pretty painful sequence of wordplay on punch, punch-up, that's the ticket, punching tickets, punch-line. We're not through yet: the accents take over again in mid battle. We try starting from "party" this time, a fair bet since the characters are having one. "Good party spirit here." "Never touch spirits, for my part." "There goes another departed spirit" – as yet another Roman is swept aloft by a mighty Gallic fist. We carry the word on into the guests' farewells – very tricky because the bubbles are extremely small, but after much phrasing, cutting and re-phrasing, we have (Briton speaking first): "I say, old fruit, you do a good line in parties." "Yes, marvel-lous party line." "Such liberality! Our tastes are conservative, but you didn't labour in vain."

Hmm ... we are fond of them all, but we can't say we're sorry to see them go, taking their accents with them.

As the scene is about to shift to Corsica, Asterix, Obelix and their Corsican friend must find transport. It so happens that they inadvertently charter the ship of their old friends the pirates, and here we have yet another, though slightly different, comic accent problem. The black pirate employs the accent of the people of the former French colonies, omitting the letter "r". This is acceptable and funny in France, but years ago we decided that it was *not* acceptable to make a comic feature of a similar mode of speech in English, and ever since we have been substituting other jokes for that lost "r". Here, the pirate captain is gloating over the prospect of robbing his rich passengers, whose identity he does not yet know, and making them walk the plank. "*O tempo'a, O mo'es*," comments the black pirate. "*À part la prononciation, tu fais des progrès*," says his ancient wooden-legged colleague, who is forever, and maddeningly, quoting Latin tags in time of disaster. We try something very complicated about committing bodies to the deep, lucky dips, dippy – we throw it out and start again. Keep things simple if possible. After a long time, we give the pirate his "r" back – "O tempora, O mores" – and have Pegleg, with reference to the prospective loot, add, "And more's the word."

As the Gauls board the ship, a couple of passwords are exchanged. "*Qui va là?*" "*Vienivienivieni.*" "*Aie aieaieaieaie.*" Tino Rossi again: both phrases are from his songs. We have to scrap them, too, and start afresh.

"Try this: I know it's painful. 'Who goes there?' 'Corsican, with friends. Can he come on board?' 'Course he can.'"

Groan.

"Well, you're not meant to *laugh*." A groan is the correct response, and I should know, as daughter of the man who composed the first *Times* crossword puzzle ever and has been at it for fifty years now. If your parent appears at breakfast inquiring, "Die of cold?" (ice cube), or suggests that the literary alternative to a storied urn is a lively smash (animated bust), you get accustomed to producing the appropriate groan.

"Now for the rest of the Corsicans – any amount of them." They have an assorted bunch of -ix names. One is Figatellix, from *figatelli*, a Corsican sausage. We don't think we can keep it – not well known in England, but our thoughts stray to Italianate foods. Moreover, Derek has just been to Italy, and waxes eloquent about the pasta he has been eating.

"Of course, this is the nearest we'll ever come to Italians, because of the genuine Italians of the time being Romans...."

"So if we're ever to use words like spaghetti and macaroni, it's now."

How many pasta names do we need? We count up: quite a number. Again, we canvass our families to see which are best known to the young. Top of our list will be Macaronix, Spaghettix, Vermicellix, Raviolix. We go to Elizabeth David's books. Her *French Provincial Cooking*, which would be well-thumbed anyway, has become even more so over the years as we look up, and try out, the various dishes Asterix and Obelix, who are fond of their food, encounter during their adventures (naturally we have cooked and eaten Mrs. David's excellent recipe for pork to taste like wild boar). This time, however, we go to her *Italian Food*, for all the pasta types are there. We realize we shan't have quite enough ending in -i, despite dividing Gnocchix into two characters, Potatognocchix and Semolinagnocchix; we must take a liberty and employ a few like Lasagnix and Tagliatellix, properly ending in -e.

And round about this point a name turns up, as we hoped it would, for that keen young recruit, who recklessly plunges into the maquis in pursuit of the Corsican resistance. As his superior tells him, "You're Courtingdisastus."

Here, at last, is the page where the French contains a genuine Napoleonic joke, as the Corsican chieftain musters his clans. "*Regardez là-bas, la colonne qui arrive en retard ... ah, Osterlix, son chef, a du mal à se lever tôt...*" And, in the next frame, with the rising sun behind him, the chief adds, "*C'est qu'il est célèbre chez nous, le sommeil d'Osterlix.*"

Now, given that English-speakers do know about Napoleon, and even about Austerlitz, you'd think this would be easy, but it turns out surprisingly hard. How many people will recognize an allusion to Napoleon's "*Voilà le soleil d'Austerlitz*", especially in the attempt we must make to twist it as the French has done? We think this one over for ages. In the end, we come up with two versions. One sticks fairly close to the French. "See that column over there? Led by the son of one of our most famous names ... the son of Austerlix." The other, after all the extra Napoleonic references we have worked in earlier to compensate for lost French jokes, breaks away from Napoleon entirely. Where else, we ask ourselves, do you also find clans, and a good bit of feuding? We could extract one of the pasta people from the main body of Corsican clan chiefs and use him here. "Yes, we're full of clan feeling ... see that column over there? Those are the Corsicans whose chief married into a Caledonian clan ... the clan of Macaronix."

It is a choice between the more sophisticated Austerlitz reference, for which you really need to be approaching A-level standard in history and/or French, and the simpler joke which we hope may appeal to more of the younger readers, and in the end we opt for the latter alternative.

This isn't the course we would – or indeed could – always adopt. We think of such sustained sophisticated jokes as the superb page in *Le Cadeau de César*. In the original, Asterix takes on a belligerent Roman soldier in the village pub, and as he launches into a swordfight simultaneously assumes the mantle of Rostand's Cyrano de Bergerac, composing a *ballade* as he fights. "*Ça, c'est envoyé!*" ("That's the stuff!") cries the innkeeper's daughter, as Asterix, like Cyrano, delivers the winning swordstroke on the last line of the *envoi*. In French, this is obviously not one for the youngest readers: it would, we felt, be wrong to simplify. Necessary, then, to substitute something. Most famous swordfight in English literature? Probably Hamlet and Laertes. Lead into it as the innkeeper's wife tells her husband to take no notice of the soldier – have her add, in English, "Act with disdain." Then the Roman can reply, with perfect truth, "I am more an antique Roman than a Dane," and we proceed to assorted quotations from *Hamlet*, with the girl commenting, "A hit, a very palpable hit!" for the *envoi* reference, and going on over the page, where opportunity offers, "He's made a hit with me all right." Inevitably, our version fell short of the lovely stylishness of the French, but we had to do something along those lines, since the passage cried out for a literary allusion.

Here, however, we did have a choice – so the one genuine Napoleonic joke of the original text of *Astérix en Corse* went by the board. ... How is it, we wonder in passing, we've never yet been able to work in "go by the board", among all the wild boar jokes? We've tried so hard to find variations on the inevitable line "This is a bit of a bore", our rough equivalent to the recurrent French joke about *sangliers* (wild boars) and *cochonneries* (rubbish).

But somehow the occasion for "go by the board" has never come up.

We're approaching the end of *Corsica*. There's another sequence involving the black pirate's accent, requiring, as our French student would have said, *"une compensation"*. The Governor and the pirates are anxious to put out to sea as fast as possible, so "cast off" seems a possible starting point, and we come up with a string of knitting references, beginning with the pirate captain's well-founded suspicion of the Governor's haste: "A bit of plain dealing first. Where's the loot you've purloined?" The pirates sink for the umpteenth time: "Well, do we cast off?" "No point casting pearls before swine." "Was that meant to have us in stitches?" "Cap'n, with due regard, you're a silly knit." And pretty soon afterwards the Gauls are home, indulging in their usual banquet and giving an account of the beauties of Corsica, which now include "some interesting Roman remains, dating from the time of our visit."

I type THE END. We look at it. Forty-four pages of typescript; we can never say exactly how long it takes to translate an *Astérix* album, since one is mulling over the problems of wordplay at all sorts of odd times before coming up with the final version. But it doesn't look much, for all that work and thought. Is anyone going to laugh at the English version? We're far too close to it to know. And we also feel a personal sadness that this is the second English *Astérix* translation René Goscinny will not read; we valued his interest and sympathetic understanding of our problems enormously.

There is still *Astérix Chez Les Belges* to come. Goscinny had just finished its text before his death. Needless to say, it is thick with Belgian accents ... our thoughts are already turning that way.

"What would you say is the sum total of English general knowledge about Belgium?"

"Gallant little."

"Brussels sprouts."

"Maybe the E.E.C., these days."

"Waterloo. Napoleon."

Back to Napoleon....

The Cinderella Story 1724–1919

IRENE WHALLEY

Irene Whalley is Assistant Keeper of the Library at the Victoria and Albert Museum, where she has special charge over the Museum's important collections of children's books. She is the author of *Cobwebs to Catch Flies: Illustrated Books for the Nursery and Schoolroom 1700–1900* (Elek, 1974). The following article was published in the May 1972 SIGNAL.

Although the well-known version of the story of Cinderella and her glass slipper only dates from its publication in Perrault's book of tales at the end of the seventeenth century, the spirit of the story goes back as far as the division of society into classes of rich and poor, ruler and ruled. There is no doubt that following the publication of Perrault's version, Cinderella quickly became one of the most popular of romances. Apart from being published in collections with other fairy tales, it is frequently found as a work on its own. This article is a study of some of the copies in the National Art Library, Victoria and Albert Museum, showing the types of illustration used over a period of nearly two hundred years, and the changes and embellishments undergone by the original story during that time.

The first publication of *Histoires ou contes du temps passé* was in 1697, with an engraved frontispiece containing the words *Contes de ma mère l'oye*, and it is as *Tales of Mother Goose* that we frequently find the fairy tales published in England. The earliest copy in the Library of *Cendrillon; ou, la petite pantoufle de verre* appeared in a work entitled *Contes de Monsieur Perrault, avec des moralitez, nouvelle édition*, which was published in Paris in 1724. This version was unillustrated, but it was soon appreciated that the *contes des fées* provided admirable illustrative material. At this period, of course, the tales were still primarily intended for adult reading, as Perrault had made obvious; they were a reflection of the artificial world of court life, though each story was dutifully provided with a moral.

Before considering the English version of Cinderella, it is useful to look at the original French version. One of the great charms of the story is its simple directness: "Il étoit une fois un gentilhomme qui épousa en secondes nôces une femme, la plus hautaine et la plus fière qu'on eut jamais vûë." The story proceeds in this direct fashion and is in fact very short, ending with equally satisfying directness: "On la mena chez le jeune prince, parée comme elle étoit; il la trouva encore plus belle que jamais, et peu de jours après il l'épousa. Cendrillon qui étoit aussi bonne que belle, fit loger ses deux soeurs au palais, et les maria dès le jour même à deux grands seigneurs de la cour." Nevertheless, within this simple directness, Perrault found room for certain detailed touches, shown in the description of the sisters' apartment and in the reaction to Cinderella's ball dress by the grand court ladies.

We will now pass on to the English versions of Cinderella, the earliest in the Library being included in *Stories or tales of passed times, with morals. Written in French by M. Perrault, and Englished by R.S., gent. The second edition, corrected.* This was published in London in 1737, and gave parallel texts in English and French. The French title-page reads: *Histoires ou contes du tems passé, avec des moralitez. Par M. Perrault. Augmentée d'une nouvelle, viz. L'adroite princesse. Troisième edition.* Each of the stories in the collection has an engraved illustration at the beginning, and this is repeated on the opposite page at the head of the French version. The phrasing of the English version of the story was to remain remarkably consistent throughout its transmutation into chapbook or rhyme.

The description of the sisters' chamber, mentioned above, is given in these words: "Her sisters lay in fine rooms, with floors all in-laid (chambres parquetées), upon beds of the very newest fashion, and where they had looking-glasses so large, that they might see themselves at their full length, from head to foot." These same details reappear in later editions of the story, but certain phrases were subsequently brought up to date: "Elles faisoient

From *Histories or Tales of passed times, with morals*. Written by M. Perrault, 2nd edition, with parallel texts in English and French, 1737 (enlarged from 4 cm × 6.5 cm) (See text page 141)

grande figure dans le pays" was rendered as "they cut a very grand figure among the quality", in which the final word had a definite period flavour. Likewise there was a need to modernize the details of the clothing worn: "it was she who ... plaited their ruffles" meant nothing to a nineteenth-century reader who no longer wore them. It was in the discussion concerning the dresses for the ball that further interesting points were to be seen: "I will wear my red velvet suit with the French trimming" – a trimming which had appeared in the original as "garniture d'Angleterre". And as if to prove that the fruit is always sweeter on the other side of the fence, "on fit acheter des mouches de la bonne faiseuse" became in English "they had their red brushes and patches from Mademoiselle de la Poche", an intrusive lady who continued to feature in the English versions of the story for many years. Other interesting points reveal themselves in this early version, where "citrouille", having been rendered as "pompion", took some time before becoming the familiar "pumpkin", while the form of "Cendrillon", having been translated as Cinderilla, speedily became the Cinderella by which we know her today.

As Cinderella prepared for and went to the ball, a few more delightful touches appeared. The rat who turned into the coachman was chosen on account of his large beard, and he became "a fat jolly coachman, who had the smartest whiskers eye ever beheld", while when Cinderella entered the ballroom in her beautiful fairy-made clothes, "all the ladies were busied in considering her cloathes and head-dress, that they might have some made next day after the same pattern, provided they could meet with such fine material and as able hands to make them". The two morals provided by Perrault are also instructive. The first one, after saying that the importance of beauty cannot be underestimated, continues: "But that which we call good grace / Exceeds by far a handsome face", and it "prevails much more (you'll find it so) / T'ingage and captivate a heart / Than a fine head dress'd up with art." This is a moral none could cavil at, but what are we to make of the second: "But none of the rich graces from above / To your advancement in the world will prove / Of any use, if godsires make delay / Or godmothers, your merit to display"?

The nineteenth century took up the Cinderella story with enthusiasm, judging by the number of different editions that exist in the Library. But Cinderella was not an improving tale, for its moral tailpieces soon fell away, and it joined the substrata of popular reading matter in the pedlar's pack. Here in chapbook form it could be read and enjoyed by children, but unofficially, and would most likely infiltrate the nursery by means of the servants' hall. Since the original story of Cinderella was quite slight, it was eminently suited for chapbook production, and needed little abridgement. All the chapbook versions kept remarkably close to the original, with just an occasional updating of word or phrase, while the story also lent itself to verse form. Many of the early nineteenth-century chapbooks, though they may appear to us to have been aimed at children, were not necessarily so: their size was conditioned by their method of sale and their illustration was typical of other chapbooks which were definitely meant for an older though unsophisticated reading public.

There was of course a great deal of hack illustration in the contemporary children's book, but there were so many incidents in Cinderella relevant to that tale alone, that it escaped much of this.

A hand-coloured illustration to an edition in verse, published by Griffith & Farran about 1860. The woodcuts had been used many times before so that the costumes were very out of date by 1860.

The early illustrations were usually crude woodcuts, since this was the cheapest form of book illustration, though occasionally engravings are found, especially in the first few decades of the nineteenth century. Some are hand-coloured, possibly by the usual method of child labour. Named artists are rarely recorded at this period, and old blocks are frequently recut or merely re-used. The figures in the illustrations usually wear contemporary dress, always allowing for the fact that, stylistically, children's books tend to be out of date as far as fashion is concerned – a fact which, together with the re-use of old illustrations, makes dating different editions extremely difficult.

The nineteenth century made certain amendments to the story, sometimes reducing it to a mere commentary on the pictures, sometimes offering it in verse. Occasionally the tale was embellished with details unknown to the original – Cinderella became fatherless as well as motherless, and the fairy godmother was painted in greater detail; while the more genteel tone of the mid-century demanded "Cinder-wench" for "Cinder-breech". Nevertheless, Cinderella had already run into trouble at the very beginning of the century, when Mrs. Trimmer had published her indictment of fairy tales. These, she said, "were calculated to entertain the imagination, rather than improve the heart or cultivate the understanding". Chief among the sinners was Cinderella, for here are to be found "some of the worst passions that can enter into the human breast ... such as envy, jealousy, a dislike to mothers-in-law and half-sisters, vanity, a love of dress etc., etc." Poor Cinderella!

However, as the reign of Victoria progressed there came a change in the attitude to the child and his books. One of the earliest to lead the way here was Sir Henry Cole, a man who had a finger in many of the pies baked in the middle of the nineteenth century, a friend of the Prince Consort, and first Director of the Victoria and Albert Museum. He felt that nursery rhymes and fairy and folk tales were part of every child's heritage, but he was appalled at the standard of illustration when he came to provide such books for his own children. His dissatisfaction prompted the "Home Treasury" series, published by Cole under his pseudonym of Felix Summerly. Gradually children began to be allowed to read for pleasure and not just for improvement, and Cinderella also benefited from this change of attitude, though she was not yet free of trouble.

There were two versions, both published by well-known people, in the 1850s, which are worth considering in greater detail. In 1854 Miss Julia Corner published *Cinderella and the glass slipper; or, pride punished* as "an entertainment for young people" in the form of a play. The text of the story, as had happened before, was transposed into rhyming couplets, and stage directions were given for domestic production of the playlet by young people. In this version both sisters were given names: one, Charlotte ("Javotte" in the original), had received hers from Perrault, but the second, usually anonymous, was here christened "Ulrica". Although known to us as "the ugly sisters" from pantomime versions, neither sister is ever described as such in the early editions of the tale, the "ugliness" being of the mind rather than of the person; and pride being one

A colour printed illustration from a "toy book" edition of *Cinderella* published by G. Routledge & Sons in 1872. Note the medievalism of the costumes. (See text page 149)

of the seven deadly sins the point was considered obvious to the Victorian child. The play was illustrated by Alfred Crowquill (a pseudonym for A. H. Forrester) with a few of this artist's less distinguished woodcuts, but the tone of this version of the story is shown by the change made by the author to the original ending: wickedness must never go unpunished, not even when the forgiveness of it adds to Cinderella's goodness. No marriage to court gentlemen for these sisters! "You / Will meet the punishment that is your due / Scorn'd and neglected it shall be your fate / To envy Cinderella's happier state."

The second version of the story to be considered in some detail is the one by George Cruikshank, published as part of his "Fairy Library" in 1854. This is a much expanded story, and Cruikshank's

Etched frontispiece from George Cruikshank's "temperance"
version published in 1854 (reduced)

reasons for altering the original are given in a postscript: "upon
looking through several books (of Cinderella) I found *some* vulgarity mixed up with so much that was useless and unfit for children, that I was obliged (much against my wish) to re-write the whole
story." Cruikshank's etchings which illustrated the story were some
of the most charming it has inspired. The story itself not only has
his personal imprint upon it but also that of his period, with its
"genteel" aspect and its facetiousness in the relationships, including
that between "Cindy" and her godmother, who is a dwarf in this
edition. A surprising departure comes towards the end of the story,
when virtue is triumphant and the marriage between Cinderella and
the prince is about to take place. The king, in true fairy-tale tradition, orders "that there should be running 'fountains of wine' in

A gen-tle-man well to do in the world, liv-ed in an old house, in coun-try, and all he lov-ed on the earth, his wife, his fond lit-tle girl, hi

From *Cin-der-ella and the Lit-tle Glass Slip-per*. Printed on one side of the sheet only, with the text below the hand-coloured cuts, G. Routledge & Co. (c. 1860)

the court-yards of the palace, and also in the streets". But the fairy godmother begs he will omit this tradition; the king needs some convincing, and so there follows over a page of "temperance tract" on the virtues of total abstinence. The fairy points out that "this same drink leads to quarrels, brutal fights and violent deaths ... if it had been necessary for man to take stimulating drinks the Almighty could have given them to him free from all intoxicating qualities". It is all a far cry from the world of Louis XIV to that of Dickens! It will be seen that, though the morals appended by Perrault had disappeared, the moral vacuum had been more than adequately filled by subsequent adapters. Another version, published about 1860, with a text carefully broken up into syllables for the convenience of very small children, ends up: "Proud peo-

Centre-page spread from Walter Crane's colour-printed "toy book" published in 1873 (reduced). (See text page 150)

ple and sil-ly peo-ple and cru-el hearts are ma-ny in the world to crush down good-ness and gen-tle-ness, but I never knew God to leave the gen-tle and good with-out a just reward."

But by this time the whole style of children's books was changing, in both content and format. Lear had already introduced nonsense to the nursery and *Alice* would follow in the next decade. Colour printing was beginning to replace the hand-coloured woodcut or the steel plate as techniques improved. Moreover, the importance of the child market for books was more fully realized. Children's books shared in the general improvement in standards of book production that characterized the 60s, and children's book illustrators began to append their names to their work. The firm of Routledge, which published many "toy books" in the 1850s and 1860s, made no pretence of anything but entertainment in their boldly illustrated *Cinderella*, printed in colour in 1872. Another fact is also obvious in this particular version, namely the interest in revived medievalism, a characteristic of the Victorian period, and one which shows itself here in the depiction of costume and background. The "toy book" style was the one chosen by Walter Crane for his famous set of children's books, which also included a *Cinderella* (the same illustrations were used for his *The Children's Musical Cinderella*). Here we have an artist of high repute designing the illustrations for the old story – and the rhyming text in consequence took up a very small part of the whole, being merely an accompaniment to the pictures. The bright and colourful illustrations reflected contemporary artistic trends, with their mixture of conscious archaism and the influence of the Japanese print, so popular at the end of the century.

Perhaps it is fitting to end this survey of the Cinderella story with

The frontispiece illustration by Arthur Rackham, published in 1919, shows the wistful romanticism of a well-established "fairy story" tradition (reduced)

one of the longest versions, where the original tale became a small novel. "Retold by C. S. Evans", this work was illustrated by Arthur Rackham; it was published in 1919, when kings and princes were going out of fashion and fairy godmothers were being overtaken by the wonders of science.

The pure narrative of the original was here treated much more subjectively, and much was made of Cinderella's feelings at various stages in the story. Nevertheless, even with all the additional padding which the twentieth-century author added to the story, certain original features remained embedded in the text. The long mirrors are mentioned, and floors and the trimmings, even as they had been in the first English edition. Rackham's illustrations differed from those of previous artists in that they were mostly in silhouette form; they also showed a romantic "period" approach, placing the figures in something like their original seventeenth- or early eighteenth-century setting.

Though this is the last Cinderella to be considered in this article, she is by no means outmoded. The pantomime versions keep her before our eyes in a modernized form, while Perrault's tales continue to enchant children and attract artists. The "rags-to-riches" theme and the miraculous transformation of circumstance have outlived the fallen thrones of reality, and each generation moulds its Cinderella to its own taste.

Silhouette illustration by
Arthur Rackham (reduced)

A SELECT LIST OF COPIES IN THE NATIONAL
ART LIBRARY, VICTORIA AND ALBERT MUSEUM

Early French Copies

Contes de Monsieur Perrault, avec des moralitez. Nouvelle édition. Paris, 1724

Histoires ou contes du tems passé, avec des moralitez ... Nouvelle edition augmentée d'une Nouvelle ... Suivant la copie de Paris, à Amsterdam, 1742

Histoires du tems passé; ou, les contes de ma mère l'oye, avec des moralites ... Nouvelle édition, augmentée de deux Nouvelles ... à Londres, et se trouve à Bruxelles, 1786

Edition with woodcuts published in Edinburgh
about 1805 (enlarged from 4 cm × 5 cm)

English Copies

Histories, or tales of passed times, with morals, written in French by M. Perrault, and Englished by R.S., gent [R. Samber]. The second edition, corrected. London, for R. Montagu, 1737
  Title-page and text also in French ("troisième edition"); an engraved illustration at the commencement of each story (repeated for the French text).

Cinderilla: or, the little glass slipper. London, G. Thompson, 1804
  Engraved throughout, with movable flaps to show transformation underneath. 6d plain, 1s coloured.

Fairy tales of past times from Mother Goose. Edinburgh, G. Ross, 1805 (Tale IV: Cinderilla; or, the little glass slipper)
Chapbook, with a woodcut for each story; bound in cover lettered "Price twopence from Ross's Juvenile Library, Glasgow, J. Lumsden & Son".

The adventures of Cinderella and her glass slipper. To which is added the popular story of Puss in Boots (London, G. Martin) [c. 1810?]
No cover, title-page mutilated; folding engraved frontispiece and illustrations in the text.

The curious adventures of the beautiful little maid Cinderella; or, the history of a glass slipper. Colchester, I. Marsden [c. 1810?]
Chapbook with cuts; price one penny.

The entertaining tales of Mother Goose for the amusement of youth. Glasgow, J. Lumsden [c. 1820?] (Cinderilla; or, the little glass slipper)
Engraved illustration including frontispiece and one on title-page; on cover:"Lumsden & Sons. New edition of Mother Goose". Watermark 1817.

Adventures of the beautiful little maid Cinderilla; or, the history of a glass slipper. To which is added An historical description of the cat. York, J. Kendrew [c. 1820?]
Chapbook with cuts ("penny books").

Cinderella; or, the little glass slipper. [London] J. Catnach [c. 1820?]
With a few crude cuts; on back cover: "books published by J. Bysh". Price sixpence.

The history of Cinderella. (Ottley) printed for the booksellers [c. 1840]
In verse, with crude cuts and colour wash.

Cinderella; or, the little glass slipper: a fairy tale. . . . A new edition corrected and adapted for juvenile readers, by a lady. London, Dean & Munday [c. 1840?]
With eight hand-coloured cuts, two to a page. An endpiece states "The history of Cinderella is founded upon a fairy tale, which conveys a very pretty moral to the youthful mind, and shows the advantage of meekness and good behaviour".

History of Cinderella; or, the little glass slipper. Glasgow, printed for the booksellers, 1852. (New and improved series no. 45)
With "Hop o' my Thumb"; crude cuts; "penny tracts".

Cinderella and the glass slipper. Edited and illustrated with ten subjects, designed and etched on steel by G. Cruikshank. London, D. Bogue [1854]. (G. Cruikshank's Fairy Library)

Cinderella and the glass slipper; or, pride punished. An entertainment for young people. By Miss Corner, and embellished by A. Crowquill, Esq. London, Dean & Son, 1854. (Little plays for little actors)
price 1s.

Cinderella; or the little glass slipper. With thirteen illustrations by M. J. R. London, Nelson & Sons, 1858.
Cuts including pages bordered with branches and leaves; hand-coloured, probably by a former owner.

Cinderella; or, the little glass slipper. London, Griffith & Farran [c. 1860?]
In verse form, mounted on linen, with hand-coloured cuts of a much earlier style.

Cin-der-ella and the lit-tle glass slip-per. London, G. Routledge & Co. [c. 1860?] (Second series of Aunt Mavor's picture books for little readers)
Printed on one side of the sheet only, with the text below the hand-coloured cuts. Price sixpence.

Cinderella and the little glass slipper. n.p., n.d.
Panorama style, opening lengthways, with crude cuts printed in colour and brief captions only to tell the story.

Cinderella; or, the little glass slipper. London, Cassell, Petter & Galpin [1869?] (Cassell's fairy story books)
Illustrations hand-coloured and mounted on linen; text in the form of extended captions. Cover colour printed. Price 1s.

Cinderella; or, the little glass slipper. [London] G. Routledge & Sons [1872?] (Routledge's shilling toy books)
Colour printed by Kronheim & Co., and with large clear text.

Cinderella. [London] G. Routledge & Sons [1873]. (Walter Crane's toy books)
Colour printed by Edmund Evans; price 6d, 1s mounted on linen.

The children's musical Cinderella. Told in familiar words to familiar tunes by W. Routledge and Louis N. Parker. With pictures by W. Crane. [London] G. Routledge & Sons, 1879
Same illustrations as the one above; price 1s.

Cinderella. Retold by C. S. Evans and illustrated by A. Rackham. London, W. Heinemann, 1919
Full length "nòvel", with coloured illustrations as plates, and text illustrations in silhouette form, including title-page and end-papers.

WORKS ON THE PERRAULT TALES,
WITH GOOD BIBLIOGRAPHIES

New York, Pierpont Morgan Library: *Perrault's Tales of Mother Goose: the dedication manuscript of 1695* ... with introduction and critical text by J. Barchilon, 1956

Soriano, Marc: *Les contes de Perrault: culture savante et traditions populaires.* Paris, Gallimard, 1968

SIGNAL QUOTES

Erik Christian Haugaard in "The Simple Truth"
(Signal 11, May 1973)

Somewhere truth exists: it can be found; all we need to do is search hard enough. This is probably the one illusion which we all share and which man cannot live without. But how shall we recognize truth when we find it? By its simplicity. Again we all agree, knowing that truth is something you stumble upon or over; and there you are. I think that the wide appeal of the fairy tale lies in its undisputed and sole ownership of "the truth". You may doubt the wisdom of Socrates, Aristotle, or the *Sunday Times*; but not a story which twenty generations of illiterate peasants have told each other through the long, dark winter nights.

I am as addicted to the fairy tale and the folk tale as anyone else; and I, too, believe that if truth can be found, like a nugget of gold, then this is the place to search for it. But why? Would not novels, plays, or poetry offer as promising ground? I don't think so, for novels are often written to please, plays to amuse, and poetry for the sake of beauty or love – and the latter can make the wisest of men into fools. But the fairy tale has only one purpose: it lets out a little truth in a world of lies when the pressure gets too great. In a very short tale by Hans Christian Andersen called "The Little Green Ones", Dame Fairy Tale herself exclaims: "One ought to call everything by its right name; and if one does not dare to do it in everyday life then, at least, one should do it in a fairy tale!"

The fairy tale belongs to the poor. It is both their weapon against those who oppress them and their means of making that oppression bearable. You laugh with a knowing wink of the eye as you tell the tale; and having told it, you feel a sense of relief, for you know that even though you live in a world that is unjust, you can still conceive of justice. It is not surprising that a Danish actor during the German Occupation, in 1943, lost his liberty for having read aloud at a public meeting Hans Christian Andersen's "The Evil King". I know of no fairy tale which upholds the tyrant, or takes the part of the strong against the weak: a fascist fairy tale is an absurdity.

Alan Tucker in "Andersen Complete", a review of
The Complete Fairy Tales and Stories
of Hans Christian Andersen *translated*
by Erik Christian Haugaard and published by Gollancz
(*Signal 16, January 1975*)

Andersen took the folk tale, in his day only recently made respectable (that is to say, worthy of notice) by Scott and the Grimms, and transmuted the form by substituting for the brutal and pagan element of arbitrary chance the more civilized concept of meaningful coincidence. The people and objects he writes about are woven into a pattern of events so real that the events themselves are like characters, which have existed and will exist for ever. His protagonists are not subjected to, but encounter these events. It follows that the people and the objects do not alter; their appearance may change, but they remain steadfastly themselves. They are not degraded. What they have in common – the Tin Soldier, the bottle neck, the dung beetle, the nightingale, and the fir tree – is that they fit into their histories like the keystone of an arch, the final clinching piece of a jigsaw. They demonstrate meaningfulness....

Andersen's gentleness and humour are universally recognized. That his philosophy is equally civilized is less apparent. Above all, Mr. Haugaard's book shows that Andersen can be trusted – his imagination is not only superb, it is entirely sane. It is a very rare gift to demonstrate free will and the workings of fate at one and the same time. Can any other children's writer claim such kinship with Shakespeare?

For clearly Andersen's is not a fantasy world, but a microcosm reflecting with delightful precision our everyday surroundings. Forget all about children, and fairy tales, and read them as you would read, say, short stories by T. F. Powys: but what a sharper mind and wit, what a much more universal genius Andersen has. Stopping to consider which living writer most resembles Andersen, I suggest it is Kurt Vonnegut, who, particularly in his earlier (and best) books, manipulates coincidence with the same marvellous quirky style of humour and storytelling. Andersen does not belong with the old tradition of Grimms' tales, with their baroque and Bach-like piling up of incident. He is the first modern writer for children, a perfect precursor, like Mozart, combining classical poise with romantic idealism.

The Puffin Years

ELEANOR GRAHAM

Before she began Puffin paperbacks for children, Eleanor Graham was in charge of the Children's Room in the famous Bumpus bookshop in London; her first writing for SIGNAL was about those days. She also had a regular review column on children's books for the *Sunday Times* during the 1930s. She received the Children's Book Circle's Eleanor Farjeon Award for outstanding services to children's books in 1974, soon after this article appeared in the September 1973 SIGNAL.

By the time Penguin Books started in the mid 1930s, I had already met Allen Lane and his brothers. I remember I was on holiday on the Yorkshire moors when the first Penguins came out, staying at a small inn where walkers stopped for the night. I noticed that practically everyone who came in had one of the little orange books sticking out of a pocket. The first question always was, "Which one have you got?"

It was such fun to watch this going on from day to day that I sent Allen a note about it. When I returned to town, he told me how, on the day of publication of that first batch, he and his two brothers sat round the telephone waiting desperately for repeat orders. According to Allen, they hadn't a bean left! The day wore on. But in the afternoon an order came in for another thousand – from either Smith's or Selfridge's, I'm not sure which. The brothers breathed again. Penguins were on their way.

I am not quite certain when Allen introduced himself to me, but it was quite early in the thirties. He was going to all the meetings about children's books that I went to, and after one of them he told me he had known my brother Stephen in New York. John

Lane (Allen's uncle) had published my brother's first two books, *A Vagabond in the Caucasus* and *Undiscovered Russia*, and when he sent Allen (then aged sixteen) to have a look round in New York, he gave him a letter to Stephen, who was there at the time. So Allen and I were on easy terms very early.

One day, after another children's books meeting, he told me that he wanted to start a series of children's Penguins. Would I be interested to edit it? It must have been a curious moment, for he was paying me something of a compliment: and I was regarding him searchingly, rather doubtfully. I had seen too many cheap series of children's books – out-of-copyright "classics", badly printed on rough paper, unillustrated. Of course, Allen Lane would not turn out a series looking like that, but at that time no one knew *what* Allen Lane might do in the different circumstance of children's books. To make myself quite plain, I told him I should not want to have anything to do with paperbacks on that level; but if he was thinking of a series comparable with his Penguins, with the best of the *new* work then being done for children ... why, then *I'd be on* – my goodness, I'd be on! He seemed to give a sort of leap at that and said emphatically, "That's exactly what I want," adding, "with you as Editor."

It was a thrilling moment, for I knew what an amazing burgeoning of quality in children's books there had been during the thirties: a burgeoning of talent, originality, and freshness of writing. It was in this context that Allen Lane proposed to publish a series of sixpenny paperbacks for children. That was the standard we were agreed upon from the very start.

I should mention here that Allen Lane had intended to produce also a series of educational books alongside the Story Books. This he discussed with Rhoda Power, who was working for the B.B.C. on historical programmes for schools. However, when the war became imminent, she was whisked away to Bristol, from which the B.B.C.'s educational series was to be run during the war years. In 1940 her famous sister Eileen (the historian) dropped dead in Oxford Street, a blow from which Rhoda found it hard to recover. Eileen had been the vigorous, go-ahead member of the family, and Rhoda depended on her greatly. She remained in Bristol for most of the war years, and her historical series for Puffins never materialized. Shortly after her return to London after the war, she too suddenly dropped dead, as she was talking to a friend over a glass of sherry in her own flat.

In the autumn of 1940 Allen Lane rang me to say that he was finally ready to start Puffins, and would I come down and talk things over. I explained that I had a war job, but he said to come after work and stay the night. He promised to get me back in time the next morning.

I set out in a raid, and when I reached Hounslow West station, it was absolutely pitch dark. There was no car that I could see, and no other side of the road either, but the ticket collector had told me that anyone from Penguins would be waiting in the pub opposite. With the feeling of wading in blackness, I picked my way across to it and was soon driving off, with flack flying overhead, to Allen's new home, Silverbeck, still only partially furnished, but warm and comfortable.

I had prepared a very long list of books I wanted for Puffins, many of them ones I had known well in my days at Bumpus's. Allen and I had already agreed in general terms the shape Puffins were to take: definitely not a series of out-of-copyright classics. What we wanted was the best of the *new* classics of the new generation, so that Puffins could be a worthy partner to the now established Penguins. I realized Allen might have difficulty in getting rights. I knew also from other publishers that there was very little paper to spare – or printing capacity either, for that matter. It was a curious, courageous, and very tough moment to start.

I soon heard how indignant some publishers were that I should embroil myself in this attempt to get their best titles (which they themselves were unable to reprint) for a miserable series of paperbacks! Some said they would never, never, never ... and so on. In fact, we got very little at that stage: refusals were almost wholesale. The librarians were indignant too, considering that I was undermining their good work for large, well-bound, well-printed books. I did not worry about that. I knew what Stead's *Books for the Bairns*, at a penny each, had meant in my childhood. In fact, Allen Lane had also had those in mind. No, I did not worry about the librarians, but I had to do some hard thinking about the publishers' refusals. Fortunately, a few realized that, if their books were kept alive by Penguins during the period of the war – and no one knew how long that would go on – they could easily be picked up again afterwards.

All dealings with publishers were carried on from the Penguin office, which meant that I made none of the direct approaches for the books I wanted. This seemed necessary at the time, but as a result permissions were obtained where they could be, and not always for those books I should have liked to see first in Puffins. I have had to think back over this, recalling – and actually handling again – that first little batch: Barbara Todd's *Worzel Gummidge*, Derek McCulloch's *Cornish Adventure*, Mrs. Molesworth's *The Cuckoo Clock*, Herbert Best's *Garram the Hunter*, and Will James's *Smoky*. (There is a nice story of someone taking a blue pencil to *Smoky* and setting out to translate it into good English. For years and years no one in Penguins – except perhaps Allen Lane and myself – recognized the reputation it had, and how justly. It has won prizes galore in America through the years. But the general staff at Penguins considered it a mere cowboy yarn and a blot on the list.) When I saw the finished copies my heart sank, for I could see the bookseller's dilemma. You couldn't make a show of five thin little books, however good. But so we got off, to a not very rosy start!

For number seven we had Eve Garnett's Carnegie Medal winner, *The Family from One End Street*. Number sixteen was J. B. S. Haldane's *My Friend Mr. Leakey*, a book for which I had a great affection. But, again, elements in the Penguin office told me it should not have been on the list. I never knew why they felt so about it. To me it was as much a classic as *Alice in Wonderland*, and issuing somehow from the same kind of mind. There was, in short, a good deal of criticism in the Penguin office about the early Puffin selection. It worried me, but not because I doubted my own choices. Allen always said genially, "Pay no attention to them!" and I took him at his word – uneasily.

Allen Lane and I had spoken often about *A Child's Garden of Verses*, which we both wanted in the series. He said he would pay for a beautifully illustrated edition, and I chose Eve Garnett for it. A lot of care was taken over the printing; indeed, the blocks were made more than once before the final form was achieved. I was afraid that something might be lost in this refining, but very little was. The cover always delighted me, with the wreath of pink-tipped daisies so in harmony with Stevenson's verses. To this I wrote the first of my prefaces on *How the Book Came to be Written*. It was number twenty-two in the series, and came out in 1948, seven years after the first Puffin saw print.

Somehow Puffins took root. Many items in the list were generally little known, but practically all were good reading. I was frequently urged by other members of Penguin's staff to put in more old favourites for the sake of big sales. I quite saw their point, but I knew also that it would have been fatal for people to feel: *There they are, just the same old out-of-copyright "classics"*. I knew parents who bought all the Puffins, as they came out, for their children. Allen himself always took early copies home to his elder daughter, without comment, and awaited her verdict. She was a treasure and liked practically all of them – by Allen's accounts to me – and I was warmly grateful.

Our real difficulty lay in getting booksellers to show Puffins properly. They did not want to sell "wretched paperbacks" instead of the old reward types: and who would buy hard-cover editions if the same books could be got for about a shilling each? The early question of their making a sufficient show in bookshops solved itself, of course, in time.

To my delight Allen asked one day if I would like Henry Williamson's *Tarka the Otter*, adding that we would get good illustrations for it. I had seen it at Bumpus's when it was first published and always had a pile of it in the Children's Room. *Tarka* became a jewel in our crown. There were beautiful decorations by Tunnicliffe, and again I wrote an introduction to it. Oddly enough, I recently received a letter from Henry Williamson, who had just seen the latest edition and read my preface with pleasure, finding it "correct and true". (I had, of course, submitted my script to him before our Puffin went into print and had his O.K. for it, but that he had forgotten.)

As time went on, I commissioned more books, notably a telling of the King Arthur stories by Roger Lancelyn Green. I knew his work and his mind pretty well by then, and he gave us a really excellent telling of the old tales. We had it most strikingly – and,

I think, fittingly – illustrated by Lotte Reiniger in her own peculiar style, which was so well suited to knights in armour and strange woodland scenes in a land of castles. It was a long book and cost a lot of money to produce, but we brought it out at half a crown. I am happy to say that it has remained one of the most appreciated of Puffins.

I had been thinking for some time about a poetry anthology when Allen spoke about our having one. He was quite happy for me to make my own, though again there were murmurs from within the Penguin office that someone "known" should do it. However, I went ahead, and *A Puffin Book of Verse* resulted. It still sells, edition after edition, most satisfyingly. I felt it should have a good deal of standard classic poetry in it, but also – most important – unexpected pieces scattered all through.

Later, wishing very much to have some of Eleanor Farjeon's poetry, but finding that her publishers would not allow us to have a whole volume of it, I devised *A Quartet of Poets*, to which her publishers, Oxford University Press, consented – at Eleanor Farjeon's urgent request. It proved rather fun, as I was able to have four poets, with a nice little collection from each. In addition to Eleanor Farjeon, I chose E. V. Rieu, James Reeves and Ian Serraillier. I remember feeling qualms as to whether the poets would get anything like enough out of it financially, for the Puffin price was 3s. 6d. with a $7\frac{1}{2}$% royalty, and that split four ways! However, they were all as charming as could be, and I never heard even an echo of a grumble. I wrote a short introduction to each section, showing something of the way each poet composed, as I found they worked so very differently. It was delightfully produced, and is now in its ninth edition – and Puffins have to be produced in large editions!

As we approached our hundredth Puffin, Allen Lane asked how I would like to celebrate it. After some cogitation and discussion we decided on *The Puffin Song Book* with Leslie Woodgate providing the material. He was delightfully unexpected about it and asked me to come to his house one evening to choose the contents. He sat at his piano, played a few bars and sang a verse or two; then like some sentencing judge from the wilds I gave a thumbs up or down on each item. It was a long session, but it gave us another winner.

Many of our best books just fell into our hands. Jean Sutcliff, who was doing a series of *Listen with Mother* programmes on the B.B.C., sent me – at Methuen, where I was also editing children's books – a sackful of manuscripts to look through. From them I picked *My Naughty Little Sister* by Dorothy Edwards and Leila Berg's *Little Pete Stories*. After doing a hardback edition of both for Methuen, I put them into Puffins, where they continue to flourish.

In 1951 I had the satisfaction of getting rights for Patricia Lynch's masterpiece, *The Grey Goose of Kilnevin*. She was a rare storyteller with that special gift of the Irish for atmosphere. It was a long book and I could not bear to cut it. So, instead of having it illustrated, we gave it the most beautiful cover I think we ever had, discarded now in favour of something very commonplace. But the original is as beautiful as ever, showing the child and her goose, with a trail of wild geese flying behind her. I have always liked the old gander's warning: "Don't go next or nigh a fox! Don't go pokin yer gobs into holes: yez never can tell what'll be in them! An keep away from dogs. Walk on the grass when yez can: tis aisier on the feet, an, whatever Jim Daly ses, take yer time; take yer time!" A lovely book!

In the mid fifties, Allen Lane asked me how I felt about doing a story of Jesus in the series. I had had the idea in mind for some time, but did not know anyone I could trust to do it. In the end, rather bashfully, I decided I must do it myself. Penguins, as a whole, did not think I would do it well enough, and I had my own misgivings. But I *knew* what I wanted – and more, what I simply could not have borne to have in Puffins! Allen said, "Go ahead," and I did.

That was a strange and wonderful experience, for material seemed to come into my hands from all sides. There were lectures of all sorts: archaeological, historical, religious. I heard – at All Saints, Margaret Street – a series of talks by Trevor Huddleston which were so vivid and inspiring that they might have been specially provided for me. It was a long job, and a testing one. I had no contract for it with Penguins, who were plainly holding themselves ready to reject it. It was an uneasy situation, and I would not let anyone see the book till it was done. When at last I sent the finished manuscript to Harmondsworth, I awaited their comments uneasily, but feeling quite sure in my own mind that they would be lucky to get a better book. I knew that, having asked for something of this sort, Allen himself would understand it. To my amazement, a guardedly appreciative report was returned to me from the office, and its fate was settled.

Then came the question of illustration. At the very moment when I had to decide, Brian Wildsmith rang and asked if he could come and show me his work. I wasn't sure, seeing his sample illustrations for ordinary children's books, how he would cope with what I wanted for my book; but I found him a wonderful collaborator, and absolutely the right person for the job. He took the manuscript away, read it – and liked it. For the next three months, he came in with little groups of drawings. We sat together, and I talked about the scenes. Sometimes he drew a little here or altered a little there. When he came again, there was always something I could recognize as the counterpart to what I had written. I still can't think of anyone who could have illustrated the book better, and I was profoundly grateful to see it start off so perfectly equipped. I shall always value and prefer the first edition with its full text, and its blue cover, with the picture of Christ staggering under the great cross.

Penguins took great trouble over that book. The paper was the best possible, the type was chosen with care, the blocks were really black, and the whole was beautifully designed and carried through. It had some wonderful reviews, and the first edition sold out in reasonable time.

Looking back at my Puffins, I don't find much that I regret. Some were certainly not best-sellers, but that was not what Allen had asked me to provide. We had failures – *Tents in Mongolia*, for instance, which I still think had vitality and considerable interest for the Puffin reader as an account of a party of young Danes who went forth to look at the prospects for colonization in that uneasy land. The young men were gay, light-hearted – and it was a true tale of adventure. But it was not a seller! That was Puffin number ten, and something of a counterblast to those who were thinking in terms of Angela Brazil and Enid Blyton. But with the Penguin background, it might have got across! I was, of course, frequently urged to get some Blyton on our list, but I never did. It was not intended for that kind of public.

I had a cut-down version of Jennie Lee's *Tomorrow is a New Day*, her autobiography, very well handled by Doris Estcourt: an inspiring story, I thought, of a poor family who were quite magnificent in their courage and determination. In between we had *Jungle John, Flaxen Braids, Starlight, a Wolf, Treasure Island* and *Kidnapped, Alice in Wonderland*, and so on. We had one of those Russian stories written to help produce a literate people quickly in that country after the Revolution. It was *Cranes Flying South*, a wonderful account of the birds and their migration.

We had Belloc's *Cautionary Verses, Black Beauty*, Eleanor Doorly's life of Mme Curie, *The Radium Woman* – an early Carnegie Medal winner – and *The Secret Garden* ... but I could go on and on. The Puffin list was a good one by any standards. I edited it for twenty years, and look back on all the books with happiness – and pride!

Dorothy Butler in "Book Post Returns":
a correspondence feature
(Signal 25, January 1978)

I believe that, in books for the very young, the words are more important than the pictures. Modern children are bombarded on every side by the visual image; meanwhile, they may be suffering from language impoverishment. I believe that the language of picture books should have the sort of clarity and strength which comes from precision. It may be vigorous or restrained as necessary, with every shade of feeling within this framework; but always economical, never bulky or contrived. It should use the resources of the English tongue wisely and sensitively, recognizing and accepting its own awesome power to mold the taste and sensibilities of the young.

From *Each Peach Pear Plum*
written by Allan Ahlberg and illustrated by Janet Ahlberg

"Get, while you are young, the gift of English words" was Eleanor Farjeon's advice. The mass of modern children might be expected to ask "How?"

Elaine Moss in "Accepting the Eleanor Farjeon Award"
(Signal 24, September 1977)

There is really no room for complacency. You who write for children, illustrate for children, and publish with infinite care and attention to detail the enormous range of enticing books for young readers, are, it seems to me, writing, illustrating and publishing into a bottleneck. You are selling your books, or you wouldn't be surviving this period of economic crisis. But you are selling your books in the main *to* adults *for* libraries. In public libraries shelves full of well-reviewed books await the avid reader who comes and is well served. So far, so good. A little wine (orange squash doesn't seem quite the right idiom!) is being poured through the neck of the bottle and being consumed by the thirsty child – by the child who *knows* he is thirsty.

But tucked tidily away in schools up and down the country there are hundreds of kids, thousands of kids (but perhaps not Wanda Gág's "Millions and billions and trillions" of kids) who are also thirsty but don't even know it....

Even assuming, as alas one cannot, that all primary schools have some kind of reading-for-pleasure book stock, there is still a major obstacle which prevents the right book from meeting its natural reader at the crucial moment. That obstacle, I am sorry to say, can be lack of knowledge on the part of the class teacher: but let me hasten to add that the fault does not lie entirely with him or her. It lies with all of us, but largely, I think, with the colleges of education whose courses on the value of children's literature in the classroom, where such courses exist, appear to have little impact on the emerging teacher. If a knowledge of children's books (books that can help children want to learn to read) on the part of student teachers is being assumed, then the assumption today is altogether false.

American Dispatch

JOHN DONOVAN

Between May 1973 and January 1979 *American Dispatch* was a regular SIGNAL feature. In it John Donovan, Executive Director of the Children's Book Council in New York, reported informally on books and events and issues that seemed particularly important to the children's book world in the United States. The following items are taken from columns published in the middle years of the decade and represent the range of subjects touched on. The Children's Book Council is a non-profit association of seventy American children's book publishers. It encourages interest in reading and the enjoyment of children's books.

1973

1972 was a year in which children's books and intellectual freedom were much discussed in the United States, mainly by librarians, but by publishers, children's literature specialists in colleges of education and by authors and illustrators as well. The discussion began on a harmonious note, with the Children's Services Division (C.S.D.) of the American Library Association (A.L.A.) endorsing with enthusiasm a statement by A.L.A.'s Intellectual Freedom Committee (I.F.C.), which recommended that American libraries not try to keep minors away from controversial books in the adult collections. Individual librarians had opened their shelves to children in the past, but to have collections usually termed "closed shelf", "locked case", "adults only", etc., declared in violation of the spirit of A.L.A.'s Library Bill of Rights was a dramatic advance for libertarians in the library community.

A second issue, brought to the attention of I.F.C. by the Children's Book Council, grew out of a practice in some libraries of

"altering" Mickey in Maurice Sendak's *In the Night Kitchen*. As
everyone knows, Mickey is naked, his modest privates clear to the
reader. Some librarians dressed the helpless little fellow; rumour
has it that others did more. The first reports seemed funny; but
as we thought about it, it seemed less funny and even dangerous.
A.L.A.'s Council has agreed; it has told American libraries that
material, once purchased, may not be "expurgated" under the
assumption that certain sections of the work may be harmful to
minors.

A remaining issue in this area gave rise to discussion that appears
likely to continue, even though at the A.L.A. mid-winter meeting
in January this year it seemed settled. This is the matter of re-
evaluating children's book collections in libraries. Librarians have
long regarded "weeding" as important. For years, in libraries and
in children's literature courses in library schools, there has been
emphasis on weeding collections. Obsolete fact books, it was felt,
have no place in a collection; a mediocre novel that no child ever
took home to read was using valuable shelf space that could be
filled by another title. No one seriously suggested that re-evaluation
of this sort should not go on.

At A.L.A.'s Annual Convention in 1972 the C.S.D. Board of
Directors adopted a statement designed to guide children's
librarians in weeding old books judged socially obnoxious. That
statement read, in part:

Most materials, whether intentionally or not, reflect the social climate and
conscience of the era in which they were produced, and at the time of production their users accept this reflection without noticing it. But social climate
and conscience and man's state of knowledge are constantly changing. Therefore, librarians must continually re-evaluate their old "standard" materials
in the light of current progress. In the process of re-evaluation, it may be
found that an old title is still accurate and fresh, an asset to the collection,
or even that it was produced ahead of its time and now has a new relevance,
so that it should be more heavily purchased and more actively promoted.
It may also be found that a highly respected title presents hitherto unnoticed
misinformation, or stereotypes in character, plot, dialog, illustrations, or
expressions that are inaccurate in the light of current knowledge or beliefs
and are demeaning to some segment of our society ... when it is not clear
from the context that the material belongs to a past era, when it apparently

fosters for the present day concepts which are now deemed to be false or
degrading, then, despite the title's prestige, the librarian should question the
validity of its continued inclusion in the library collection....

Foul! cried I.F.C. Should a librarian decide, in the words of
Dorothy Broderick of Dalhousie University, that "the whole concept of social responsibility implies value judgments – some things
are right and some things are wrong and it is that simple"?

C.S.D. and I.F.C., reviewing C.S.D.'s 1972 statement, were able
to agree that re-evaluation is justified, if the librarian remembers
that:

In making his decision [that a book no longer serves a useful role in the collec-
tion], the librarian has a professional obligation to set aside personal likes
and dislikes, to avoid labelling materials, to consider the strengths and weaknesses of each title, and to consider the work as a whole with objectivity
and respect for all opinions. Only after such consideration can he reach a
decision as to whether the title is superseded in coverage and quality, and
should be discarded, or should be kept in the collection.

*   *   *

The Children's Book Section of the Library of Congress has
observed its tenth anniversary. The occasion is in itself a remarkable testimonial to its first and only Head, Virginia Haviland, who
has developed the Section. The Library's vast holdings of children's
books, and the Section's services and publications, are of major
importance to us.

Many assume that the Library of Congress is the U.S. National
Library; in fact, there is no such establishment in this country.
L. of C. performs most of the functions of a national library, however, and this had led to repeated suggestions that it be declared
our national library. Now, it belongs to and is financially supported
by the U.S. Congress. If it were to become a national library, its
destiny would no doubt be controlled by the Executive Branch, i.e.,
the President, of our government. Mr. Nixon's government has
proposed that virtually all Federal support for book-related government programmes be eliminated. His proposals in this field coupled
with an accumulation of various other insensitivities suggest that
the time is not right for a change in L. of C.'s status.

*   *   *

The 1973 National Book Award in the Children's Books category has been given to Ursula K. Le Guin for *The Farthest Shore*, the concluding volume of a trilogy that began with *A Wizard of Earthsea*, published by Parnassus Press in the U.S. The second book, *The Tombs of Atuan*, like the third, was published by Atheneum in the U.S. All three titles have the Gollancz imprint in Britain. Mrs. Le Guin's three books have had a splendid press in this country. Her writing has, in the words of Zena Sutherland in the *Bulletin of the Center for Children's Books*, University of Chicago, "a majestic intricacy; to appreciate it the reader must enjoy ornate language, the grave discussion of life and death and love and courage, and the tongue-rolling exotic names of a legendary land".

The National Book Awards (N.B.A.) programme gives awards in ten categories. Mrs. Le Guin's award is the fifth for a children's book. Meindert DeJong, Isaac Bashevis Singer, Lloyd Alexander and Donald Barthelme are the earlier recipients. Mr. Barthelme's 1972 award for *The Slightly Irregular Fire Engine*, published by Farrar, Straus & Giroux in the U.S., was not a wildly popular one in children's literature circles. Paul Heins, editor of the *Horn Book* and one of the three judges for the award, registered a firm dissent, and there was some grumbling that the N.B.A. programme was headed for a rocky future if books as idiosyncratic as Mr. Barthelme's were to take the honours in the future. The 1973 award is a popular one, however, although Sada Fretz writing in the *Washington Post* suggested that, "Ironically, *The Farthest Shore* lacks the organic multi-dimensional reality of its predecessors, but if the prize can be considered a tribute to the whole three-volume fantasy, then the choice is hard to fault."

The N.B.A. awards ceremony is the most splendid occasion in America's literary year. The awards' recipients, who must be Americans, gather for three days of hobnobbing with book reviewers, who come from all over the country for the ceremony and related events. The awards began in 1950. On many occasions they have served to introduce to a wide public writers – particularly novelists – who had been cult figures until receiving the award. The judges are as often as not writers themselves, and there has always been private and public sniping about literary feuds, literary politics and literary jealousies. These comments, combined with sometimes newsworthy events at the awards ceremonies, combine to make New York book people shudder nervously when N.B.A. time arrives each year.

It is interesting to observe that, in the five years when there has been a children's book award, at least three of the recipients have been the undisputed "stars" of the awards ceremony.

Mrs. Le Guin's acceptance remarks include some comments on writing fantasy:

We who hobnob with hobbits and tell tall tales about little green men are quite used to dismissal as mere entertainers, or sternly disapproved of as escapists. But I think that the categories are changing like the times. Sophisticated readers are accepting the fact that an improbable and unmanageable world is going to produce an improbable and hypothetical art. At this point realism is perhaps the least adequate means of understanding or portraying the incredible realities of our existence.

A scientist who creates a monster in his laboratory; a librarian in the Library of Babel; a wizard unable to cast a spell; a spaceship having trouble getting to Alpha Centauri; all these may be precise and profound metaphors of the human condition. The fantasist, whether he uses the ancient archetype of myth and legend or the younger ones of science and technology, may be talking as seriously as any sociologist – and a great deal more directly – about human life as it is lived, and as it might be lived, and as it ought to be lived.

For, as a great scientist has said and as all children know, it is by the imagination, above all, that we achieve perception, and compassion, and hope.

1974

The book of 1973 for the children's literature community in America is *The Juniper Tree* (Farrar, Straus in U.S.; Bodley Head, autumn 1974, in Britain), twenty-seven tales from Grimm. Lore Segal translated most; four were translated by the late poet Randall Jarrell. It is Maurice Sendak's pictures that have made the book an event, however. All of the adjectives we have become accustomed to reserving for Sendak are being dusted off again, and while no one has commented in print on the book as of this writing, enough people saw press sheets and advance material so that the rumblings began as early as June at the American Library Association Convention in Las Vegas, Nevada. The Sendak pictures in *The Juniper Tree* are close in spirit to his illustrations for MacDonald's *The Light Princess* and *The Golden Key*. But they are imbued with a kind of ghoulishness – Sendak appears to have robbed a grave for his inspiration – and also a sense of freedom and abandon that are startling. That Sendak has been a major illustrator has been

From *The Juniper Tree and Other Tales* translated from the Brothers Grimm by Lore Segal and Randall Jarrell and illustrated by Maurice Sendak

certain for a dozen years; that he continues to startle suggests something about both us and the disciplined obsessions of this artist.

*   *   *

The U.S. Supreme Court has become a force in the children's book
community, and in a most curious way. During the late 1960s, virtually every major American city, and many small communities as
well, had movie houses showing movies involving sex acts. People
paid five dollars to see films that were, before, privately screened.
At the same time a number of so-called underground newspapers
and magazines became freely available. Many of these publications
would not have been sold at newsstands in an earlier day, but in
many cities in the U.S. there is only one local daily newspaper available, and people selling newspapers "have to make a living, like
everybody else". Newspaper stands began to sell *Screw*, *The East
Village Other*, and a number of other publications that occupied
space that used to be filled by the *New York Herald Tribune*, *Washington Star*, *Boston Herald* and countless other publications that
had expired. In due course, people showing films portraying sex
acts, and selling books and other publications with sexual incident
or language thought prurient, were brought to courts for violating
local ordinances. In June of 1973 the Supreme Court handed down
five decisions that said, in effect, "obscenity" is not protected by
the First Amendment to the U.S. Constitution, which guarantees
"freedom of speech". Before the 1973 decisions, it had been our
law that if a work could be shown to have "redeeming social
value", it could not be suppressed. Now, if "taken as a whole"
a work can be shown to appeal to prurient interest in sex, and
"taken as a whole" the work does not have redeeming social values,
and if it portrays sex "in an offensive way", it can be suppressed.

Several months passed, or so parochial New York publishers
believed, without response from communities. But as the 1973
children's books were being evaluated around the country, and as
the prize-winning children's books published in 1972 were being
bought in schools and libraries, publishers began to receive nervous
letters from people who bought children's books for institutions
supported by public funds. Somehow the Supreme Court's pro-
nouncements about "dirty" movies and its dictum about local

mores had made itself felt in many areas. Librarians, who see the new books sooner than teachers, told publishers that they were getting inquiries about books accessible to children and young people from concerned citizens in their towns and cities. A children's librarian from a large mid-western city reports that she was sent more inquiries in 1973 than she had received in her twenty or so years, combined, of being responsible for administering her city's children's and young adult book collections.

Both the American Library Association and the National Council of Teachers of English have developed procedures to help librarians and teachers faced with a person or groups wanting to keep books out of collections. Both groups recommend that schools and libraries establish written criteria for buying books, films, and so on, and that they publicize the existence of their criteria. Each association has developed a form for citizen complaints; it urges institutions to ask people to put their objections in writing, on this form, so that they may be reviewed. Until recently protesters generally would not take the time to cope with forms, complaint procedures and the like, and nothing happened after a first irate telephone call. Recently, however, institutions – nervous for fear of losing support (most American schools and libraries are financed out of local taxes, assessed on the value of real property owned and/or personal income) – have begun to withdraw attacked books from collections. The withdrawal is frequently accompanied by a statement saying that the book has not been removed, only taken away until it can be judged. If these statements weren't so sad, they would be funny. We live quite comfortably with "double speak", however; in fact, the National Council of Teachers of English has a Committee on Public Double-Speak that has gained national prominence during the Watergate year.

In addition to withdrawing attacked books from collections, librarians are now electing not to purchase books that might be controversial. And controversy is not where one finds it, we discover, but where one looks for it. So moral and human a book as Johanna Reiss's *The Upstairs Room*, recipient of brotherhood awards and a 1973 Newbery Honour Book, is a particular target for its "more than 50 irreverent expletives and the one four-letter word in the book", according to an article by a North Carolina

177

school librarian in the *School Library Journal* for December 1973. An elementary school principal in Michigan wrote to the Children's Book Council, stressing that publishers should realize that "most of our young people are wholesome, and we want to keep it that way ... common sense tells me that some things are corrupting to morals and/or bring out kinds of thinking and actions not desirable". The illustrations in a prize-winning early 1973 book were thought too suggestively sexual in some communities that asked both the illustrator and publisher to give them reasons for purchasing the book "because of recent Supreme Court rulings and concerned parents".

Most of us are deeply if quietly fearful that these incidents of censorship will multiply. The irony is that the Supreme Court decisions stressed that works should be "taken as a whole" when evaluated; a portion of the children's book community appears to be picking at parts, and most aggressively.

*   *   *

As SIGNAL readers no doubt know, Richard Adams's *Watership Down* was published in the United States by Macmillan, but not as a children's book, even though it originated here as a project of the Macmillan children's book department. Susan Hirschman, who directs that department, read a copy of the British edition on a flight from London to New York at the time it was being published in England, and decided immediately that Macmillan must offer to publish it in America. She succeeded in securing the American rights. As her Macmillan colleagues began to read the book, their enthusiasm was such that everyone in the trade book division of the firm soon heard of it. In due course a decision was made to present the book quite simply as a book: not an adult book, not a children's book, but a book.

The decision was a wise one. It comforts children's book partisans, for they are able to say with some satisfaction that *Watership Down* is, after all, *really* a children's book, while at the same time people who haven't read a standard children's book since they were ten years old are comforted by thoughts that it really *isn't* a children's book. Whichever, it is an enormous success.

The first tangible sign of the appeal here of *Watership* was the

pre-publication licensing of the U.S. paperback rights to Avon
Books for an unprecedented amount of money. It's impolite and
vulgar to make observations about money, except when, as in the
case of the arrangements with Avon Books, the amount calls attention to itself. For what they are worth, published reports indicate
that the Avon advance payment is calculated from a base of eight
hundred thousand dollars. Customary escalation clauses having
to do with a book's presence on *The New York Times Book Review*
best-seller list will raise the advance considerably. At the time the
agreement was concluded the advance was the highest ever paid
by a paperback publisher for rights to a hard-cover book here.
Records of this sort are short-lived, of course, and within ten days
or so after this one was established another paperback house paid
a good deal more for a new novel by Frederick Forsyth. Word of
Watership had circulated in the children's book community here
as soon as it was being reviewed in England, and hundreds of copies
of the Puffin edition were being read and loaned throughout 1973.
It was an exception if an American children's book person visiting
England at that time did not carry back *Watership*. As soon as the
Avon Books purchase became known, the book became part of
publishing legend, just as, if one understands the accounts correctly, it is part of British publishing legend, if for other reasons
entirely.

It is instructive to read again the major notices *Watership* received on publication. The children's book critics were unanimous
in praise. Newspapers and general-interest magazines wrote of the
book with a slight note of embarrassment and apology, but not
condescension. Reviews began in this fashion: "Straight faces,
please, and no tittering from the back of the room. Because the
subject today is rabbits – yes, bunny rabbits –..." (*New York
Times*, 6 March 1974); "I'll make a deal with you: if you won't
say anything dumb like 'I'm not interested in a story about rabbits,'
I won't say anything dumb like 'this is a great novel'" (*Newsweek*,
18 March 1974). The quality in the book that seemed most frequently remarked upon by all reviewers is its unsentimentality. All
the reviews mentioned Richard Adams's narrative skills. The only
major review that I have read that seems essentially negative was
by Richard Gilman in *The New York Times Book Review*, 24

March 1974. Mr. Gilman found the book lacking "the high wit and imaginative force of 'Alice in Wonderland' or the triumphant (if occasionally purple) lyricism of 'The Wind in the Willows'..." He mentioned the Lapine language device as "symptomatic of what is wrong with 'Watership Down', or rather what keeps it from being wholly right. There is a subtle indecisiveness or doubt on Adams's part as to just how convincing his fiction is. This is manifested partly by his tendency to do too much (the Lapine, the rabbit myths) and also by the frequent occasions when he steps outside the narrative to serve for a moment as a naturalist...." Another negative notice, though to my mind a funny one, more revealing of the class(less?) snobbery of the reviewer than illuminating of the book, appeared in *The Village Voice*, 21 March 1974: "They [the rabbits] have many of the values and anxieties of public-school England ... something within me balks when an author tries to teach me how to turn into a British rabbit."

With the passing of months, the comments on *Watership Down* will be more composed. I have read one by Dennis Flanagan, editor of *Scientific American*, that will appear in the annual children's books issue of *Wilson Library Bulletin* in October. Entitled "To Each Generation Its Own Rabbits", the Flanagan article explores *Watership Down* "for what it represents [rather] than what it says. It is a significant expression of the current state of relations between the literary culture and the scientific one ... [It] is a scientific novel, a work that embraces two cultures."

Watership Down has become 1974's most popular novel. When it first appeared on *The New York Times Book Review* best-seller list on April 14th it occupied the fourth spot on the fiction list. This is quite unusual: a book customarily starts quite far down the list, gradually edging up towards the top, a spot that, once occupied, is usually occupied for several weeks, or even months. *Watership* made it to the top in four weeks, deposing Gore Vidal's *Burr*, and at the top it remains as summer begins. That it has been totally absorbed by Americans there can be no doubt: *Publishers Weekly*, our book trade magazine, reports that a San Francisco bookseller listing the book as the best-selling novel in its shop for that publication's June 10th Best Seller list, called the book *Watergate Down*.

*   *   *

We appear to be publishing fewer children's books, by title, each year. As recently as five years ago about three thousand books were published annually; the figure for 1973 was just under two thousand. This is a dramatic drop, attributable in part to the uncertainties associated with our government's support for federal programmes involving libraries. In the late 1960s, in particular, federal funds became available to libraries, mainly school libraries, for the purchase of books, and of films, filmstrips, recordings, etc. For about a two-year period, best estimates suggest, almost seventy-five million dollars a year made its way to children's book publishers. Subsequently, as book collections acquired depth, libraries bought as much audio-visual material as books. In the most recent years there has been an annual contest between the U.S. Congress, which makes our laws, and the President, who has the power to authorize the expenses required by Congress's laws. Each year, recently, President Nixon, who in the past appears to have regarded Federal programmes of this sort ill-conceived, has created major obstacles that would have killed these particular programmes were it not for the vigorous lobbying efforts of the educational community and the responses of the Congress to those efforts. By use of a variety of complicated legislative devices, funds have continued to be available, though in smaller amounts than previously. Mr. Nixon has had other things on his mind for the past year, however, so it is possible that if he should serve his full term in office he will not be as aggressively hostile to social legislation as he has been in the past. Given the revelations surrounding Mr. Nixon's re-election, it amuses one to speculate about how these programmes might never have had to be in jeopardy if the industries servicing the programmes – publishers, let's say – had had their heads in the same place certain other industrialists did in the early seventies. Fortunately, they did not.

It was common in the late sixties to hear librarians, teachers and reviewers urge publishers not to publish so many books. It was impossible, they seemed to feel, to keep up with the literature. In retrospect, the request – and it was made often and seriously – appears ridiculous. Now that the day of publishing less has come, the sort of book that isn't around any more is the very sort of marginal title that made our children's books here such a varied, vigorous and idiosyncratic lot. The marginal book is disappearing. An excellent example is the novel first published abroad in a foreign language and then translated into English. If there is one kind of book young Americans need almost more than any other, it is the foreign novel. As a people we are notoriously inward-looking; anything, including our literature, that would help to temper our cultural isolationism makes a significant contribution. Five years ago, when it was asserted there were too many books being published, there may have been about 150 young persons' books a year that had been translated from another language; in 1973 there were approximately thirty. In a time of abundance a peripheral book – a book that doesn't have universal appeal, whatever that is – has a place. Of course, it always has a place, but if it is not published, that place, alas, is as a manuscript in the author's desk drawer.

1975

At a children's book conference in Providence, Rhode Island, in October of 1974, sponsored by a joint committee of the Association for Childhood Education International and the Children's Book Council, the children's book author Alvin Tresselt alluded amusingly to the matter of "language" in editions of books published in both the United States and Great Britain. It is boring to discuss differences in U.S. and British spellings of such words as "colour", "defence", "catalogue", etc. For many years, U.S. and English editors went to the trouble of changing spellings so that words youngsters read would conform to nationally accepted spellings. Here, book discussions relating to English-language titles from abroad inevitably mention English spellings if the American publisher has concluded it was not important to "convert" certain words. This is a tedious subject.

Mr. Tresselt's remarks related to a different problem. He attempted to convey the thought that a word, by its nature, may mean one thing here, and something else, or nothing, there, wherever "there" might be. An example he cited was from a text of his, *Hide and Seek Fog*, illustrated with great sympathy and skill by Roger Duvoisin. (The book is published by Lothrop, Lee &

Shepard in the U.S., World's Work in England.) "In the fog book," Mr. Tresselt observed:

I said the children spoddled in the lazy lapping waves on the beach. Shortly after the book came out I began getting letters wanting to know what this word [spoddled] meant. It was a word I had known all my life. My mother would say, "Stop spoddling in the sink and finish washing those dishes." ... So it seemed a perfect word to use in the book. I confidently went to the dictionary, but it wasn't there. Then I recalled that my mother had grown up in England, and thinking it might be a British word, I ... checked the O.E.D. It wasn't there, either ... a dictionary of regional English words [revealed that] *spuddle* means to dig idly in dirt, related to spud, a potato, peculiar to two counties in England. My mother had grown up in an adjoining county, and apparently the pronunciation had changed slightly when it crossed the county lines. When the British edition of the book came out I looked through my copy and noted that some of the spellings had been changed: *gray* was *grey*, *vacation* had become *holidays*. Then I checked out *spoddle* and found that my good English word had been changed to *paddled*. Some time later I met the British editor and asked why. "We thought it was one of your strange American words," was the answer.

*   *   *

Children's rights is an area of increasing interest here. The Association for Childhood Education International, with which the Children's Book Council and other groups work closely, has singled out children's rights as a top priority concern during the years ahead. The past decade has been one in which the rights of our many races, persons from diverse ethnic backgrounds and women and girls have been asserted vigorously. Children's books have been deeply and positively affected by each of the rights movements. One reason is that critics find in this branch of literature a body of work easily identifiable and thought to have a deep effect on those who read and look at it. The criticism has been mainly constructive. Authors, illustrators and publishers have welcomed it and have, indeed, been major contributors to it. In certain instances, the criticism has been hysterical and destructive, taking the form of irrational attacks that have given enormous satisfaction to the attackers and nihilists clustered round them.

It will follow, as new books are written and old books reread, that the dignity, respect and concern with which children are portrayed will be closely examined and commented upon. Lists of approved and disapproved books will proliferate; conferences will take place; presumably children will be increasingly more involved. In general, writing and publishing books will be a far more lively enterprise than it presently is.

A book sure to be on anyone's approved list in the children's rights area would be Florence Parry Heide's *The Shrinking of Treehorn*, illustrated by that genius Edward Gorey (published here by Holiday House; in Britain by Kestrel and Puffin). "Something very strange was happening to Treehorn," it begins. "The first thing he noticed was that he couldn't reach the shelf in his closet that he had always been able to reach before, the one where he hid his candy bars and bubble gum." Then Treehorn discovers that his clothes are getting too big and that he's tripping on them. "'Too bad, dear'" says his mother. At dinner, as Treehorn shrinks below the table top, his father urges him to sit up. "'I can hardly see your head,'" his father says. Arguments ensue. Treehorn insists he is

From *The Shrinking of Treehorn*
written by Florence Parry Heide and illustrated by Edward Gorey

shrinking. "'Don't argue with your mother, Treehorn,'" his father says. "'Nobody shrinks.'" Treehorn continues to shrink; he can't post a letter in the mail box; he can't climb onto the school bus; he can't reach the water fountain in the corridor at school; the principal at school thinks Treehorn is shirking, not shrinking. Well, Treehorn finally gets back his size but it's not because anyone helped him!

The book is delicious. It doesn't attack adults, but it certainly observes them closely and to their detriment.

1976

This note is by way of being a cautionary tale, for the area with which it deals is one that I do not see much written about in Britain – at least not in the fair sample of Commonwealth children's literature serial publications I see regularly. These observations relate to criteria for judging children's books, and they suggest themselves by virtue of the publication here of a volume titled *Human – and Anti-Human – Values in Children's Books: A Content Rating Instrument for Educators and Concerned Parents: Guidelines for the Future*, published by the Racism and Sexism Resource Centre for Educators, a Division of the Council on Interracial Books for Children. It does not matter that this volume is unlikely to be available for your scrutiny – interesting though you may find it – for its significance is that it suggests that people who evaluate children's books must judge children's books for their social usefulness, in addition to traditional judgements about literary and artistic quality, enjoyment by children, and use in some pedagogical situation. This objective has been sought by the Council on Interracial Books for Children (C.I.B.C.) since its founding a decade ago; it has never been as effectively stated, however, as it is in *Human – and Anti-Human – Values in Children's Books*.

It is possible to dismiss this matter as a mere extension of the old didacticism-in-children's-books argument that was much talked of when the "new realism" became an issue in children's books, also about a decade ago. However, I believe that the activities of C.I.B.C., particularly as expressed in this new volume, suggest a closeness in both fact and spirit to the Gorky pieces on the function of children's literature in a socialist state. Straightaway, let me say that I don't make the comparison to Gorky for purposes of labelling C.I.B.C. in an inflammatory way; not at all. I think the questions and issues posed by the volume are profound, and involve serious issues and disagreements as to the nature and function of both children's books and children's book publishing in a society that labels itself "democratic". It is beyond the scope of this little piece to go into the true nature of American society, though it is this very evasion that friends at C.I.B.C. would suggest is the root of the problems and differences of opinion.

Some background facts are necessary in order to bring perspective to what must, I suppose, pass as a serious problem.

That America is a pluralistic society is certainly not new information to SIGNAL readers, and that England has become one somewhat similar to ours in the last two or three decades is not news to us. *Human Values* insists on capitalizing the word "Black" while "white" always appears in lower case. As I do not comprehend the reasoning behind this decision, it is simpler for me to use both words in lower case. In America, the black population is either 15% of our total population, or may account for 20% of us; various statistics-compiling sources differ and none, it seems, is authoritative enough for there to be a definitive statement on the matter. In any event, there has never been a time in American children's book publishing history when blacks, or themes and subjects having to do with "blackness", occupied 15–20% of publishers' lists. However, as early as 1941, Augusta Baker of the New York Public Library System was able to compile a list of children's books portraying blacks positively. That listing has been recompiled and revised on numerous occasions since that time; just as a similar listing prepared by the Chicago librarian Charlemae Rollins for our National Council of Teachers of English has gone through numerous revisions. Both of these listings have consistently emphasized in introductory matter the necessity of there being children's books not only *for* black children, but for all children who would hope to understand and value both the "black experience" and the black contribution to American life.

While each of these bibliographic activities – and many others were taking place under the auspices of local librarians and such organizations as the National Conference of Christians and Jews – had its impact, there appeared in 1965 an article in *Saturday Review*, a magazine with a general (i.e., public) readership, that has had a continuing and perhaps permanent effect on children's book publishing in America. Nancy Larrick's "The All White World of Children's Books" suggested that most children's books reflected a sort of narrowness, middle-classness, and sterility – particularly in fiction for the middle and upper age reader – that was truly damaging to children not a part of the majority culture. In our little world, the article has become famous. I had occasion to refer to it in 1975 at a National Council of Teachers of English meeting as the piece that inspired the "black gold rush", for in the late sixties and early seventies there emerged an outpouring of children's books that attempted to make up for the deficiencies Nancy Larrick, and others too, had identified. During this bizarre time in American children's book publishing, some awful books emerged. Many were written and published by well-intentioned, liberal writers and publishers; someday there will be a doctoral thesis analysing the whole phenomenon to us. Meanwhile, it became clear that publishers wanted to be responsive to what seemed a clear social need, and with something for which there was obviously a market.

As time passed, it was evident that books created to satisfy a market would be, at best, ephemeral and, at worst, dangerous.

At the beginning of this period C.I.B.C. emerged as a constructive critical force, quick to identify racist manifestations in popular and little-known children's books alike. In due course C.I.B.C. published a *Bulletin*, with articles, reviews, and – a marvellous service – examples of art work by black and other non-white artists that publishers might not otherwise see. C.I.B.C. also sponsored a contest for unpublished black writers. Many of the winners of these contests – other minority groups are now eligible to enter it – have become well-known authors, published regularly.

With time, most American publishers got the message, hammered home to them by the Larrick article and subsequently elaborated on by many sources. Certainly, events in our political and social lives in the past decade – totally apart from children's books – have had a lasting effect on the children's books published today. I asked a publisher friend not long ago if he would publish a book in "black" English without first knowing if the author is black. He said that he probably would not, even though the manuscript (if one existed) might convince him to think otherwise.

Now I approach, but do not yet come to, *Human Values*. It seemed to me that C.I.B.C. – its initial reason for being having been achieved – might logically retire from the children's book scene. There is an informed and perhaps over-sensitive body of editors and publishers who now understand needs and interests that their predecessors may have been aware of only dimly, if at all. Mistakes in judgement will occur, but so do they occur in every aspect of our public and private lives.

C.I.B.C., however, elected to identify – selectively – other isms. Blacks were joined by the Hispanic cultures (we have at least three – probably more – Puerto Rican, Cuban and Mexican-American, or Chicano); Asians or Asian-Americans; women, including girls, and men and boys; old people; divorced people; persons who abuse drugs and alcohol; ill, handicapped and dying people; adopted persons; athletes; Jews; and "non-fiction". It is a broad spectrum.

And, perhaps, as an organization geared to attack, C.I.B.C. could not confine itself to children's books alone, but expressed deep concern over television programmes that utilized children's books as source material. A particular target happens to have been the televised version, here, of Theodore Taylor's *The Cay*, a story of interdependence between two humans shipwrecked together on a Caribbean island during World War Two. One of the persons is a black adult man, the other a young white boy. They grow to understand, depend on and, I suppose, love each other. However, because the adult is perceived by some to defer to the young white, C.I.B.C. elected to confront the broadcasters with charges of racism, and suggested that concerned T.V. viewers express their displeasure to the network (American T.V. has three national networks, and numerous local stations) broadcasting *The Cay*.

I am getting closer to *Human Values*.

Curiously enough, until *Human Values*, it was not C.I.B.C. that made it clear to American publishers that there are forces that can be impressed upon them that will influence their children's book publishing. The group that most effectively dramatized this stance was the Task Force on Gay Liberation of the American Library Association's Social Responsibilities Round Table. This organization prepared the document "Guidelines for Treatment of Gay Themes in Children's and Young Adult Literature", which suggested that any book dealing with homosexuality should be evaluated, before publication, by "a consultant who is proudly identified as gay ... to point out negative stereotypical attitudes when they occur".

The consideration in this matter is *when* it is appropriate for a special-interest group to impress itself on creators. Alas, I am not familiar with the British laws in this respect, but in America, the First Amendment to our Constitution assures us – all of us – a voice if we choose to exercise it. In a society – ours – that has been subject to weird and fortunately disastrous attempts to arrest "free speech" in the past few generations, it seems to me both reckless and dangerous to suggest to authors and publishers that they have some function, which is to serve an ideology. The time to criticize and evaluate books – children's books – is after they exist and not beforehand.

Human Values evaluated 235 of the approximately 2,500 children's books published in this country in 1975; 34 were found "noteworthy"; 85 "neutral"; and 93 "negative". Ironically, many of the evaluations, which are terse reviews that accompany a fixed rating scale, are frequently devoted to assessing the literary and graphic merits of books rather than to placing a book in its proper political position. Most make interesting and illuminating reading.

The rating scale for evaluating books involves many factors. The best books are anti-racist, anti-sexist, anti-elitist, anti-materialist, anti-individualist, anti-ageist, anti-conformist, anti-escapist, they build positive images of women and minorities, and they inspire action. Books that take no positions in these areas are innocuous, and therefore dangerous because they support prevalent lifestyles. Many books – lowest in this scheme – are considered positively racist, sexist, etc.

I do not wish to denigrate the positive intentions of people who evaluate children's books on charts, forms and diagrams that have been prepared for them in advance. But it is difficult to understand the purpose of such an endeavour. That American society is less than perfect is obvious; anyone who denies it misunderstands American life. That, however, the creators of children's books need to be warned thus – "four hundred years of racism on this continent have left book writing and publishing primarily in the hands of a white, college-educated elite"; "... at this point in history, directly or indirectly, one serves either the racist past or a humanistic future"; "the old publishing ratio, used by the industry for years, was three boy characters to one girl character"; and that "we are, in fact, highly concerned with norms; the need is for new ones, *not* the elimination of norms ..." – suggests an adversary relationship between originator and evaluator that is certainly unhealthy and could prove fatal.

"Change", that desirable eventuality, is not, after all, imposed, except in a totalitarian society.

SIGNAL QUOTES

Robert Leeson in "Faces over my Typewriter"
(Signal 30, September 1979)

All children should be told stories at home and in school. The lack of them is one of the primary deprivations children can suffer. And they ought to be told stories not late on Friday afternoons when the rest of school work is done or abandoned, but first thing Monday morning, Tuesday morning and so on. We often say that the oral tradition is dying and the book has taken its place (not without some loss for many of our population). But it's not entirely true. Many of our classics are as widely known as they are partly because the oral tradition is maintained in our schools. There are books like *Alice in Wonderland* or *Wind in the Willows* which I know as well as the next person, but which I never read as a child. They were read to me by devoted teachers. Indeed I never actually read those two books until I came to read them to my own children. But I knew them all right. And I can go into any school and ask children about the Cheshire Cat and Long John Silver and get a response from readers or non-readers. If we relied on self-reading to transmit our heritage, it would have withered on the vine. Children need stories; they will rarely come to reading without them. And writers are glad (those who have done it) to play the part of go-between linking story and book in the mind of the child.

Rumer Godden in
"Opening the Children's Books of the Year Exhibition"
(Signal 21, September 1976)

It takes courage to tell a story, to endure the discipline of writing it, and doing that for children is a far more difficult art than writing

191

a novel: courage not to listen to what people tell you, to what your publishers say will sell. Even they do not always know. It is difficult not to think about money when one is writing. We keep one eye on the critics, the other on the grownups who after all buy the books – but we shouldn't even think about the child. Only about the story; to let ourselves be entranced by it, not be ashamed to be rapt away.

From *Mr. Gumpy's Outing* written and illustrated by John Burningham

Standards of Criticism
for Children's Literature

JOHN ROWE TOWNSEND

John Rowe Townsend is a well-known author and critic of books for children and young people. This article has been slightly edited from the text published in the May 1974 SIGNAL. It was a reprint of the 1971 May Hill Arbuthnot Honour Lecture first published by the American Library Association in its Children's Services Division publication *Top of the News* for June 1971. Mr. Townsend's book *A Sense of Story*, which is mentioned in this article, has recently been revised and retitled *A Sounding of Storytellers* (Kestrel, 1979).

To give the May Hill Arbuthnot Honour Lecture is the greatest privilege that can fall to a commentator on books for children. It is with some idea of matching my response to the size of the honour that I have decided at last to attempt the largest and most difficult subject I know in this field: namely, the question of standards by which children's literature is to be judged. This is not only the most difficult, it is the most important question; indeed, it is so basic that none of us who are professionally concerned with children and books ought really to be functioning at all unless we have thought it out to our own satisfaction and are prepared to rethink it from time to time. But, as in many other areas of life, we tend to be so busy doing what we have to do that we never have time to stop and consider why and how we do it. True, Mrs. Arbuthnot herself had a good deal to say on the subject of critical standards, but she would not have claimed to say the last word.

It seems to me that the assessment of children's books takes place in an atmosphere of unparalleled intellectual confusion. There are two reasons for this. One is a very familiar one which I need not elaborate on. It was neatly expressed by Brian Alderson in an article in *Children's Book News* of London for January/February 1969, when he said that "everyone in the children's book business subsists in a slightly unreal world, where time, brains and energy are expended on behalf of a vast and largely non-participating audience". It has been pointed out time and time again that children's books are written by adults, published by adults, reviewed by adults, and, in the main, bought by adults. The whole process is carried out at one, two, three, or more removes from the ultimate consumer.

This situation is inescapable, but it is an uneasy one. Most of us think we know what is good for ourselves, but the more sensitive we are, the more seriously we take our obligations, the less we feel sure we know what is good for others.

The second cause of confusion is that children's literature is a part of the field, or adjoins the field, of many different specialists; yet it is the *major* concern of relatively few, and those not the most highly placed in the professional or academic pecking-order. Furthermore, the few to whom children's literature is central cannot expect, within one working lifetime, to master sufficient knowledge of the related fields to meet the experts on their own ground and at their own level. And yet, while the children's literature person obviously cannot operate at a professional level in all these various fields, the people operating in the various fields can and quite properly do take an interest in children's reading as it affects their own specialities, and quite frequently pronounce upon it. But, understandably, such people are often unaware of or have not thought deeply about the aspects of children's literature that do *not* impinge upon their own field. The subject is one on which people are notoriously willing to pronounce with great confidence but rather little knowledge. Consequently, we have a flow of apparently authoritative comment by people who are undoubtedly experts but who are not actually experts on *this*.

I am not here to quarrel with those who see children's literature in terms of social or psychological adjustment, advancement of deprived or minority groups, development of reading skills, or anything else. I have said in the foreword to my book, *A Sense of Story*, that "most disputes over standards are fruitless because the antagonists suppose their criteria to be mutually exclusive; if one is right the other must be wrong. This is not necessarily so. Different kinds of assessment are valid for different purposes." I would only remark that the viewpoints of psychologists, sociologists, and educationists of various descriptions have rather little in common with each other or with those whose approach is mainly literary.

We face, in fact, a jungle of preoccupations, ideas, and attitudes. I should like to begin my discussion by clearing, if I can, some small piece of common ground which will accommodate most of us who care about children and books.

Let me borrow a phrase used by Edgar Z. Friedenberg in a book entitled *Coming of Age in America*, published in 1965. I do not agree with all that is said in the book, but I think the phrase I have my eye on is admirable. Friedenberg used it to describe the true function of the schools; I would use it to describe the duty of all of us, either as parents or, in a broad sense, as guardians. This aim, he said, was "the respectful and affectionate nurture of the young, and the cultivation in them of a disciplined and informed mind and heart".

Extending this formulation to cover the special interest which has brought us here today, I should like to add that in furtherance of these ends we would wish every child to experience to his or her full capacity the enjoyment, and the broadening of horizons, which can be derived from literature. Diffidently I invite my hearers, and my readers, if any, to subscribe to this modest and unprovocative creed. What it asks is the acceptance of literary experience as having value in itself for the general enrichment of life, over and above any virtue that may be claimed for it as a means to a nonliterary end. Anyone who cannot accept the proposition is of course fully entitled to stand aloof; but I cannot think of anything to say to such a person, because if literature is *solely* a means to an end, then the best literature is the literature which best serves that end, and the only matters worth arguing about are whether the end is a good one and how effectively it is served. Furthermore, those points cannot be argued in general terms, but only in relation to a particular cause and a particular book.

I wonder if from the tiny clearing we have made we can begin to find a way through the tangle that surrounds us. Let us try to consider what literature is, what it offers and what is children's literature. I do not want to spend a lot of time on questions which, although they may present theoretical difficulties, are not really perplexing in practice. I am going to define literature, without appeal to authority, as consisting of all works of imagination which are transmitted primarily by means of the written word or spoken narrative – that is, in the main, novels, stories, and poetry – with the addition of those works of non-fiction which by their qualities of style or insight may be said to offer experience of a literary nature. This is a rather loose definition, but in practical terms I think it will do.

What does literature offer? Summarizing ruthlessly, I will say that it is, above all, enjoyment: enjoyment not only in the shallow sense of easy pleasure, but enjoyment of a profounder kind; enjoyment of the shaping by art of the raw material of life, and enjoyment, too, of the skill with which that shaping is performed; enjoyment in the stretching of one's imagination, the deepening of one's experience, and the heightening of one's awareness; an enjoyment which may be intense even if the material of the literary work is sad or painful. I should add that obviously not all literature can offer such a range of enjoyments; that no work of literature outside such short forms as the lyric poem can offer these enjoyments throughout; and that the deliberate restriction of aim is often necessary in children's literature as in much else.

What in particular is children's literature? That is quite a hard question. There is a sense in which we don't need to define it because we know what it is. Children's literature is *Robinson Crusoe* and *Alice* and *Little Women* and *Tom Sawyer* and *Treasure Island* and *The Wind in the Willows* and *Winnie-the-Pooh* and *The Hobbit* and *Charlotte's Web*. That's simple: but it won't quite do. Surely *Robinson Crusoe* was not written for children, and do not the *Alice* books appeal at least as much to grownups?; if *Tom Sawyer* is children's literature, what about *Huckleberry Finn*?; if the *Jungle Books* are children's literature, what about *Kim* or *Stalky*?; and if *The Wind in the Willows* is children's literature, what about *The Golden Age*?; and so on.

Since any line-drawing must be arbitrary, one is tempted to abandon the attempt and say that there is no such thing as children's literature, there is just literature. And in an important sense that is true. Children are not a separate form of life from people; no more than children's books are a separate form of literature from just books. Children are part of mankind; children's literature is part of literature. Yet the fact that children are part of mankind doesn't save you from having to separate them from adults for certain essential purposes: nor does the fact that children's literature is part of literature save you from having to separate it for practical purposes (in the libraries and bookshops, for instance). I pondered this question for some time while working on *A Sense of Story*, and came to the conclusion that in the long run children's literature could only be regarded as consisting of those books which by a consensus of adults and children were assigned to the children's shelves – a wholly pragmatic definition. In the short run it appears that, for better or worse, the publisher decides. If he puts a book on the children's list, it will be reviewed as a children's book and will be read by children (or young people), if it is read at all. If he puts it on the adult list, it will not – or at least not immediately.

Let us assume that we have found, in broad terms, a common aim; that we know roughly what literature is and the nature of the experience it offers: that we have a working definition of children's literature, even if it is more pragmatic than we would wish. Can we now make some sense out of the question of differing standards? So far I have tried to examine what exists rather than to project a theoretical system out of my own head. We all know how often the application of a new mind to an old problem will fail because the new thinking is insufficiently grounded in what has been thought and done before; indeed, it often overestimates its own originality.

When we look for individual assessments of actual books (as distinct from general articles on children's literature and reading) we find that most of what is written comes under the headings of (a) overwhelmingly, reviews, (b) aids to book selection, and (c) general surveys. There is little writing that I think could be dignified with the name of criticism, a point to which I will return later. While examining reviews, selection aids, and surveys, in both the United States and Britain and in relation to imaginative literature, I asked myself not whether they were sound and perceptive or whether I agreed with them, but what they were actually doing and what their standards appeared to be. I was aware that similar enquiries had been carried out by others, and more thoroughly; but I was aware, too, that my findings would be matters of judgement which were not of simple fact, and the scheme of my over-all study required that the judgements should be my own. I will spare you the raw material of my investigation and will keep my conclusions brief. I found, naturally, some differences between reviews in general and specialist publications, but from my point of view they were not crucial.

What the reviewers and selectors were largely concerned with, more often than not, it seemed to me, was telling you what the story was about: a necessary activity, but not an evaluative one. I came to the conclusion that where they offered judgements the writers always concerned themselves with one or more of four attributes, which I do not place in order of importance or frequency. These were (1) suitability, (2) popularity, or potential popularity, (3) relevance, and (4) merit. "Suitability" is rather a blanket term, under which I include appropriateness to the supposed readership or reading age or purpose, and also attempts by the reviewer or selector to assign books to particular age groups or types of child. "Popularity" needs no explanation. By "relevance" I mean the power, or possible power, of theme or subject matter to make the child more aware of current social or personal problems, or to suggest solutions to him; where a story appears to convey a message I include under "relevance" the assessment of the message. Finally, by "merit" I mean on the whole, literary merit, although often one finds that what might be called undifferentiated merit is discerned in a book.

Of the four attributes I have mentioned (please remember that my classifications are arbitrary and that there is some overlap) it may well have occurred to you that the first three are child-centred: suitability to the child, popularity with the child, relevance to the child. The fourth is book-centred: merit of the book. This is an important distinction: failure to perceive it has given us a great deal of trouble in the past, preventing us from understanding each other and understanding what we are about. In an article in *Wilson*

Library Bulletin for December 1968 I rashly coined a phrase about "book people" and "child people". "Book people," I said, were those primarily concerned with books: authors, publishers, a great many reviewers, and public librarians. "Child people," I said, were those primarily concerned with children: parents, teachers, and (in England at any rate) most school librarians. This division was useful in a way, because it helped to account for two diametrically opposed views of the state of English children's literature: that it was in a very healthy state, with so many good books being published; and that it was in a very unhealthy state, because so many children didn't find pleasure in reading. "Book people," I thought, tended to take the former view; "child people" to take the latter. Incidentally, it was reflection on the fact that such totally opposite views could be held that led me to feel we needed an examination of standards and, in part, led me to offer my present hesitant contribution to that formidable task.

However, I did not and do not intend to set any group against any other group, and I must say at once that all children's "book people" I know are also "child people" in that they care about children; and all the "child people" I know who are interested in books are on that account "book people". And I will repeat here what I said earlier in another context: that different kinds of assessment are valid for different purposes. Not only that, but different standards can co-exist within the mind of the same person at the same time. This is why we get mixed up. Our judgements are rarely made with a single, simple purpose in mind, and we do not stop to separate our purposes any more than we normally stop to analyse our own processes of thought. Because we are both "book people" and "child people" and because we care about both books and children, book-centred and child-centred views are all jumbled together in our heads. Is it a good book, will children like it, will it have a beneficial effect on them? We ask ourselves all these questions at once, and expect to come up with a single answer.

It is easy for mental sideslips to occur, even when we are writing for publication. A simple instance (one of many that could be cited) is in the London *Times Literary Supplement* of 16 April 1970, where the anonymous reviewer of a book of verse by Alan Brownjohn discusses the book with much intelligence in the language of literary criticism, and finishes by saying that "this is a book all children will most definitely enjoy". The statement is unrelated to the rest of what is said and, unfortunately, cannot be true. Nobody has yet found a book that "all" children enjoy, and if there were such a book I do not think it would be a book of poems. The reviewer cannot have *thought* before writing that; he or she has made the remark either as a general expression of approval or as an unrealistic inference: "It is good, so they will all enjoy it."

There are people – Brian Alderson in an article provocatively entitled "The Irrelevance of Children to the Children's Book Reviewer"; Paul Heins, if I understand him correctly, in two articles in the *Horn Book* called "Out on a Limb with the Critics" and "Coming to Terms with Criticism", in June and August 1970, respectively – who maintain that reviewing should be strictly critical. Alderson says: "It may be objected that to assess children's books without reference to children is to erect some absolute critical standard relating neither to the author's purpose nor to the reader's enjoyment. To do much less, however, is to follow a road that leads to a morass of contradictions and subjective responses."

I do not wish to prolong my discussion of a subject already so much discussed as reviewing. On the whole I agree with Heins and Alderson, whose positions, I think, can fairly be described as purist. I would prefer the reviewer to address himself sensitively to the book which is there in front of him, rather than to use his space for inevitably crude assessments of suitability for some broad notional category of child or speculations that the book will or will not sit long on the shelf, or that it will or will not help its readers to adjust to reality or understand how the other half of the world lives. Readers can use their intelligence and make these assessments or pursue these speculations for themselves. I suspect that library systems can manage the practical task of book selection without undue dependence on the individual reviewer. What they need to know from him, if they need to know anything from him (and if it isn't too late anyway by the time the review appears), is: does the book have literary merit?

Suitability, popularity, relevance – are these not questions for the buyer, and perhaps above all for those who are closest to the ultimate consumer? "Will this be suitable for *my* child, will this be popular with *my* class, will this be relevant for children in the area served by *my* library?" Surely only the parent, teacher, or librarian there on the spot can find the answer. He will find it in his own judgement and experience. And he will soon learn whether he was right.

I hope I have cleared the ground sufficiently to allow myself to move on to a discussion of critical principles in relation to children's literature. I am not sure whether I have sufficiently indicated the *usefulness* of the critical approach. If I have not, then I ought to do so; for although some of us would no doubt practise it quite happily for its own sake, if it is not useful we cannot reasonably expect others to give their time and attention, their paper and print, to the result of our endeavours. So I will suggest first that a standard of literary merit is required, and indeed in practice is accepted, as the *leading edge*, so to speak, of book assessment since non-literary standards relate so largely to specific aims and situations, times, places, and audiences. Literary standards are not fixed forever, but they are comparatively stable; that is part of their essence. Without this leading edge, this backbone if you prefer it, there can only be a jumble of criteria, a haphazard mixture of personal responses. And I have found in my own numerous discussions with people concerned with various aspects of books for children, that even those who most strongly condemn what they consider to be an excessively literary approach do in fact take it for granted that there is some independent standard of quality other than what children like or what is good for them or what brings them face to face with contemporary issues. "Wonderful stuff, but not for *my* kids" is a frequent comment.

I would suggest, too, and have suggested in the introduction to *A Sense of Story*, that a critical approach is desirable not only for its own sake but also as a stimulus and discipline for author and publisher, and, in the long run, for the improvement of the breed. Donnarae MacCann, introducing a series of articles in the *Wilson Library Bulletin* for December 1969, made this point and quoted from Henry S. Canby's *Definitions* (second series, 1967):

Unless there is somewhere an intelligent critical attitude against which the writer can measure himself ... one of the chief requirements for good literature is wanting.... The author degenerates.

Donnarae MacCann goes on to say that "there is no body of critical writing to turn to, even for those books which have been awarded the highest literary prizes in children's literature in Britain and America". That seems to me to indicate a serious lack, and to suggest a further use for the literary criticism of children's books: to help them to achieve their proper status. There is a parallel between the standing of children's literature now and that of the novel a hundred years or so ago. Listen to Henry James in *The Art of Fiction* (1884):

Only a short time ago it might have been supposed that the English novel was not what the French call "discutable" ... there was a comfortable, good-humoured feeling abroad that a novel is a novel as a pudding is a pudding, and that our only business with it could be to swallow it.... Art lives upon discussion, upon experiment, upon curiosity, upon variety of attempt, upon the exchange of views and the comparison of standpoints.... [The novel] must take itself seriously for the public to take it so.

We can apply Henry James's statements to children's literature today. As yet, it is barely discussible at a respectable intellectual level. But if we are to move onward from kiddy lit and all that the use of that squirmy term implies, then children's books must be taken seriously *as literature*, and this means they must be considered with critical strictness. Vague approval, praise for the work of established writers because they are established and, above all, sentimental gush will get us nowhere.

I have suggested, diffidently, what I consider to be literature and what I believe in broad terms to be the nature of literary experience. From the latter it would be possible to derive, in equally broad terms, an elementary criterion for the assessment of literary merit. But we need something more detailed and sophisticated, which could hardly be drawn by legitimate processes of deduction from my simple premises; and I feel even more diffident when I think of the amount of distinguished American and British literary criticism in print. Is this even a case where the construction and application of abstract rules are proper? Perhaps we ought to see what some of the critics say.

We find in fact that the literary critics, both modern and not-so-modern, are rather reluctant to pin themselves down to theoretical statements. In the introduction to *Determinations* (1934), F. R.

Leavis expresses the belief that "the way to forward true appreciation of literature and art is to examine and discuss it"; and again,
"out of agreement or disagreement with particular judgements of
value a sense of relative value in the concrete will define itself, and,
without this, no amount of talk about values in the abstract is worth
anything". The late T. S. Eliot was elusive about critical standards,
but when he did make a firm statement it could be startlingly down-
to-earth. He said, in *The Use of Poetry and the Use of Criticism*
(1933):

The rudiment of criticism is the ability to select a good poem and reject a
bad poem: and its most severe test is of its ability to select a good *new* poem,
to respond properly to a new situation.

I should mention that Eliot, like many other critics, sometimes
used the word "poem" as shorthand for any work of imaginative
literature. Whether he was doing so here I am not sure, but his
statement is a statement about criticism, not about poetry, and if
for "poem" you substituted "novel", "painting", or "piece of
music" it would be equally true.

In the same book, Eliot remarked that "if you had no faith in
the critic's ability to tell a good poem from a bad one, you would
put little reliance on the value of his theories". I do not recall that
Eliot ever explained by what standard you were to judge whether
the critic could tell a good poem, but obviously it was some standard other than the person's own theory and, in fact, I am fairly
sure that it was the consensus of informed opinion over a period
of time. And that comes originally from Dr. Johnson, who said
in the *Preface to Shakespeare* that the only test that could be applied
to works of literature was "length of duration and continuance of
esteem"; and also, in the *Life of Gray*, that "it is by the common
sense of readers uncorrupted by literary prejudice that all claim to
literary honours is finally decided".

Matthew Arnold in *The Study of Poetry* (1880) proposed, as aids
to distinguishing work of the highest class, not rules but touch-
stones, examples from the great masters. Arnold says:

Critics give themselves great labour to draw out what in the abstract con-
stitutes the character of a high quality of poetry. It is much better simply
to have recourse to concrete examples; – to take specimens of poetry of high,

the very highest quality, and to say: The characters of a high quality of poetry are what is expressed *there*. They are far better recognised by being felt in the verse of the master than by being perused in the prose of the critic.... If we are asked to define this mark and accent (of "high beauty, worth and power") in the abstract, our answer must be: No, for we should thereby be darkening the question, not clearing it.

Here Arnold was undoubtedly talking about poetry and not using the word as shorthand. His touchstone principle could be extended to prose, although it strikes me as not entirely satisfactory anyway since it would not help you to judge really original work. The main point is, however, that Johnson, Arnold, Eliot, Leavis – and Henry James, too, if I correctly interpret his critical writings – are reluctant to prescribe an abstract framework against which a work of literature can be measured. They see the danger. "People are always ready," T. S. Eliot said, "to grasp at any guide which will help them to recognize the best poetry without having to depend upon their own sensibility and taste." Once establish a formula (this is myself speaking, not Eliot) and you open the door to bad and pedantic criticism by people who rely on rules instead of perceptions. Not only that but you risk creating a structure within which writers can be imprisoned. Writers should never be given the idea that there is one approved way of doing things. Far better to keep an open critical mind and encourage them with the words of Kipling:

> There are nine and sixty ways of constructing tribal lays,
> And – every – single – one – of – them – is – right!

Am, I, you may ask, suggesting that there should be no formal standards at all? Well, not quite that. It depends on the critic. Some find formal principles helpful in organizing their thought. Mrs. Arbuthnot did; and I am sure the "criteria for stories" which she sets out on pages 17–19 of *Children and Books* have been valuable to a great many people, especially those who are feeling their way into the subject. Mrs. Arbuthnot suggests looking at stories with an eye to theme, plot, characters, and style, and that is excellent; it gives you somewhere to start; it gets you moving. The guidelines for the award in England of the Carnegie Medal are almost identical and are laid down with staccato brevity; they are not expanded and explained, as Mrs. Arbuthnot expanded and explained hers. But I believe that Mrs. Arbuthnot's standards are less valuable than her example, as seen in the perceptive, practical literary criticism and, I might add, art criticism all through her book. It may well be that the British Library Association realized that what mattered for the Carnegie were not a few bald words about plot, style, and characterization, but the knowledge and judgement of the people who were appointed to apply them. The terms of the *Guardian* award for children's fiction, with which I am associated, say only that it is to go to an outstanding work; everything else is left to the judges, and I see nothing wrong with that. A good critic will indeed be aware of theme, plot, style, characterization, and many other considerations, some of them not previously spelled out but arising directly from the work; he will be sensitive; he will have a sense of balance and rightness; he will respond. Being only human he cannot possibly know all that it would be desirable for him to know; but he will have a wide knowledge of literature in general as well as of children and their literature, and probably a respectable acquaintance with cinema, theatre, television, and current affairs. That is asking a lot of him, but not too much. The critic (this is the heart of the matter) counts more than the criteria.

He will have his standards, but they will have become part of himself; he will hardly be conscious of them. Certainly he will not cart them around with him like a set of tools ready for any job. He will, I think, if I may now quote myself again from *A Sense of Story*, approach a book with an open mind and respond to it as freshly and honestly as he is able; then he will go away, let his thoughts and feelings about it mature, turn them over from time to time, consider the book in relation to others by the same author and by the author's predecessors and contemporaries. If the book is for children, he should not let his mind be dominated by the fact, but neither, I believe, should he attempt to ignore it. Just as I feel the author must write for himself yet with awareness of an audience of children, so I feel the critic must write for himself with an awareness that the books he discusses are children's books.

This last point gives me my cue to return very briefly to an issue which I touched on but put aside at its logical place in my discussion, because I wanted to keep some edges clear and I feared it might blur them. I think I can now safely go back to it. When I indicated that a critical approach was book-centred rather than child-centred, when I said I agreed on the whole with the purists, I did not, emphatically not, mean to imply that the book exists in some kind of splendid isolation, and that whether it actually speaks to the child does not matter. Rather, I think that purists can go too far in their apparent disregard for popularity. There is a sense in which the importance, the value even, of a work, is linked with its capacity to appeal to the multitude. To take some exalted examples: does not common sense tell us that part of the greatness of a Beethoven, a Shakespeare, a Michelangelo lies in the breadth of their appeal, the fact that their works are rewarding not only to a few cognoscenti but to *anyone* in possession of the appropriate faculties? A book is a communication; if it doesn't communicate, does it not fail? True, it may speak to posterity, if it gets the chance; it may be ahead of its time. But if a children's book is not popular with children here and now, its lack of appeal may tell us something. It is at least a limitation, and it *may* be a sign of some vital deficiency which is very much the critic's concern.

Those of us with purist tendencies are also perhaps too much inclined to turn up our noses at the "book with a message". For the message may be of the essence of the work, as in the novels of D. H. Lawrence or George Orwell. The revelation of the possibilities of human nature for good or ill is a major concern of literary art, probably *the* major concern of literary art. If the writer engages himself with a contemporary problem, he may be engaging himself most valuably with the mind and feelings of the reader; and to demand that he be neutral on the issues raised is to demand his emasculation. Nevertheless, it needs to be said from time to time that a book can be good without being immensely popular and without solving anybody's problems.

You will have noticed that in this talk, now drawing to a close, I have refrained from discussing specific contemporary books for children. This has been a self-denying ordinance. We would all rather talk about books than principles. But to illustrate adequately – not just casually – the various general points I have made would require reference to many books and to many pieces of writing about them; it would be the task of a course of lectures, not a single one. And so, having reluctantly maintained a somewhat abstract level throughout, I want to finish, as it were, on the theoretical summit of children's literature. T. S. Eliot, in the book already cited, remarks that:

In a play of Shakespeare you get several levels of significance. For the simplest auditors there is the plot, for the more thoughtful the character and conflict of character, for the more musically sensitive the rhythm, and for the auditors of greater sensitiveness and understanding a meaning which reveals itself gradually.

Now authors cannot all be Shakespeares, nor for that matter can critics all be Eliots. And even within our own limitations we cannot aim at the peaks of achievement all the time. But no one compels us to be modest in our ambitions; no one has compelled me to be modest in making claims on behalf of children's literature, nor have I any intention of being so. Let's all remember with pride and pleasure that children's books of the highest merit will work on several levels; they will work indeed on the same person at successive stages of development. The best children's books are infinitely rereadable; the child can come back to them at increasing ages and, even as a grownup, still find new sources of enjoyment. Some books, a few books, need never be grown away from; they can always be shared with children and with the child within. The writer for children need feel no lack of scope for high endeavour, for attempting the almost but not quite impossible. For of books that succeed in this comprehensive way, that bind the generations together, parents with children, past with present with future, we are never likely to have too many.

To the Toyland Frontier

ROBERT LEESON

Robert Leeson is Children's Books Review Editor for the *Morning Star* and a novelist for children and young people. He has written several provocative articles for SIGNAL; this one appeared in the January 1975 number.

In the provincial (and rather noisy) capital of Toyland a diplomat from neighbouring Academia drafts a report recommending his government to undertake full *de jure* recognition, to replace the present unsatisfactory *de facto* situation between the two countries. To his draft he attaches a statement from one of the many authors who have been slipping across the frontier to get published: "Diplomatically Toyland barely exists (like China before Kissinger discovered it). No long reviews, no STUDIES. But can they sell books! Back home in Academia they discuss you all right. But do they read you? Pity we can't shift the border: it's embarrassing travelling on a Toyland visa."

This flight of fancy was inspired as I read John Rowe Townsend (SIGNAL, May 1974) on "Standards of Criticism for Children's Literature", which was a reprint of a lecture given some little while before, but very well worth reading. It is, as far as I know, the most comprehensive – and best – statement of what might be called the purist position in children's book criticism. He says well what some say not so well and others think without saying so publicly. It is a point of view I'd like to dispute.

Mr. Townsend makes a complex and interesting case for the non-existence of a specific children's literature. (It is a point of view as widely held in theory as it is ignored in practice, and he indeed falls back on the basic fact that publishers go on publishing "children's" books.) He emphasizes the extensive border zone between children's and adult literature and the universality of the best writing.

He argues further for an "independent [critical] standard of quality other than what children like or is good for them or what brings them face to face with contemporary issues". The alternative to standards based on "literary merit" is, in his words, a "jumble of criteria, a haphazard mixture of personal responses". He quotes also the "purist" Brian Alderson, who speaks of a "morass of contradictory and subjective responses". The critic, says Mr. Townsend, should not be concerned with "suitability, popularity, relevance", which should be left to the parents, teachers, librarians: those "closest to the ultimate consumer". His critical system would be book-centred rather than child-centred, changing the centre of gravity, thus: "Just as I feel the author must write for himself yet with an awareness of an audience of children, so I feel the critic must write for himself with an awareness that the books he discusses are children's books."

The reform is needed because, so far, children's literature has been "barely discussible at a respectable intellectual level", and has not been "taken seriously as literature". Its few specialists are not "highly placed in the professional or academic pecking order".

Well, let's agree: Academia should recognize Toyland. Let's further agree that there is great disagreement over criteria in children's literature. Pressure groups concerned about class, racial, sex bias, add new vigour to the old moral-versus-entertainment argument.

If the criteria are jumbled, it is because children's literature is in a state of expansion and change greater than at any time in its history. To bring together these disparate elements into a comprehensive (let alone unified) critical theory will take time and effort – and be worth the trouble. It will happen, I think, through a process of synthesis, not by the total rejection of non-literary criteria, nor by standing aloof from the consumers and those nearest them. Even less will it be done by a retreat into an aestheticism developed in the field of adult literature (these days, turning to adult lit-crit is like asking to be rescued by the *Titanic*); still less will it be done by turning to an aestheticism which represents only *one aspect* of literary influences.

But Mr. Townsend has chosen his company well. Dr. Johnson said that the writer must "divest himself of the prejudices of the age ... disregard present laws and opinions and rise to general and transcendent truths that will always be the same". Matthew Arnold thought practical considerations "the bane of criticism", which should be "absolutely and entirely independent" of partisan interest and lead men to "what is excellent in itself and the absolute beauty and fulness of things". Despite the restating, in each generation, of eternal truths, Saintsbury was still complaining in 1907 of critics with "the ethical twist". The battlefield on to which Mr. Townsend rides is strewn with corpses which constantly spring to life and lay about them.

Children's literature has had a lifetime of centuries, closely linked, as Mr. Townsend notes in his excellent *Written for Children* (Kestrel), with the rise of the bourgeoisie and the large-scale development of printing. He uses the term "middle class" and I'll follow him in that, though I think (and the present day seems to confirm) that much of the middle class is disturbed about the fruits of the bourgeois age. Indeed the literary tradition Mr. Townsend draws on is in part a reaction to crude pragmatic capitalist calculation of the past – an opposition to Gradgrindism.

It is also an attempt – which has gone on since the modern book age began and the middle class first dominated the cultural scene and invented children's literature – to pass on the precious gift of literacy and education imbued with its own ethic; an attempt to provide a universal and lasting standard of judgement on writing. Mr. Townsend is dubious about eternity and settles for a "comparatively stable" standard. Now, for a universal (never mind a lasting) standard you need either a social consensus ("we all know what we mean") or an intellectual community floating above "present opinion" on a sort of hover-cushion of transcendental truth. This kind of intellectual consensus has always been illusory. More than ever today, when the hegemony of the middle class is challenged and the workers tread so close on their heels they "gall their kybes", is it *seen* to be illusory. Speaking of world social changes, of the shocks to the old imperialism that have affected the appeal of writers like Ballantyne, Mr. Townsend says "we have suffered ... a fatal loss of confidence". We?

A kind of cultural consensus might have existed in the pre-printing world, when lord and commoner alike depended on the spoken word and Sir Philip Sidney's definition of the good story was one that appealed to young and old alike. In that far age of greater cultural oneness (though we shouldn't be romantic about it) literary standards and present politics were expected to mix. When the skald broke the flow of verse with "*that* was a good king", no critic rose from the other side of the fire to complain. Nor did Sir Philip Sidney himself hesitate to defend poetry on the grounds of relevance and suitability. (Indeed, aesthetes united, please note: the first mass printed work, the most sublime prose-poem in our language, the Authorized Version, was motivated by relevance and suitability, commissioned by the state and written by a committee.) But print was tied to power. The middle-class martyrs went to the rack for it (just as later they savagely punished the working-class newssheet mongers who followed their good example). It's interesting to note that the same king who encouraged Caxton gave the official minstrels' guild a unique nationwide monopoly, to expel from the story business "rude husbandmen and artificers of various crafts".

Print, reading were a means to freedom, but also, without social consensus, a means to inequality. Children's books which grew out of this divided situation bore the middle-class stamp. In the early nineteenth century, the Nonconformist craftsmen and labourers began to teach their children letters and see universal education on the skyline. But they had no control over book publishing. They hardly had paper. The Primitive Methodist pottery workers taught their children in sand-boxes, smoothed over after each finger had traced the letters. When their children came to read books, the literary reality of these (even of the best) was at one remove from their lives, reality as seen by the eye of the middle class.

The power to assume consensus among middle-class educated people is impressive. In his delightful *The Enchanted Places* (Methuen), Christopher Milne, speaking of "the air of snobbishness" about his father's *When We Were Very Young*, says A. A. Milne was writing "to entertain people living in the 1920s, and those were the attitudes current at the time". People – and people. As a child

I looked on Christopher Robin as a creep. (I'm relieved to find the real person a very amiable bloke.) "Hush, hush, nobody cares; Christopher Robin has fallen downstairs." But in the Pooh books I hardly noticed C. R. We were down to the roots of the universal in the child's world. A literary critique which judged the Pooh books superior to the poems would have a sociological underlay, whether the critic recognized it or not.

Times have changed. As Brian Alderson noted in *The Times* (13 March 1974): "*The Family From One End Street*, famous enough in the thirties, now reads like a dim comedy at the expense of washerwomen and dustmen; *Magnolia Buildings* – its equivalent for the sixties – is going the same way." This verdict is shared by Mr. Townsend in *Written for Children*, a book, I might remark, both relevant and suitable for those nearest the consumer.

How pure are the purists? How influenced by non-literary criteria in a world where the events of the 1940s and 1950s upset the stable judgements of the 1920s and 1930s? In face of change, in face of the pressure of outsiders forcing their criteria upon you, what does the consensus-assumer do?

There was "no malice" in Hugh Lofting's lapses into racialism, says Mr. Townsend. Lofting was "sincere". So indeed was Enid Blyton when she protested that she had "good and bad golliwogs" in her stories. There's the rub. Critical judgement of Lofting in the 1970s cannot be what it was in the 1920s – or the 1960s – even if we reach for a non-literary criterion like sincerity to defend him from the harshest blows. When Brian Alderson pressed home his critique of Enid Blyton in *The Times* last October, he used Beatrix Potter and Barbara Willard as his yardsticks – not on literary grounds (such comparisons would be odious) but on grounds of suitability, adding for good measure that "to get a lot out of a book, you may have to put a lot in". Matthew Arnold might scratch his head over that one, but Janeway would like it.

Like Mr. Townsend, Mr. Alderson is indeed a pragmatic purist. When in his catalogue for the 1973 *Looking at Picture Books* exhibition, he speaks of "the norm of family portrayed tending very much towards an average gentility", we see him absorbing the non-literary criterion into the literary. But he also suggests that "for all" the "crude and paternalistic attitude towards coloured families", seen in Helen Bannerman's *Little Black Sambo*, it has an "immediacy of appeal". Here the non-literary intrusion is warded off but without conviction. Indeed: "for all" pursued to its logical end, the book-centred judgement separated from the child-centred, arrives finally at the system of criticism enshrined in the popular song of thirty years ago – "It ain't what you do, it's the way that you do it." This is roughly where the aesthetic party may arrive in its flight from the "morass of subjective responses" – by a paradox inherent in such flights – at a position of extreme subjectivity.

This position is associated with that remarkable figure of dogma who has slipped across the Toyland frontier recently: the writer who writes for himself. Mr. Townsend generously equips him with an awareness of the audience, but I don't think this creature is redeemable by any qualification. He's a monster, the quintessence of bourgeois egoism, ever ready to abuse the public when it takes him at his word, ever ready to pocket the proceeds when it doesn't.

The pursuit of individualist perfection by author and critic has taken them farther and farther away from the reader. It has contributed to the present parlous state of the adult novel.

The bourgeois contribution to literature was to take the tale with its moral-action-character, and to add psychological depth to the last. At its greatest this made the novel a supreme vehicle for moral and action, beautifully interrelated. In modern times, the wholly subjective pursuit of psychological insight, the search for truth within the consciousness of the author rather than in the world at large, has led to the near-expulsion of moral and action from the most "advanced" novels. Moral and action flee to Genre-land, where they dwell with varying fortunes in its provinces – SF, romance, the thriller. Or they cross the border into Toyland where they have always been welcome.

In children's literature moral and action have been secure because the best (and the worst) authors have always been conscious that they were writing for children (whether their *essential* child was within themselves or not). Their inspiration for writing was children, even when the world at large, still children deep down, took the book to heart. Within the children's book the basic elements of the eternal story have remained, refreshed by the changing times just as the old folk tale renewed itself.

The basic element in a definition of children's literature is indeed the title of Mr. Townsend's book, *Written for Children*. Books not written for children (distinguishing between author's intention and publisher's marketing) can be adopted by them. The child is becoming the adult and will, in growing older, reach out specifically for the adult view of the adult world. But the virtue in children's books is that they speak direct to children, affording them free passage in and out of their children's world, enriching them, preparing them for the future.

The first motive is entertainment, reading belonging with playing, but play belongs also to learning and preparation. Left to themselves, children base their play not on a retreat from the world, but a tentative reaching out for it. They "escape" to explore, trusting to return safely. And the value in good children's literature is the helpful role it plays in the child's own play-exploration.

We do not successfully help them in and out of the world by waving the moral stick at them. A novel for children, as for adults, is a story about people for whom life has some problem or experience, not the exposition of problems that can happen to people. But a story which does not take true account of life is spineless, like a jelly fish. All books have their message, either at the start, or by the end. Reformers tend to be more conscious message-bringers, and status quo supporters more conscious message-hiders. When I see yet another story of a cosmic struggle between good and evil, I wonder whether the author votes Tory. But seeking to rescue the children's book from the opinions of the time will not help reader or writer any more than slipping out by the back door when the librarians are at the front will help the critic.

Children's literature is undergoing an enormous change, from minority interest to something like a mass movement, involving not just writer, editor, critic, but large numbers of librarians, teachers and the public. And the lobby from the women's and children's rights movement is part of the public, let the professionals forget at their peril.

You may say (as I heard at a conference last summer) "if you don't like what we do, go and publish your own books", thus conveniently ignoring economic realities. But if pressure groups do publish their own, and they certainly will, this will simply enlarge the field of the critic and challenge critical criteria the more. The demand for suitability and relevance – whether its form is convenient for the critic or not – is part of the general movement. Together the book trade and the public are acquiring the will, and more slowly the means, to bring books for pleasure and benefit to every child. Thus the hitherto unfulfilled dream of the pioneers of the printing press begins to come into real view at last. Perhaps with that growing realization of a common humanity, through the children and the world we, bit by bit, hand on to them, we may aspire to a new universality in literature, not the narrow and apparent universality of a social group in complacent occupation of the commanding heights of culture, who imagine that "everyone" is like them and that what they like is good for everyone.

Can critics hold aloof from this movement? At their peril, I should say. Rather than purge criticism of non-literary elements, let us renew and enrich literary standards with those elements, that literature may better reflect and in its turn enrich life. Critics may well reject a narrow and didactic "end justifies the means" stance. But not, surely, to rush to the other extreme, discarding relevance, suitability and all the albeit volatile elements of actuality, and separating oneself off not simply from the child readers but those nearest them as well. To do so would in the end force the critics to a kind of voluntary retirement from all useful employment.

To what? Retreat perhaps to some dry-rotted cottage, where, sharing the expense with the writer who writes for himself, to operate a hand press, one to produce books, the other to comment on them. The end product, of course, would be the distillation of absolutely unadulterated independence of literary judgement upon the perfect individual expression of imagination, uncorrupted by ethical, moral, sociological influences, the definitive verdict on the ultimate creation, freed from time, space, existence and every other extraneous factor. Naturally, neither writer nor critic would read what the other had written because this would be against all the rules of the game.

But I cannot believe it. Looking to the future I see something rather different. I see a recognition of Toyland by Academia rather like Nixon's of China, because it is too important to ignore. I see the critics merrily crossing and recrossing the frontier, suitcases packed, tidily or not according to upbringing, with a new range of criteria, some of them (let's be frank) borrowed from people with whom they are not on speaking terms.

Though they may greet the customs official with a bland "Nothing to Declare".

Chorister Quartet

CHARLES SARLAND

Charles Sarland is head of English at a Bedfordshire middle school.
This article was published in the September 1975 SIGNAL.

William Mayne is the great "problem" amongst modern children's
writers. Everyone seems agreed that he is a writer of great subtlety
and complexity, that he has an uncanny knack of seeing the world
through the eyes of children, and that he is the most assured stylist
of all modern children's authors. Yet he remains obstinately unread
by children, and short of saying that he is a very sophisticated
writer, which he is, no one has satisfactorily explained why. I do
not intend, in this article, to question his critical standing, though
I will declare a personal bias towards *Choristers' Cake* and *Words
and Music* and some of the shorter books he has written about
younger children like *The Big Wheel and the Little Wheel* and *The
Last Bus* as opposed to *Ravensgill*, *Earthfasts* or *A Game of Dark*.
Whatever their relative merits, however, I intend to confine myself
to the four Cathedral Choir School books for they contain elements
that are common to everything that he has written, from *Follow
the Footprints* to *A Game of Dark*. I want in particular to look in
some detail at the writing style, for it seems to me that valuable
clues are to be found in it that go a long way to explaining precisely
why many children find it difficult to come to terms with a writer
who, on the face of it, would seem to have so much to offer.

On first reading the earliest of the Chorister books, *A Swarm
in May*, one is struck by three things: the meticulously detailed descriptions of the physical environment; the uncanny insight into
a small boy's concerns; and the wordplay, the witty allusions and
puns that inform the book. These three aspects of Mayne's work

turn out to be characteristic of his whole output and all three things relate to his style. First and foremost then, he is concerned to show exactly what it feels like to be a small boy in a choir school. He does this by detailing the physical environment from precisely the point of view of such a small boy, re-creating for the adult reader that forgotten time when the immediate physical environment was a continual source of interest and even wonder. Consider for instance the climax of the book, the passage where Owen collects the bees with the aid of a strange-smelling globe attached to a large key by a chain that they have found.

Owen went alone into Dr. Sunderland's house, feeling unusual walking about outdoors alone in cassock and surplice. He went through the yard. He was about to lift the top of the hive when he remembered that the white globe, ready in his hand, had no smell or attraction when it was cold. He took it into the house again, and ran Dr. Sunderland's gas geyser over it until he smelt the strange smell of it through the burnt gas. He left the bubbling water, and waited to see whether the smell vanished. It stayed so he opened the back door again. There was immediately a crowd of bees on the globe, and from each of the three hives they came flying until the weight of them began to pull the key into his skin again, where the chain hung through his fingers. Owen stepped back and closed the back door against the rest of the bees. He had hanging from his hand a swarm as big as the one he had carried on Thursday. They hung in an egg-shaped brown lump, with a faint buzz coming from them; but they were perfectly docile. Owen did what he had seen Dr. Sunderland do: he touched them. They were yielding, but they had hard backs, and their wings were smooth. They took no notice of his hand.

It is the tiny detail that is telling; for instance, "he smelt the strange smell of it *through the burnt gas*", "where the chain hung through his fingers", or the description of the swarm. Furthermore it is immediately clear that the insight into Owen's concerns is achieved precisely by this concentration on detail. But something else also emerges from a consideration of this passage, and that is Mayne's handling of pace. The book is here nearing its climax, and the reader's concern is that Owen shall successfully negotiate the ordeal of the service. Yet the detail slows the pace deliberately: instead of warming the globe in his hand as he approaches and letting the bees gather until he has a fair-sized swarm, he must forget to warm it, take the globe back to the house, and even then he doesn't run, and then further detail is presented, the bubbling water, the weight of the swarm, the feel of the swarm, and so on. The reader must forget the action and concentrate instead on the sensations of the moment.

If one examines the wordplay of the same book one gets some idea of the mental processes that Mayne expects his readers to apply. For instance, one of the teachers, Mr. Sutton, has a nickname, Brass Button. At one point Owen puns on his name: "'No fear,' said Owen, 'Brass Button's come quite unsown with me'" and later in the book he develops the metaphor in answer to Dr. Sunderland, "'He won't for me, sir,' said Owen. 'I weaken his threads too much.'" And here is Trevithic, the head chorister, with two musical puns in the same breath, the one obscure and the other more obvious, "'You are burbling out the dullest passages I ever heard,' said Trevithic. 'I think you must have gone slightly decomposed in the afternoon.'" In order to appreciate such jokes – indeed in order to understand them, for their metaphorical applications have specific meaning within the narrative and emotional context of the book – the reader must stand back and make the connecting links that Mayne deliberately leaves out. In other words the wordplay alienates the reader from the drama of the narrative and draws his attention instead to the formal linguistic elements that serve to unite Mayne's delineation of character. In the above example on the two occasions that Owen puns on Mr. Sutton's name the reader is reminded of Owen's apprehension of Mr. Sutton but remains objective in his consideration of that apprehension.

Once again the technique is devoted to dissipating the immediate dramatic impact and replacing it with a contemplative consideration of the situation. The Brechtian term "alienation" would seem to fit the bill very precisely here, for Brecht's alienation devices were conceived with similar purposes in mind. I am not suggesting that Mayne is a Brechtian writer, merely that he has adopted and adapted the technique for his own use. In passages of dialogue the same result is achieved by somewhat different means. Take for example a crucial interchange in *Cathedral Wednesday*. A dayboy, Andrew Young, finds himself acting head chorister because of illness. He has a lot of trouble with the two boys next below him in seniority. Finally he puts them on the prefect's "list", a grave step. There follows this conversation when he meets one of them:

> "Is it ...?" said Silverman and stopped. "Hmn," he said, and shook his head.
> "Better line up," said Andrew quietly.
> "Yes," said Silverman. He looked fully round at Andrew. "Is it Book Boys?" he said.
> "What do you think?" said Andrew.
> "But honestly," said Silverman, "we...."
> "Line up," said Andrew. "Attention, left turn, quick march, left, left, left."

This is, potentially, a highly dramatic exchange in which Andrew, for the first time in the book, asserts his authority. Yet the conversation is interrupted by passages of description, "He looked fully round at Andrew" and "said Silverman and stopped.... he said, and shook his head", so that the passage takes far longer to read than it would have done to say. And even if it is objected that these would have been legitimate details under any circumstances, one still has to explain why there are so many "he saids" in the latter half. The passage might well have gone:

> "Is it Book Boys?"
> "What do you think?"
> "But honestly, we...."
> "Line up," said Andrew.

and immediately there is an increase in pace and drama. So clearly Mayne wishes to prevent his readers from becoming emotionally involved either in Silverman's desperation or in Andrew's triumph and they are encouraged instead to take a more objective view.

On other occasions he will deliberately create a situation in which he is forced to break off the narrative in order to explain what is going on. Here is Mr. Lewis, late for breakfast in *Words and Music*: "'... go and make the toast for me. It's my breakfast.' He didn't mean that the toast was for him, but that he should have been downstairs seeing that everyone else got it in time." Instead of a clear exposition of the total situation within which the drama can unfold, Mayne gives the reader little snippets of exposition in order to clear up the puzzlement that he himself has created.

If the opening section of *Choristers' Cake* is examined in detail it will be seen to exemplify all these points. It is the description of one of those games where a ball is rolled down between the legs of teams of boys standing in long lines. If the ball gets outside the legs it has to be fetched back to the same place. The game is never described directly, however; instead a number of sense impressions are presented which, as it were, move inside the structure of the game rather like a planet moves inside an orbit, and the reader has to posit the structure from internal evidence, rather as man posits a possible orbit from observation of related phenomena. Thus we start with a totally unrelated sense impression, an inscription, which is then related to a viewer, Sandwell, who himself is then related to the over-all situation.

"Sometime Dean of this Cathedral Church," said the two lines of carved letters just below Peter Sandwell's eyes and between the next boy's feet. Whoever had put them there had not thought that one day the Cathedral choir boys would be standing on it during their PT lesson. Standing was not the right word: Peter Sandwell had both heels on it, and so had Meedman, just in front, but their knees were wide apart and their heads were between their knees: they were waiting for the football to be rolled along through the arches of legs, so that it could be raced round to the front of the team again.

Meedman felt Sandwell's head butt against his seat, so he sat as much as anyone can sit who looks for the time being like the two legs of a wishbone. Sandwell resisted the weight, but his head was pushed lower and lower. "Sometime Dean of this Cathedral Church" slid out of sight. He found he was looking down the rest of the sometime Dean's inscription, reading a Latin verse from above.

The football came down the tunnel, being paddled along from above by hand, slapping along the stone floor over the inscriptions, bringing with it a shadow that was not round, but pointed like an arch and graded from dark to light grey, with the different depths of the grey moving among themselves as the ball ran through the alternate shadow and light from the openings of the cloisters. It rolled along a little tunnel (of boys) inside a larger one (the north walk of the cloisters). Meedman guided the ball along his yard of tunnel, and passed it to Sandwell, who hit it a two-fisted biff when it rested for a moment on a cherub's tombstone face, and set it flying down the cloister alone.

What is in fact being described here is a competitive game, but none of the excitement of such a game gets into the words. Instead we have the visual description of the ball and its attendant shadows, and when Sandwell commits his crime by sending the ball outside the line of legs it is not explained that it is a crime, though such can be deduced from the conversation which follows.

"Perfect fool," said Trevithic, loudly, from the head of the team.

"Don't tell him," said Lowell, who had come up from the back of the other team and was now leading it.

"He's an augmented fool," said Madington, brushing his hair more on to the top of his head in case Trevithic barged into him bonily again.

"Sandwell," said Trevithic, "fetch it."

"Run, Sandy," said Meedman, removing his weight from Sandwell's shoulders.

"Me?" said Sandy, sitting down on the Latin verse and exchanging his view of the sometime Dean for one of the bright coats of arms in the cloister vaulting.

The whole team lifted their heads and turned their bodies without moving their feet, and urged him to hurry. Sandy thought they looked like a row of startled looper caterpillars. The ball lay quietly against the door to the Bishop's garden. Sandy fetched it and ran forward to the head of the team with it. They bent themselves down as he ran past them. "Like the backbone skeleton of an animal," he thought; and fed the ball to Trevithic.

The point of course is that, within the context, it would not need to be explained to Sandwell that he had boobed so Mayne does not explain it; rather, he gives us the next aural impression that Sandwell would have had, Trevithic's comment.

The conversation itself bears close examination. It is the dramatic core of the scene yet the drama is held at arm's length. In the first place there is the musical pun of perfect/augmented fool. Secondly, there is the apparent meaninglessness of Lowell's remark until the reader works out for himself that it is because Lowell is in the opposing team that he does not want Sandwell told. Thirdly, there is the puzzlement about Madington brushing his hair to the top of his head, for nowhere in the passage previously has it mentioned that Trevithic has barged into him. Of course Mayne's "again" carries all the implication that he wants. Fourthly, there is the whole little episode of Meedman removing his weight from Sandwell's shoulders, an episode which has to be considered in the light of the second paragraph to be fully understood. In fact here, as with Madington's hair, there is a concealed causal relationship. What in fact happens is that Meedman has virtually been sitting on Sandwell, and Sandwell has been pressing upwards in compensation. Thus when Meedman removes his weight Sandwell overbalances and sits on the floor. Mayne does not make the causal link, the reader has to do it; and even then he has Sandwell sit on the Latin verse, not the floor, and looking not immediately at the ceiling but first at the coats of arms which are then placed in their correct context. In order to appreciate fully what is going on, the reader must carry Mayne's wealth of detail in his head because it is within the matrix of this wealth of detail that the structure of the book will unfold.

There is then this irony: that a more conventional author would give the reader an objective view of the situation, and by doing so, assuming a degree of competence on the writer's part, would engage him in the action, while Mayne, by presenting a subjective viewpoint, forces the reader to a more dispassionate consideration of what is going on.

In *Choristers' Cake* the central character, Sandwell, is unsympathetic. He is conceited, obstinate and foolish. At various points in the story he makes the wrong decisions. Yet he remains the central character, and it is through his eyes that we perceive the action. If it were not for his alienation techniques Mayne would never be able to handle such a delicate situation and retain an objective moral viewpoint. But the book requires a degree of sophistication in the reader that would not normally be found in children of the same age as his characters. It is clear from the way that he uses pace, dialogue, causal relationships, puns and wordplay that the last thing that he wants is that the reader should be carried along on the tide of the narrative. Always the requirement is that out of the sense impressions that he supplies the reader should construct his own pace, his own drama, his own causal and verbal links, and it is a measure of Mayne's mastery that they are there to be constructed. He admits no ambivalence of response, but the reader must work hard to pick up all the cues that are laid down for his guidance.

There are a number of conclusions that present themselves. One is that Mayne will quite simply remain a minority taste. Another is that perhaps the publishers could usefully look at the age range for which they are intending his books. There is a case for saying, for instance, that *Choristers' Cake* is suited to a thirteen- or fourteen-year-old audience rather than a ten-year-old audience. Certainly *Ravensgill* would seem out of place in a list of books for eight- and nine-year-olds. One hopes that the fact of his unpopularity will not discourage publishers from ensuring that the best of his books remain in print.

Books by William Mayne referred to in this article published by Oxford University Press: *Follow the Footprints* (1953), *A Swarm in May* (1955), *Choristers' Cake* (1956), *Cathedral Wednesday* (1960; now republished by Brockhampton); published by Hamish Hamilton: *The Last Bus* (1962), *Words and Music* (1963), *The Big Wheel and the Little Wheel* (1965), *Earthfasts* (1966), *Ravensgill* (1970), and *A Game of Dark* (1971).

The Good, the Bad and the Indifferent
Quality and Value in Three Contemporary
Children's Books

PETER HUNT

Peter Hunt, who lectures in English at the University of Wales Institute of Science and Technology, has made several contributions
to SIGNAL on the subject of the criticism of children's books. The
following article, written especially for this book, is an attempt to
specify ways in which adult thinking about children's books may
be made more rigorous. Page references for quotations from the
three books discussed are given in brackets at the end of each quote.
The editions used are: Richard Adams: *Watership Down* (Puffin,
1973 [original hardback edition, Rex Collings]); Leon Garfield:
The Pleasure Garden (Kestrel, 1976); William Mayne: *IT* (Hamish
Hamilton, 1977).

There is a good deal of conventional wisdom around children's
books, largely on which authors are good and which are less good.
Yet there is little consensus on whom or what the books are for,
or on what "good" and "less good" are supposed to mean. The
distinctions between usefulness, quality, and value have become
hopelessly blurred.

One example of this is the annual argument over the Library
Association's Carnegie Medal, summed up by the dispute over
K. M. Peyton's 1969 award. In reply to Dominic Hibberd's "The
Flambards Trilogy: Objections to a Winner", Colin Ray wrote:

The real trouble, I think, is that we are up against Mr. Hibberd's "critical
standards". These are not defined, but appear to be those of *literary* criticism.
If he will refer to the terms of the Carnegie Medal, he will find that the award
is for an "outstanding" book. I would personally criticize that adjective as
being vague: but one thing it does not explicitly mean is that the Medal is
a literary award.[1]

Some of the problems implied by this dispute might be solved if we attempt to define the terms which give so much trouble.

Quality implies a judgement within a kind, or class, or genre: something that is good of its type, good for the purpose for which it was intended, or for which it has been adopted. *Value*, on the other hand, is a judgement between classes, implying something more lasting, more profound. In texts, it implies a resonance in the words we read from levels of human significance which are not merely personal. A symphony is more valuable than a spade, however high the quality of the spade; rush matting and Persian carpets may both be useful, but one has rather more to be valued. A valuable book does not necessarily require that it be read in a certain way; it merely allows one to read according to one's capacities. This suggests that value, unlike quality, is not shackled by prescription – what somebody thinks a book ought to be like – and that value judgements can be made in terms of the resonances (or transforms) between text, structure, theme, and the basic motivations which they reflect.

The three books I would like to consider – Richard Adams's *Watership Down*, Leon Garfield's *The Pleasure Garden*, and William Mayne's *IT* – have little in common, except that the authors have all won the Carnegie Medal. But each illustrates a different approach to quality, to value, and to the technical problems of writing. They also lie, in different ways, in the no-person's land between adults' and children's books where questions of quality and value become most confused.

I must stress at once that there is no point in searching for a distinction between adult and child. The distinction is between *ways of reading* and the way in which a book allows itself to be read. Both the achieved response and the potential response are functions of an interaction between book and reader; but the first lies more with the reader, and the second more with the book. Ultimately, one is a question of quality, the other of value.

Watership Down needs scant introduction. It achieved at one point the curious distinction of being published in both adults' and children's editions; as a world bestseller it has suffered inevitably from the schizophrenic critical response accorded to *The Lord of the*

Rings: extravagant praise followed by round condemnation. In retrospect, it is easy to apply Adams's observation on Kipling – that he had "a certain insensitivity and banality – even vulgarity"[2] – to his own book; but it is equally easy to overlook his impressive technical achievement. Set the twin tasks of making rabbit behaviour into an interesting narrative, and of telling the story in such a way as to integrate this with necessary factual information, he was more successful than he is sometimes given credit for. The blemishes, as we shall see, often derive from unsureness about the validity of the narrative contract between author and reader.

The reactions to the book – as adult novel and as children's book – have been significant. Perhaps the shrewdest review appeared in *Newsweek* (18 March 1974): "I'll make a deal with you. If you won't say anything dumb like 'I'm not interested in a story about rabbits', I won't say anything dumb like 'This is a great novel'". Quite so; *Watership Down* is good of its kind: that is, an adventure narrative, efficiently told and sufficiently unusual to make it distinctive. It does not, generally, pretend to be more than this; although when it does, the pretensions show. Yet when we turn to Alec Ellis's comments on the book in connection with its Carnegie Medal award for 1972, we might get a different impression. "*Watership Down* is a phenomenon the like of which only appears once or twice in a lifetime, and one could not reasonably ask more of a treasure so scarce."[3]

The implications here should give us pause. Is there a value scale running unbroken from adults' classics down to children's rubbish, with the acceptably second-rate adult books and the very best possible children's books sharing the same rung? Possibly not, but while that assumption is detectable, it is difficult to get a clear view of the books themselves.

Watership Down was, of course, a first novel and might be forgiven some of its defects on that score. Leon Garfield has, however, been a successful "quality" children's author for some years, with a string of awards and serializations behind him. As with many of his contemporaries, his books have more or less steadily tended to move up the notional age-appropriateness range, to the point at which *The Pleasure Garden*, originally published by Kestrel, has appeared under Penguin's young-adult Peacock imprint alongside

Drabble's *The Millstone* and Salinger's *The Catcher in the Rye*. The most obvious reason for this ambivalent placing would seem to be the content; Garfield is dealing with themes (appearance/reality, good/evil, childhood/adolescence, identity) and subject matter (transvestitism, voyeurism, murder) which either require a certain maturity to comprehend or relate to, or will sell to a given age group, or both. Or it may be that the kind of reservation expressed by Rhodri Jones in *The Use of English* has had some effect: "These were crude and violent times, and foul language can be justified in terms of character, but are such things suitable reading for children?"[4]

Apart from this, Garfield's reputation has been built upon distinctiveness as much as on distinction. Whereas Richard Adams's style is, by and large, unexceptional – possibly as a result of the base material he is working on – Garfield's is quirky and erratic, and has been said to accord with the version of the eighteenth century (Hogarth out of Smollett) in which many of his books are set. It has come in for some immoderate praise: "Leon Garfield can do anything with words and his touch is very sure." "Never are the metaphors forced ... for their outward form and their inward meaning co-exist with no conflict, fusing into a perfect work of art [of *The Drummer Boy*]."[5] Thus John Rowe Townsend and Richard Camp, and even Rhodri Jones seems to accept the reputation as read; the reputation of a writer of quality who is, by virtue of the fact that there is patently more in his books than mere narrative, producing books of *value*. His works are in the higher echelons of children's fiction (useful, successful) and thus, as they edge over the frontiers, they may be compared toe-to-toe with any book. The confrontation with deeper significances and motivations may increase the books' ambivalence in the market place, but must also allow of greater potential for ultimate value. A close look at *The Pleasure Garden* may show us whether this is actually so, and perhaps whether Garfield's status is entirely warranted.

In William Mayne, whose name may by now inspire little more than apathy in view of the protracted arguments about his work, we have a writer much admired by some adults and, it is said, little read by children. This may be, of course, because he is an adults' writer masquerading under a children's imprint. The problems with his books are: how far do they allow an adult way of reading and how far do they *require* it?

From his impressive output (if only numerically) of around sixty books, I have selected *IT*, a novel which is typical of his work to the point of self-parody. This book certainly has those characteristics of style and narrative stance that have so neatly divided opinion about him. He has been described as

...a watcher rather than an ally. Even his dramatic technique seems deliberately designed to alienate the reader from the events and from the people described. This attitude to story is so little to be found in children's books that even children who have grown up as frequent and thoughtful readers find Mayne at his densest and best very difficult to negotiate.[6]

Aidan Chambers's use of the word "best" here is interesting, in that it implies a stance on the dichotomy between quality and value which I have defined. Mayne is different from Garfield and Adams in that his books are not generally thought to be *good of their kind*, although they may have manifest qualities, and perhaps value.

But what *is* their kind? *IT* might seem to be clearly a children's book, and not merely because of the imprint. It does not, like Mayne's *The Jersey Shore*, deal with problems of adolescence or growth. If it is about the possession of a twelve-year-old by a spirit, there is nothing of horror in it – or *IT*. No issues seem to be confronted; there is a treasure hunt, a minster complete with choir, an ancient ritual, a tightly observed family – all the familiar Mayne ingredients. The narrative stance modulates almost the whole book through one child's perception of events, allowing us to know no more than she knows, and expressing this in words and thought patterns she might have put together. Mayne has a problem similar to that of Adams: to present faithfully the actions and reactions of a species with which we are not too familiar – children (or *other* children) – and to provide enough information to make obscure family interactions comprehensible.

So far, all very obvious. Yet the technique by which Mayne integrates these elements is, as Chambers notes, uncommon. He establishes a three-way narrative contract between author, protagonist, and reader, a method far more sophisticated than that of Garfield or Adams, and his fidelity to it is reflected in the surface language. As an example, the heroine's family are consistently referred to as

Mum, Dad, and Grandpa – not because Mayne is allying himself with the child reader, or because he is being patronizing, but because those are the terms in which Alice comprehends her world. Mayne is only a watcher in the sense that his characters are watchers. We are not watching things happening to them. We are watching them watching things happening to them. In *IT*, we are very rarely required to dissociate ourselves from what is happening; we are involved. Consequently, significances cannot – as in Garfield, and occasionally in Adams – be pointed out. They exist in the apparent inconsequentiality of the detail. Alice scarcely distinguishes between trivial and momentous events; and that is precisely the point of the book. *IT* is almost an essay in relativity. If this seems to be a thoroughly pretentious reading of the book, we might reconsider what is meant by a child's *way of reading*. It may well be that Mayne's message is so obvious (to a child) as to be uninteresting; just as his fidelity to the state of childhood is too exact. The adult may learn a great deal – and a great deal of value – about childhood; possibly a child knows it already. Perhaps the conventional wisdom about Mayne may be just as misleading as that about other authors; not one of these three authors, or these three books, can be called entirely good, or bad, or indifferent – nor are they directly comparable.

Attempting to analyse the books, therefore, shows up a structure of paradoxes in the relationship of value and response, and quality and response: apparent quality and actual quality – of what is commonly perceived and what is actually there; of what is proclaimed and what is prescribed. These paradoxes are not unique to children's books, or even particularly acute in them. But it can hardly be denied that those involved with children's books tend to strike attitudes to novels like these which are partisan, or vague, or simply in reaction to everyone else: and these stances have made the paradoxes seem important. We will see that the key to recognizing *value* very often lies in the quality of the surface language: something readily accessible. This fact makes it easier to arrive at a judgement which is at least less subjective than most.

In an interview Leon Garfield observed that *Watership Down* was, like many significant children's books, "a freak book by somebody who is not naturally a writer".[7] Certainly this shows on the surface of the text on occasion. Fred Inglis has written that it is "by turns, clumsy, portentous, longwinded, and magnificent";[8] he did not add that the vast majority of the book is also efficient (if not exactly elegant), unassuming, economical, and undistinguished. It is true that Adams is capable of surface felicities: "Then it was gone, and Bigwig's fur was blowing in the whack of wind that followed it down the hedges." (59) "He sat still and his words seemed to come crawling up the sunlight, over the grass." (125) And equally, of awkwardnesses: "'. . . . but I thought that first of all I ought to tell you how it is that we four – Silver, Buckthorn, Strawberry and I – have come back without any does.'" (239)

But it should be noted that he very rarely lapses into children's book register so that, when he does, it is strikingly out of key (and, as happens with Garfield, sometimes vulgar, as if that is a natural concomitant). "He could smell the man. The man could not smell him. All the man could smell was the nasty smoke he was making." (92) "'Well, what is the charm?' said Chervil. 'You say: O fly away great bird so white, And don't come back until tonight.'" (351)

Rather more interesting is the degree of consistency he shows in the implied narrative contract. We have noted his technical problems, and on occasion he can integrate pure information with scarcely a hiccough:

A rabbit in fear of an enemy will sometimes crouch stock-still, either fascinated or else trusting to its natural inconspicuousness to remain unnoticed . . . So it was with Fiver now. (113)

However, elsewhere, the authorial voice takes over and begins to preach:

The short June darkness slipped by in a few hours. The light returned early to the high down but the rabbits did not stir. Well after dawn they were still sleeping, undisturbed in a silence deeper than they had ever known. Nowadays, among fields and woods, the noise level by day is high – too high for some kinds of animal to tolerate. Few places are far from human noise – cars, buses, motor-cycles, tractors, lorries. The sound of a housing estate in the morning is audible a long way off. People who record bird-song generally do it very early – before six o'clock – if they can. Soon after that, the

231

invasion of distant noise in most woodland becomes too constant and too loud. During the last fifty years the silence of much of the country has been destroyed. But here, on Watership Down, there floated up only faint traces of the daylight noise below. (138)

It is noticeable that this hectoring is from the author, not the narrator; the story is put aside, the contract is broken. Along with this goes a lapse into language designed for a specific audience: "some kinds of animal", "people who", "cars, buses ..." and into cliché and platitude: "during the last fifty years ..." But cheek by jowl with this we find, perhaps, an implied resonance to a deeper level which is not actually there: "undisturbed in a silence deeper than they had ever known". Possibly both intent and effect here are literal – but the slight deviation of "deeper" seems to suggest that Watership Down is more than just a safe place for a warren. Is this signalling an implied general truth behind the story? Perhaps the falseness can be recognized in the cliché.

Elsewhere Adams could quite justly be accused in Ruskin's terms of being a second-order writer; a man who "feels strongly, thinks weakly, and sees untruly". The rabbits rest after a hard day's travel, and the author steps forward:

To come to an end of anxiety and fear! To feel the cloud that hung over us lift and disperse – the cloud that dulled the heart and made happiness no more than a memory! This at least is one joy that must have been known by almost every living creature.

... Here is a soldier who was waiting, with heavy heart, to suffer and die in battle. But suddenly the luck has changed. There is news! The war is over and everyone bursts out singing! He will go home after all! (68–9)

And so on for half a page. Now this is not only clichéd, but untrue, and the half-borrowing from Sassoon only points it up. The depth of the story (the contact with which gives an impression of value) simply will not support such artificial significances. This is not because the story is about rabbits, or because their heroisms are small. It is that nothing in the book goes beneath theme level; and that level itself is pre-digested. As some critics have pointed out, plot and character are not greatly different from a hundred B-picture war stories; which is only to say that the surface variations (rabbits, names) are ingenious transforms of a structural element that has ceased to have any real significance. Whatever the origins, this structure has become fossilized, and now stands for nothing but itself. It is, at best, only superficially disturbing – or true. (A parallel example is the use made of nursery rhymes by Lewis Carroll. The nursery rhymes may initially have been transforms, or reflections, or resonances of very deep levels, but, denatured by adaptation and simplification, they now provide only a shallow foundation.)

Given the modest aims that Adams has insisted upon, this might scarcely seem to be a criticism; but the attempt, however unconscious, to imply that we are – or should be – reading something that has profounder levels, is not entirely honest to the narrative contract. As we have seen, the surface structure tends to betray such attempts, while elsewhere such flights end in bathos. When the rabbits first reach the River Test, Marco Polo at Cathay is invoked; or, when Bigwig is chewing the hinge of a rabbit hutch: "'By Frith, that'll do', said Blackberry, for all the world like the Duke of Wellington at Salamanca." (222)

It is also curious that Adams, who can evoke the weather so accurately and appropriately as a natural hazard and an element of naturalism, should attempt to use it as a pseudo-mystic element in the defeat of Woundwort. One might argue that the employment of such a discredited device is rather appropriate to the level of incident he is working with. Yet the concatenation of extravagantly inaccurate mixed metaphors and clichés in which it is couched, suggests that he is deliberately trying to pull the book onto a different plane.

Along the western horizon the lower clouds formed a single, purple mass, against which distant trees stood out minute and sharp. The upper edges rose into the light, a far land of wild mountains. Copper-coloured, weightless and motionless, they suggested a glassy fragility like that of frost. Surely, when the thunder struck them again they would vibrate, tremble and shatter, till warm shards, sharp as icicles, fell flashing down from the ruins. Racing through the ochre light, Bigwig was impelled by a frenzy of tension and energy. He did not feel the wound in his shoulder. The storm was his own. The storm would defeat Efrafa. (359)

Where, one wonders, does "surely" come from? The shift into the present suggests, conventionally, some cohesion with the protagonist's consciousness. That it is clearly inappropriate to Bigwig's perceptions casts doubt on the last two statements. This piece of authorial self-indulgence seems to be not only underselling the pace of the story and infringing the narrative contract, but also attempting to impose significance by sleight of hand.

Despite authorial disclaimers, it seems to me that the chapter epigraphs share something of this intent. Apart from one excellent joke ("the General's unjust interference, so far from being injurious to their felicity, was perhaps rather conducive to it..." [467]) their effect tends to be to emphasize the comparative shallowness of Adams's own writing. This is especially the case with the interpolated tales of El-ahrairah, which are for the most part inept and vulgar pastiches and are not well served by being introduced with quotations from Yeats and the Psalms. In these attempts to provide a solid, and resonating, underpinning to the rabbits, the juxtaposition of the heroic and the childish (rather than child-like) seems to indicate an ambivalence about the status of the tale.

Adams has been fairly scathing of political and social interpretations of his work, claiming – rather manifestly in opposition to Garfield's approach – that, at least in intent, such attitudes are not in the book.[9] I have some sympathy for his position (although, of course, an author is hardly in a position to judge) in that much of the writing on *Watership Down* has tended to gloss the ideas. This fashionable, endemic, and, it must be said, unarduous way of approaching books, is as common in universities as in the children's book world. It is also inherently dangerous, as it suggests that *what* is said is a great deal more important than *how* it is said. In teaching, especially, this provides a paradox, because the quality of the *how* is part of, and reflects very accurately, the depth or value of the *what*. Worse, this approach can engender an uncritical acceptance of works clearly well stocked with ideas, however poorly formulated or ill written. One suspects that it is this situation which leads to a novel such as Leon Garfield's *The Pleasure Garden*, despite Garfield's manifest talents in other books.

Richard Adams has committed himself to print as being proud of his transcription of Hampshire dialect,[10] and while he may be excused the assumption that "yore" is any different from "your", it is less easy to be charitable to Garfield's rendition of Cockney, which includes such phonetic wonders as "solumm" and "minnit". I mention this trivial point only because it is characteristic of an apparent lack of craftsmanship in *The Pleasure Garden*. An author may not be responsible for his books' categorization, but he is certainly party to it – and here Garfield seems deliberately to be striving for significance, for a quasi-adult audience, and, by implication, for "literary" status.

His quite legitimate tendency to find symbols lying around his eighteenth-century world is exaggerated in this book. Mrs. Bray and Dr. Dormann, apart from running the Mulberry Pleasure Garden ("eastward in Clerkenwell"), also selectively blackmail their patrons, getting their evidence from a team of eavesdropping urchins. Dr. Dormann's confessional approach to extortion leads his clients to regard him as a kind of malign saint, while he regards Mrs. Bray and the garden as parts of a heaven from which he might be expelled. The urchins, despite what they see, have their innocence nurtured, until knowledge and age come upon them and they are cast out.

When Garfield is not too obviously manipulating things, these elements are reasonably subtle and coherent. Into the garden comes the flawed angel, the Reverend Martin Young, much attracted to one Fanny Bush (subtlety of names is not one of Garfield's fortes). A young man is murdered in the garden ("the splash of blood in the midst of the innocent gaiety of the pleasure garden" [55]) and Martin, suspecting Fanny, conceals some evidence. Dormann attempts to blackmail him, her innocence is established, and the true murderer is, literally, unmasked. (He is acquitted, ultimately, as he was provoked by the young man's transvestitism.) Interleaved with this is the story of the chief spy, Briskitt, who tries a little blackmail of the murderer on his own account. He spends his hush money on presents for the raddled mother of one of his compatriots, is disillusioned, and leaves the garden, and what innocence he had, behind. We leave Fanny and Martin alone together, Fanny reading lengthy extracts of "The Song of Solomon" to him, while a masked ball proceeds in the pleasure garden.

Even from this filleting of the novel, some impression of the sheer richness of the materials is evident; themes and implications abound, and when these cohere with Garfield's prose, the effect can be impressive.

> Salisbury Court was a deep, quiet socket of a place, approached from Dorset Street by a narrow passage called The Wilderness. The houses were tall and cheek by jowl, forming an exclusive community of shadows into which a dim intrusion was achieved by a single lamp.... At times, it seemed as if the whole court was a convoluted shell, pressed to an invisible ear. (171)

Unfortunately, by this stage of the novel, our response to the possibilities of the prose has probably been blunted. Garfield's surface deviations from "normal" language, which usually signal more profound significances, are inconsistent. Sometimes, and most effectively, we can find sparkling ingenuity; which is satisfactory in itself, but which has no deeper meaning. "The rattle of feet and the noise of panting suggested that a small-sized hailstorm had got inside the house and panicked." (11) Sometimes there are rather heavy-handed attempts at implying deeper meanings: "The church was fathoms deep in darkness, and the long pews slumbered through sermons of silence." (69) Here the metaphor is not particularly appropriate, and the choice of vocabulary perilously close to cliché: rather as if the sound patterns are more important than the matter. Occasionally, such ingenuity can resonate down to (or up from) a thematic level; Dr. Dormann watches from the murderer's house the pursuing Reverend Young: "How had he come there? What damnable congregation of chances had led him there?" (177)

But when Garfield draws attention to the structure of metaphor and symbol, the effect is very often a false resonance as we may have seen with Richard Adams. Instead of referring down to a coherent level of ideas. or resonating up from significance to a correlative image, the text seems to imply either that he has not been able to think the consonances through, or that he has not felt it necessary to do so. In the first chapter, we are given an overview of the garden and its patrons, and the chapter ends with the evening: "Slowly and laughingly, with promises and assignations for the Friday to come, the revellers go out of the pleasure garden, out into the black garden of pain." (10) At this point, the text simply cannot support this kind of overwriting, this injection of significance. Similarly, at the end of the book, tagging the garden suddenly as "the garden of two childhoods" leaves the reader not impressed by the depth of this, but wondering whether the depths exist anywhere but in the author's hopes. The description simply does not relate to any structure which can justify it.

By far the most effective elements are those where the surface interplays with character and atmosphere, and goes no further; where ingenuity is no more than that; where it is true to itself. Thus the cameos are witty and clever, if not authentic, creations: Mrs. Gish's clothing establishment, the staymaker's ("whose name, in accordance with an ancient custom, was Wishbone"), Cuper's Pyrotechnic Factory. But almost everywhere, Garfield is prey to overwriting:

The general effect of coming into this place, with its ceaseless explosions of sparkling fire and the dark, demonic figures of the experimenting journeymen, was that one had strayed into the bowels of creation and witnessed apprentice gods trying their hands at universes. (124)

If the reader, encouraged elsewhere to relate to apparently accessible levels of significances, attempts to do so with these gratuitous instances, then disillusion soon sets in. It becomes virtually impossible – and progressively less worth the trouble – to see whether he means them or not. There is a considerable difference between this and intentional or integrated ambiguity.

As before, we can see that the narrative contract is an excellent touchstone. Martin Young, walking home with Fanny with a good deal of torment in his soul, arrives at her lodgings:

She opened the iron gate, which screamed like a soul in hell.... Her little room danced and flickered all round her in the yellow light; garments in various stages of stitching hung from pegs round the walls; shawls, caps with streamers and capes with limp hoods, like girls with broken necks, crowded the eye and suffocated the mind. (100)

Whose eye, and whose mind? Are we transposing from the thoughts of Young, or is the author supplying these images? If the latter, we do not have the contract with the character to respond to, merely an imposed assertion that relates only artificially to the action, let alone the theme.

A more difficult case is that of Briskitt. Possibly Garfield intends us to see him as an ambivalent figure, comic, sad, and – as when he leaves the garden – significant beyond himself:

He went like a sudden rushing wind. . . . Not knowing altogether from what, he ran for dear life . . . although to call it dear was not, in Briskitt's case, entirely truthful. At last he reached the gate and, with a final raucous grunt, he fled out of the garden for ever. (169)

Why "truthful" rather than "true"? Where are we standing? The biblical allusion (one of many in the book) implies that there is something more to this than the event: yet if we supposed so, we are brought up short by Garfield's self-confessed inability to resist the smart aside. Our response is undermined. But Garfield can not only break his contract with the reader; he also breaks his contract with the characters. When Briskitt, stirred by romance, prepares to visit Chops's mother in Bridewell, the narrator invites us to observe him sympathetically.

. . . Briskitt arrayed himself for the coming visit to the lady of his heart. He donned his satin waistcoat, which became him like a Crusader's apron . . . He stood, stiff and still in the stable, awaiting his squire – a burning knight diminished by a perspective of distance. (105)

This may correspond with Briskitt's view of himself, although the imagery is unlikely. But when Garfield sustains the tone as the boys enter the gaol, we rapidly arrive at parody; a betrayal of the character and of the viewpoint.

They . . . passed under a low doorway that admitted them to that part of the castle where, in nun-like seclusion, the ladies were lodged.
     They mounted the winding stair towards the airy chamber where Chops's ma, in company with six other damsels, was cruelly locked away for the weary space of the night. Upwards and upwards they toiled, with Briskitt's satin waistcoat rising and falling over the pumping of his knees like a brave banner. (105)

Grahame, in *The Wind in the Willows*, pulls this sort of parody off magnificently because – in Toad's downfall – he is writing farce. Here, Garfield is the adult observer, not so slyly laughing at a character who is undergoing a crisis, however trivial. (And, if Briskitt is central to the theme of growing and initiation, the crisis is not trivial.) The boys approach "Chops's ma": and note that, unlike Mayne, Garfield arbitrarily imposes this name on her; no three-way contract is defined.

His shadow crossed her, and the damsel, clad in her knitted shawl, her nearly new shoes and dark stockings as holey as the Pope of Rome, opened her eyes from a drowsiness that was something more than sleep. Dimly she perceived her child – the fruit of her womb – and, in a spasm of sentiment, flung wide her arms, thereby exposing her copious bosom that was scratched from some altercation she couldn't possibly have remembered. (106)

This seems to be writing of regrettable "quality". Drifting away from the parodic mode, we have a joke – a purely written joke at that – made by the author, who thereby seems not much interested in the scene if he is prepared to draw attention to his typewriter. We are then invited to nudge elbows with the author in our superior knowledge of what causes the "drowsiness that was something more than sleep". Do we then sway into consonance with the woman's consciousness – "dimly she perceived ..."? No, for we then have a phrase which takes us back to parody, "the fruit of her womb". Are we still in contact with Briskitt's traumatic moment? Hardly, when "copious" is used; and even less so when the clichéd tone of the magistrate intrudes: "some *altercation* she couldn't possibly have remembered". The casual dropping of "which" and the contraction "couldn't" strongly suggest that here the superior and almost sniggering author is inviting us to join him in patronizing what one might have supposed from the context was a tragic figure. To single out Garfield's prose as ingenious and stimulating is to overstate the case. Too often what we find is slyness rather than wit, as with the aside on Major Smith (which can hardly emanate from his character) – "all women look alike during the day ..." – emphasized by the leader.

These problems should not be overstated. His use of the symbolism of masks elsewhere in the book comes close to both coherence and significant resonance. Martin Young and Dr. Dormann are linked by the falsity of their own images ("the man possessed by a devil and the man possessed by an angel") and Dormann's awareness of his own ambivalence (expressed in a dream) and his physical manifestation of it, are very striking:

Then everyone ripped off their paper faces, leaving blood and bones to

239

the open view. This was the worst moment of all, because he knew that he must take off his own mask, and, with it, his face. (27)

> Even as Martin bent over him, the skin on his face seemed to come up in a curious, colourless rash – like roughened paper. It was almost as if he had something pasted over his whole face. (122)

But, as with the blind beggar who wanders enigmatically in and out of the story, one is more often left with an impression of casual rather than coherent substructures.

In 1971 Frank Eyre made some perceptive comments about Garfield, noting, of *Black Jack*, "the almost frenzied 'come along quickly, let's get on with action and not bother too much about what is really supposed to be going on' that is the special mark of his manner"; and of *The Drummer Boy*, "there is too much in this book that strikes false notes".[11] These are precisely the problems with *The Pleasure Garden*. The variable narrative stance implies clearly that action is not the primary concern of the book; therefore, the author has a duty first to the book, and perhaps more to the implied audience to make these other concerns coherent. If one is concerned with the audience, then a symbol, an undertone, a resonance, is a serious (although not necessarily solemn) business. If you are going to lead someone along a path merely to leave them in a bog of frustration, disillusion, or incoherence, then it might be better not to lead them at all. To say that *value* – in terms of depth and honest interaction between surface and depth – is inappropriate to a children's book is merely to suggest that the second-rate is appropriate to children; it seems to me unlikely that even the most child-centred critic would admit that.

Therefore it may be hard to suggest that Garfield has deliberately produced a book which sells short the potential of his readers, in which case it is difficult to defend him in terms of art or audience; or that he is not capable of producing a better book, in which case his publishers should look to their standards. Yet it is clear that Garfield has produced, and can produce the book of value which *The Pleasure Garden* points towards. The confusions in the minds of publishers and critics, who have been reluctant to look at the *book*, appear to have affected the author with a vengeance.

❊　　❊　　❊

In 1972 a reviewer of William Mayne's *The Incline* noted: "Perhaps it would have made a better novel for adults, for it is a book *about* children, rather than for them."[12] While we have seen that this comment could well apply to *IT*, it may seem that Mayne's books do not offer a great deal more. Their surface qualities may excel but, like *Watership Down*, there is little of interest or significance beneath this surface. At least Garfield makes an attempt to inject something other; Mayne's fidelity to the narrative contract, his apparently obsessional insistence on detail, seems to convey no more and to be ultimately self-defeating. Yet Mayne has sufficiently refined his art so that the deep resonances are echoed in virtually all the surface structures; the significance lies in the insignificance of events. To this extent, it may be that Mayne requires a subtle, possibly "adult", way of reading.

Nevertheless, good as Mayne's narrative stance is, he responds in *IT* to the practical demands of his context, with some curious results. He occasionally breaks his author–character–reader contract with omniscient interjections. The first few chapters do little more than set scenes and establish characters, and Mayne intrudes to keep the momentum going, to point out significance.

The remarks had not been about Alice at all, which was a good thing in some ways and annoying neglect in others. Alice sat alongside the case and felt she was alone. She remembered that feeling as the year went by and the next year went on into summer: today was her last day of being alone for all of that time. (11)

That is that, Alice thought. Another empty hill climbed today, and she chiefly felt hungry for missing most of lunch ... She felt safe from all visitations: no one knew where she was.

But where she was had become known, and there was a visitation. (22)

She had to stop among the later graves and whimper behind a tall stone and blow her nose and still not be rid of a lump above the mouth and behind the eyes.

I will find everything, she said, to be a pilgrim. And she was to find. (47)

This is just the portentousness which we have noticed in Adams and Garfield; the shift into received structures of children's book narrative, which allow the author to hint ahead. Mayne's use of this device is, as commonly happens, accompanied by cliché, a flaw emphasized by his consistency elsewhere. As with Garfield, he robs himself at these points of the opportunity to integrate depth through the character.

One may compare the effect of such variation with the way in which all levels of the book, from surface to deep motivation, are integrated at key points elsewhere in *IT*. The greatest difficulty of his earlier attempt at making supernatural events gel with a meticulously naturalistic setting, *Earthfasts*, was the explanation of the points at which two different sets of experience meet. The transitions tended to be cumbersome, and the same occurs in *IT* when Alice peers into the stone she has discovered on the hill near the Minster, the Eyell:

> It was something that Alice's eyes could not understand, as if they had got themselves focussed wrong and were striving to interpret. It was like looking at a photograph and its negative at the same time, all shape and depth that cannot be seen or understood; it was like the thing that happens when you stare at an object for a long unblinking time and the image goes dark and swirling. (52)

By the intrusion of the "you", we move uncomfortably away from Alice's mental fumblings with the problem. The conventional storyteller stance has been momentarily adopted, as if there is an admission of inadequacy in the carefully built-up technique. When this technique is allowed free play, as when the ceremonies are completed at the end of the book, the effect is rather different:

> She held out her hand, and from the ring there flashed the reflection of a ribbon of lightning that struck from side to side of the cloud. The ring was now the centre of all, and the weight of the world seemed to be on it. She put her other hand to it and turned it on the finger, and then drew away the hand that wore it. It was now ringless, free. In the ring was all the pull of darkness for ever encircled by it: to look at it was like looking into the opening on the stone in the Eyell, substance and not substance, place and not place, time and not time.
>
> ... The ring and the opening became one, and then became nothing, and there was only stone. The ring itself fell for ever away from her hand, down into the bottom of time, dwindling without diminishing, along a perspective of eternity. (187)

This works, if it works, because of the integration with character, and because a phrase like "along a perspective of eternity", which might in another context appear pretentious, is supported by the coherence of the resonances preceding it. If he is fudging a description of the indescribable, we can accept this because we accept the consciousness that modulates it – Alice's.

A complete shift of narrative approach is usually only successful if the detailed texture of the language has sufficient quality to overcome the jar of contrasting techniques: which is only to say that the text must continue to signal the integrity of the theme, or deeper levels. At a pivotal point in *IT*, when Alice reaches literally across time to stab the witch, Mayne steps completely and at first sight incongruously away from his character, changing stance, tense, and tone:

...she looks about and from its place where it lies on the hill she picks a thin bar of iron, some passing abandoned rubbish. With this metal she digs at the fourth opening.

At the first push there is a little tempting resistance, a satisfaction in having the metal sink in, and she feels the old rust flake off on hard edges. At the end of the thrust, when her hand has gone as far as it can and the iron has gone as far as it will, the iron quivers as if a weight had dropped away from it. She draws it out, and it comes glistening, and when it comes she feels nothing for herself but all the world round her seems to move, just a little, and just a little, and then is as it was.

She turns away from the stone and walks down among the fallen leaves. They rustle under her feet and they rustle behind her, and she takes up the basket and goes out across the field and to her home. (68)

Here we have a highly controlled and crafted piece of writing, which gives us confidence in, and gives validity to, any resonances we may detect. Such minor details as "from its place", "picks", "some passing abandoned rubbish", "this metal" convey the ambivalence of the object, its inevitability and its unimportance. The resonance down to levels of significance below plot or theme is achieved by the simultaneous resonance to other elements in plot and character which are more obvious and accessible. Details are unimportant but are constantly foregrounded. Children's games are unimportant, but are at the centre of the narrative. The Minster and its rituals, choirs, and characters are trivial in the perspectives of time which they encapsulate. Religious differences are given perspective by being seen through the eyes of Alice and Raddy: are their perceptions so inaccurate? And all these elements are drawn together by incidents which seem momentous – possession, exorcism – but which are continually deflated and understressed. Alice is "suddenly and copiously sick" at the end of her ritual: but it is largely because of a hastily swallowed potato. When the sad spirit raises an irate storm every time she goes near the Minster, Alice finds it tiresome and simply changes her route to school. "'I can't be bothered with it in the morning.'" Even potential melodrama is suppressed, and as such integrates at thematic level and below.

The stress of the book is out of key with the narrative, and this seems to be precisely the point. Hence Mayne's use of elements which echo rather closely those of his contemporaries (especially Alan Garner's *Elidor*), and which rework his own preoccupations, could be seen as either satire or derivativeness; but the crafting of the book makes such issues irrelevant. That they might be more relevant in Adams's or Garfield's work is a function of those writers' surface skill and integrity.

Whether or not one accepts these views of the authors (which have, deliberately, little or nothing to do with *actual* readership), we cannot leave Mayne without noting examples of the surface quality of his writing. His skill in conveying complex personal and family relationships has been underestimated – or considered irrelevant – partly because he has refined it to an almost casual level. It is difficult to think of any other contemporary author who can so economically suggest infrastructures, interdependence, and lack of communication, while at the same time conveying these through the eyes of a convincingly real child:

Getting home changed nothing for Alice. She was still going to be the wrong way out for everybody else. She could see it in everything around her, and she could see it in what she did herself and in what she had ever done.

"I don't know what you are thinking about these days," said Mum, when Alice had stood and watched something interesting but fatal happen to the gravy in the baking dish. "You've burnt both." Alice had, of course. She had stopped stirring and let the gas flame scorch a ring, first of innocent bubbles and then of real cinder, while she had thought about nothing she could remember in words.

"You'll clean that drip-tin," said Dad, and there was another little argument about that, with Dad using one name for one thing, Mum the other and Alice not being allowed to be on either side.

"Out of my kitchen, both of you," said Mum, when it was quite clear that no one agreed.

"Now then," said Dad to Alice as they went out of the door, "have a care."

"I have several," said Alice.

"Happen you have," said Dad. Then they went to bring their visitors to the table. (15)

There are, of course, slight slips (notably "Alice had, of course") and elsewhere Mayne can slip into simplification, or invent unlikely and unnecessary expedient explanations, as when Mum's and Grandpa's under-reaction to *IT* is shrugged off because they had encountered similar things in Africa. One would hardly claim of any author that he is perfect, but the consistency of Mayne's craftsmanship deserves rather more respect than it is sometimes accorded. There are few writers capable of precise observation conveyed in such precise words:

The wind came thin from the west and splashed drops of rain from the trees. The drops fell on the stone pavement, for a moment becoming its colour, as if the stone had lifted up rather than had something land on it; then the stone was undisturbed again, merely wet. (94)

With all its detail imperfections, *IT* seems to have a coherent root significance, reflected at all levels, up from theme, through plot and character, to the surface details of the prose. Garfield, on the other hand, plays with language, indulging whimsy – often successfully – and wit and ingenuity. But one is not left with any sense that he is in control of his medium, or that the interesting equals (or is as interesting as) the profound. Again, the quality of the surface indicates the value of the depths. Natalie Babbitt said of Mayne's *A Year and a Day*: "... the sense of something in motion behind this story, and the resonance of its telling provide a special power.... His stories come from very deep in the well."[13]

This cannot, in all honesty; be said of *The Pleasure Garden*, although it might of some of Garfield's earlier books. Whereas *Watership Down* operates very adequately on the level it sets itself, and *IT* is there to be read according to one's capacities, *The Pleasure Garden* seems uncertain in both purpose and execution.

The ways in which these three authors are customarily read and evaluated, then, seems often to have perilously little to do with the books themselves. I am not suggesting that we should pursue that phoenix The Great Book to the exclusion of all the rest; but we should beware of allowing ourselves to accept the mediocre, or the expedient, or a weak novel of a usually reliable author, as anything more than they are. To look for value in the sense I have suggested does not preclude enjoyment either of surface felicities or of competent reworkings of fossilized themes and plots. But, equally, it does not allow us to confuse the useful with the good, or the good with the great. One cannot quarrel with the dual standard which so manifestly exists – good for adults versus good for children – as long as its users realize how dangerous a premise it can be.

REFERENCES

1. Colin Ray: "*The Edge of the Cloud* – A Reply to Dominic Hibberd" (*Children's Literature in Education*, No. 9, November 1972). Reprinted in *Writers, Critics and Children* edited by Geoff Fox et al. (Heinemann Educational Books, 1976) p.139.

2. Richard Adams: "Some Ingredients of *Watership Down*" in *The Thorny Paradise* edited by Edward Blishen (Kestrel, 1975) p.172.

3. Alec Ellis & Marcus Crouch, eds.: *Chosen for Children* (Library Association, 3rd edition, 1977) p.164.

4. Rhodri Jones: "Leon Garfield" in *Good Writers for Young Readers* edited by Dennis Butts (Hart–Davis Educational, 1977) p.43.

5. John Rowe Townsend: *A Sense of Story* (Longman [Kestrel], 1971) p.103. Richard Camp: "Garfield's Golden Net" (SIGNAL 5, May 1971) p.55.

6. Aidan Chambers: "The Reader in the Book" (SIGNAL 23, May 1977) p.73. This article is reprinted in the present book on pages 250–75.

7. Justin Wintle & Emma Fisher: *The Pied Pipers* (Paddington Press, 1974) p.206.

8. Fred Inglis: "Spellbinding and Anthropology" in *Good Writers for Young Readers* op. cit. p.124.

9. Wintle & Fisher: *The Pied Pipers* op. cit. p.142.

10. Blishen: *The Thorny Paradise* op. cit. p.171.

11. Frank Eyre: *British Children's Books in the Twentieth Century* (Longman [Kestrel], 1971) pp.102, 104.

12. *Times Literary Supplement*, 14 July 1972, p.807.

13. *New York Times Book Review*, 2 May 1976, p.40.

SIGNAL QUOTES

Elaine Moss in "On the Tail of the Seductive Horse"
(Signal 19, January 1976)

What a child feels about a book as he reads it makes that book good or bad in a subjective sense whatever the objective critic may say about it; the reader is as much part of the dynamics of the written word as are the author and the story he writes. Why else should Hans Andersen have called the *Fairy Tales* his "gift to the world", and what, I wonder, would he think of those modern authors "for children" who speak of writing only for themselves? One writes a diary for oneself, a letter for oneself and the recipient – who is palpably present; a novel for oneself, of course, and for the reader who is there all the time and who will draw from the book his own unique satisfaction.

It is this isolation of the child with his book, the private communication, the seed sowing, the awakening, that makes reading so important a part of growing, and criticism so delicate a horticultural operation. None of us can know what message a picture, a piece of music, a poem or a book brings to anyone else. But what we do know is that being able to receive is vital. Channels to the young are many, wide open, but inclined to silt up if unused; if used, however, they lead in a myriad of surprising and rewarding directions.

Hugh Crago in "Cultural Categories
and the Criticism of Children's Literature"

(Signal 30, September 1979)

By focusing on the artist's creativity, critics have reinforced the assumption that it is the only kind of creativity there is. At the same

247

time, by a curious intellectual sleight-of-hand, critics have in writing about books expressed themselves in such a way that statements about their own response become transformed into statements about the work or its creator. As a critic, indeed, I was systematically trained to do this. It would not do, I found, to write a sentence like: "I feel uncomfortable and afraid when I read X's description of a child being stoned to death by thugs." Instead, I learned to translate my response into something like: "X's description of a child's being stoned to death by thugs is convincing in its mobilization of the reader's emotions." Or, at an even greater distance from the original reaction: "X's description . . . is disturbing and terrifying."

This process allows the critic to operate without taking full responsibility for his own feelings, even to judge without being conscious of them. By eliminating the "I", he casts himself in the pseudo-objective role of the omniscient predicter of other people's responses, when in fact he is speaking only of his own. And by expressing his reactions as attributes of the work in question, he suggests again that it is the art work itself (or its creator) which alone has potency. In fact, no description could move me to tears or admiration if it were not for my own experiences and my own sensibilities. This is not to claim that a literary work (or any art work) may not attempt to channel its readers' emotional responses in certain ways: a reader's experience of a text is not wholly and solely a product of his or her own psyche. But *in itself* a book cannot create *any* feeling in its audience. The locus of feeling is in the reader, not in the book.

From *War and Peas* written and illustrated by Michael Foreman

The Reader in the Book

AIDAN CHAMBERS

Aidan Chambers writes for children and young people and, for adults, about children's books. Although proprietor of The Thimble Press, which publishes SIGNAL, an article by him was not included in the magazine until May 1977. This was an edited version of a talk he gave at the University of Bristol School of Education earlier that year. In it he tries to show how some of the contemporary ways of thinking about literature in general can be applied to books for children. The article won the Children's Literature Association's first award for critical writing; the Association is based in the United States, where Mr. Chambers is known for his regular column about children's books in *The Horn Book Magazine*.

I

1. Two to say a thing ...

There is constant squabble about whether particular books are children's books or not. Indeed, some people argue that there is no such thing as books for children but only books which children happen to read. And unless one wants to be partisan and dogmatic – which I do not, having had my fill of both – one has to agree that there is some truth on both sides and the whole truth in neither.

The fact is that some books are clearly *for* children in a specific sense – they were written by their authors deliberately for children – and some books, never specifically intended for children, have qualities which attract children to them.

But we must go further than that truism, which helps us very little to deal critically with books or to mediate them intelligently and effectively to children. We need a critical method which will take account of the child-as-reader; which will include him rather than exclude him; which will help us to understand a book better and to discover the reader it seeks. We need a critical method which will tell us about the reader in the book.

For it seems to me that all literature is a form of communication, a way of saying something. Samuel Butler once observed that it takes two to say a thing, a sayee as well as a sayer – a hearer as well as a speaker. Thus, if literature is a way of saying something, it requires a reader to complete the work. And if this is so, as I am convinced it is, it must also be true that an author addresses someone as he writes. That someone has come to be called "the implied reader".

2. *The implied reader*

Let me defend myself against an obvious objection. I am not suggesting that, as an author writes, he necessarily has in the front of his mind a particular reader. F. H. Langman in a useful article, "The Idea of the Reader in Literary Criticism", puts it this way:

I do not say we need to know what readers the author had in mind. An author may write for a single person or a large public, for himself or for nobody. But the work itself implies the kind of reader to whom it is addressed and this may not coincide with the author's private view of his audience. What matters for the literary critic is to recognize the idea of the reader implied by the work. Not only correct understanding but also evaluation often depends principally upon correct recognition of the implied reader. (*British Journal of Aesthetics*, January 1967, pp.84–94)

I would go further. I would say that, until we discover how to take account of the implied reader, we shall call fruitlessly for serious attention to be paid to books for children, and to children as readers by others than that small number of us who have come to recognize their importance. What has bedevilled criticism of children's books in the past is the rejection of any concept of the child-reader-in-the-book by those people who have sought most earnestly for critical respectability. And they have done this, have set aside the reader-in-the-book, in the belief that mainstream criticism requires them to do so, when in fact literary criticism has for years now been moving more and more towards a method that examines this very aspect of literature. If children's book critics look for parity with their colleagues outside the study of children's books, they must – if for no other more valuable reason – show how the concept of the implied reader relates to children as readers and to the books they read.

The idea of the implied reader derives from the understanding that it takes two to say a thing. In effect it suggests that in his book an author creates a relationship with a reader in order to discover the meaning of the text. Wolfgang Iser, in *The Implied Reader* (Johns Hopkins, 1974), puts it this way: he says that such a critical method "is concerned primarily with the form of a work, in so far as one defines form basically as a means of communication or as a negotiation of insight" (p.57).*

To achieve this, an author, sometimes consciously sometimes not, creates, in Wayne C. Booth's words: "an image of himself and another image of his reader; he makes his reader, as he makes his second self, and the most successful reading is one in which the created selves, author and reader, can find complete agreement." (*The Rhetoric of Fiction*, University of Chicago Press, 1961, p.138.)

The author's second self† is created by his use of various techniques: by the way, for example, he puts himself into the narrator – whether that be a third-person godlike all-seer or a first-person child character; by the way he comments on the events in the story; and by the attitude he adopts towards his characters and their actions, which he communicates in various ways, both subtle and obvious.

In the same way (and let me stress again, deliberately or otherwise) the reader's second self – the reader-in-the-book – is given

---

* Iser has enlarged and refined his ideas in *The Act of Reading* (Johns Hopkins, 1979).

† The term was revived by Kathleen Tillotson in her inaugural lecture at the University of London, published under the title *The Tale and the Teller* (Athlone Press, 1959): "Writing on George Eliot in 1877 Dowden said that the form that most persists in the mind after reading her novels is not any of the characters, but 'one who, if not the real George Eliot, is that second self who writes her books, and lives and speaks through them.' The 'second self', he goes on, is 'more substantial than any mere human personality' and has 'fewer reserves'; while 'behind it, lurks well pleased the veritable historical self secure from impertinent observation and criticism'."

certain attributes, a certain persona, created by the use of techniques and devices which help form the narrative. And this persona is guided by the author towards the book's potential meanings.

Booth points out that a distinction must be made "between myself as reader and the often very different self who goes about paying bills, repairing leaky faucets, and failing in generosity and wisdom. It is only as I read that I become the self whose beliefs must coincide with the author's. Regardless of my real beliefs and practices, I must subordinate my mind and heart to the book if I am to enjoy it to the full."

3. *The unyielding child reader*

Booth expresses something mature literary readers have always understood: that a requirement of fulfilled readership is a willingness to give oneself up to the book. They have learned how to do this: how to lay aside their own prejudices and take on the prejudices of the text, how to enter into the book, becoming part of it while at the same time never abandoning their own being. In C. S. Lewis's words, literature allowed him "to become a thousand men and yet remain myself".

Children, of course, have not completely learned how to do this; they have not discovered how to shift the gears of their personality according to the invitations offered by the book. In this respect they are unyielding readers. They want the book to suit them, tending to expect an author to take them as he finds them rather than they taking the book as they find it. One of the valuable possibilities offered by the critical method I look for is that it would make more intelligently understandable those books which take a child as he is but then draw him into the text; the books which help the child reader to negotiate meaning, help him develop the ability to receive a text as a literary reader does rather than to make use of it for nonliterary purposes.

The concept of the implied reader and the critical method that follows from it help us to do just that. They help us establish the author's relationship with the (child) reader implied in the story, to see how he creates that relationship, and to discover the meaning(s) he seeks to negotiate. Clearly, such understanding will lead us beyond a critical appreciation of the text towards that other essential activity of those concerned with children's books: how to mediate the books and their readers so that individual books may be better appreciated by children and so that children are helped to become literary readers.

II

We must examine one book closely in an attempt to reveal its implied reader. But before we come to that, it may be useful to consider some of the principal techniques by which an author can establish his tone – his relationship with his desired reader – and, of particular importance in children's books, by which he can draw the reader into the text in such a way that the reader accepts the role offered and enters into the demands of the book.

4. *Style*

Style is the term we use for the way a writer employs language to make his second self and his implied reader and to communicate his meaning. It is far too simplistic to suppose that this is just a matter of sentence structure and choice of vocabulary. It encompasses an author's use of image, his deliberate and unaware references, the assumptions he makes about what a reader will understand without explication or description, his attitude to beliefs, customs, characters in his narrative – all as revealed by the way he writes about them.

A simple example which allows a comparison between the style a writer employed when writing for adults and the alterations he made when rewriting the story for children, is provided by Roald Dahl. "The Champion of the World" is a short story first published in *The New Yorker* and now included in *Kiss Kiss* (Michael Joseph/Penguin). Some years afterwards Dahl rewrote the story for children under the title *Danny: The Champion of the World* (Cape/Puffin). The original version could hardly be called difficult in subject or language. A ten-year-old of average reading ability could manage it without too much bother, should any child want to. Both versions are told in the first person; the adult narrator of the original is in some respects highly ingenuous, a device Dahl employs (following *New Yorker*-Thurber tradition) as a foil for the narrator's friend Claud, a worldly wise, unfazable character, and an exaggeration into comic extravagance of the otherwise only mildly amusing events of a fairly plain tale.

Because the original is written in this first-person, easily read narrative, which is naive even in its emotional pitch, Dahl could transfer parts with minimal alterations straight from the original into the children's version. Yet even so, he made some interesting and significant changes. Here, for example, is the original description of the entry into the story of its arch-villain, Victor Hazel (differently spelt in the two tellings), whose unforgivable snobbery and unscrupulous selfishness are justification enough in the narrator's eyes to warrant poaching his pheasants:

I wasn't sure about this, but I had a suspicion that it was none other than the famous Mr. Victor Hazel himself, the owner of the land and the pheasants. Mr. Hazel was a local brewer with an unbelievably arrogant manner. He was rich beyond words, and his property stretched for miles along either side of the valley. He was a self-made man with no charm at all and precious few virtues. He loathed all persons of humble station, having once been one of them himself, and he strove desperately to mingle with what he believed were the right kind of folk. He rode to hounds and gave shooting-parties and wore fancy waistcoats, and every weekday he drove an enormous black Rolls-Royce past the filling-station on his way to the brewery. As he flashed by, we would sometimes catch a glimpse of the great glistening brewer's face above the wheel, pink as a ham, all soft and inflamed from drinking too much beer.

Here is the recast version written for the children's telling:

I must pause here to tell you something about Mr. Victor Hazell. He was a brewer of beer and he owned a huge brewery. He was rich beyond words, and his property stretched for miles along either side of the valley. All the land around us belonged to him, everything on both sides of the road, everything except the small patch of ground on which our filling-station stood. That patch belonged to my father. It was a little island in the middle of the vast ocean of Mr. Hazell's estate.

Mr. Victor Hazell was a roaring snob and he tried desperately to get in with what he believed were the right kind of people. He hunted with the hounds and gave shooting parties and wore fancy waistcoats. Every week-day he drove his enormous silver Rolls-Royce past our filling-station on his way to the brewery. As he flashed by we would sometimes catch a glimpse of the great glistening beery face above the wheel, pink as a ham, all soft and inflamed from drinking too much beer.

Dahl has simplified some of his sentences by chopping up the longer ones with full stops where commas are used in the adult version. And he does some cutting: he takes out the abstractions such as the comment about Hazel loathing people of humble station because he had once been one of them himself. Presumably Dahl felt children would not be able (or want) to cope either with the stylistic complexities of his first version or with the motivation ascribed to Hazel's behaviour. Whatever we may think about this, it certainly reveals Dahl's assumptions about his implied reader.

What he aims to achieve – and does – is a tone of voice which is clear, uncluttered, unobtrusive, not very demanding linguistically, and which sets up a sense of intimate, yet adult-controlled, relationship between his second self and his implied child reader. It is a voice often heard in children's books of the kind deliberately written for them: it is the voice of speech rather than of interior monologue or no-holds-barred private confession. It is, in fact, the tone of a friendly adult storyteller who knows how to entertain children while at the same time keeping them in their place. Even when speaking outrageously about child-adult taboo subjects (theft by poaching in *Danny* and, in this extract, harsh words about a grown-up), the text evinces a kind of drawing-room politeness. At its most typical the style speaks of "the children" in the tale. Arthur Ransome marks a high point in that traditional manner:

So the letters had been written and posted, and day after day the children had been camping on the Peak of Darien by day, and sleeping in the farmhouse by night. They had been out in the rowing-boat with their mother, but they had always rowed the other way so as not to spoil the voyage of discovery by going to the island first. But with each day after the sending of the letters it had somehow seemed less and less likely that there would ever be an answer. The island had come to seem one of those places seen from the train that belong to a life in which we shall never take part. And now, suddenly, it was real. It was to be their island after all. They were to be allowed to sail out from the little sheltered bay, and round the point, and down the lake to the island. They were to be allowed to land on the island, and to live there until it was time to pack up again and go home to town and school and lessons. The news was so good that it made them solemn. They ate their bread and marmalade in silence. The prospect before them was too vast for chatter. John was thinking of the sailing, wondering whether he really remembered all that he had learnt last year. Susan was thinking of the stores and the cooking, Titty was thinking of the island itself, of coral, treasure, and footprints in the sand. Roger was thinking of the fact that he was not to be left behind. He saw for the first time that it was a good thing to be no longer the baby of the family. Vicky was the youngest now. Vicky would stay at home, and Roger, one of the crew of a ship, was to sail away into the unknown world.

Ransome achieves precisely the same relationship with his reader as Dahl, and by pretty much the same stylistic qualities. Ransome's style is more fluid than Dahl's, gentler on the ear, better balanced and more tuneful. But it is essentially writing for children; no one, surely, can believe that, had Ransome been writing for adults – in the sense of an implied adult reader – he would have adopted the tone of voice so evident and so well created in *Swallows and Amazons* (Cape), from which the extract is taken (pp.16–17 in the Puffin edition).

Style can, as I say, work in a much more complex and subtly effective way than these two extracts suggest – or rather than my use of them here suggests. And we will look further into this aspect of the writer-reader relationship when we come to examine a major text.

5. Intermission: What the writers say . . .

Mention of Ransome calls to mind his much-quoted words about writing for children: "You write not F O R children, but for yourself, and if, by good fortune, children enjoy what you enjoy, why you are a writer of children's books."

All very well and, obviously, what Ransome believed about himself. But it is difficult to believe on the evidence of Ransome's books that, had he really thought he was speaking to an adult audience primarily, he would have adopted the same tone of voice or would have treated his stories in the ways he does. Even a traditional critical examinnnations of his books, eschewing all thought of the reader, implied or otherwise (excepting of course the critic, who never considers himself anything but an objective, and therefore somehow never a specific reader – a matter Langman in the article already mentioned deals with very effectively), must surely reveal that Ransome's books are for children in quite specific ways, whatever Ransome himself said. Which is not to suggest that he, or any other writer who adopts this idea about himself as a writer, is dissembling. Rather, I want simply to reinforce Langman's observation: "An author may write for a single person or a large public, for himself or for nobody. But the work itself implies the kind of reader to whom it is addressed and this may not coincide with the author's private view of his audience."

Which proves one thing, if anything at all: we must be wary of using as evidence in criticism what an author says about himself, publicly or privately: a caution we have not sufficiently taken to heart in talking about children's books. Over the past five or six years there has been a fashion for calling the authors on stage to explicate themselves and their work in public and to defend it against the worst ravages of pedagogy and off-the-cuff criticism. That has been beneficial neither for the authors nor for their audiences.

6. *Point of view*

Tone of voice, style as a whole, very quickly establishes a relationship between author and reader; very quickly creates the image of the implied reader. In books where the implied reader is a child, authors tend to reinforce the relationship by adopting in their second self – giving the book, if you prefer – a very sharply focused point of view. They tend to achieve that focus by putting at the centre of the story a child through whose being everything is seen and felt.

This is more than simply a device. If literature for children is to have any meaning at all, it must primarily be concerned with the nature of childhood, not just the nature commonly shared by most children but the diversity of childhood nature too. For, like all literature, children's literature at its best attempts "to explore, re-create and seek for meanings in human experience" (the phrase is Richard Hoggart's); this attempt is made with specific reference to children and their lives through the unique relationship between language and form.

But, at the level of creating the implied reader and of an author's need to draw a child reader into his book, this narrowing of focus by the adoption of a child point of view helps keep the author's second self – himself in the book – within the perceptual scope of his child reader. And the child, finding within the book an implied author whom he can befriend because he is of the tribe of childhood as well, is thus wooed into the book. He adopts the image of the implied child reader and is then willing, may even desire, to give himself up to the author and the book and be led through whatever experience is offered.

Thus the book's point of view not only acts as a means of creating the author-reader relationship but works powerfully as a solvent, melting away a child's non-literary approach to reading and re-forming him into the kind of reader the book demands.

Some authors, feeling constricted by a too narrowly child-focusing viewpoint, try to find ways of presenting a fuller picture of adulthood without losing the child-attracting quality of the narrower focus. A few have tried to do this directly, using adult characters and a point of view that shifts between a child-focus and an adult-focus. But very few of the few who have tried have succeeded. It remains one of the major problems for children's writers now. Nina Bawden has always been exercised by this difficulty, and has gone a long way towards finding satisfactory solutions, especially in *Carrie's War* (Gollancz/Puffin). This book is well worth critical consideration as a very fine example of the way an author can deploy her craft in the creation of an implied reader, apart from her success in revealing adult characters to a remarkably complex degree without loss of definition for her young readers.

Most writers approach the problem of adult-portrayal less directly. They tend to cast their tales in the form of fantasy, usually with animal-human characters. Robert C. O'Brien's *Mrs. Frisby and the Rats of NIMH* (Gollancz/Puffin) provides a much enjoyed modern example; Kenneth Grahame's *Wind in the Willows* (Methuen) probably the best known and most affectionately regarded;

and Russell Hoban's *The Mouse and His Child* (Faber/Puffin) one of the most complexly layered and handled (for which reasons, no doubt, it is finding its most responsive audience not among children but among adolescents).

But if I wanted to select, in the context of my theme, two superlative examples that encompass a possible readership of about seven years old right on to adulthood, I would choose Alan Garner's *The Stone Book* (Collins) to demonstrate the direct approach and Ted Hughes's *The Iron Man* (Faber) as an example of the solution through fantasy.

7. Taking sides

It does not follow, of course, that a writer who places a child at the narrative centre of his tale necessarily or even intentionally forges an alliance with children. *Lord of the Flies* (Faber) is entirely peopled by children, but no one would call it a book for children in any sense. (Adolescents enjoy it – or at least their teachers have decided they shall study it; but adolescents are not children, an understanding I have so far taken for granted.) Even the point of view of William Golding's book, though it pretends as a narrative device to restrict itself to the child characters' points of view, is in fact profoundly adult in range and perceptions. And this is to say nothing about the style and the implied reader it helps create.

William Mayne, always published as a children's author but notoriously little read by children and much read by adults, may, for all I know, intend to be a writer for children. But what the tone of his books actually achieves, as Charles Sarland brilliantly uncovered in his article, 'Chorister Quartet" (see pages 217–24), is an implied author who is an observer of children and the narrative: a watcher rather than an ally. Even his dramatic technique seems deliberately designed to disengage the reader from the events and from the people described. This attitude to story is so little to be found in children's books that even children who have grown up as frequent and thoughtful readers find Mayne at his densest and best very difficult to negotiate. He wants his reader to stand back and examine what he, Mayne, offers in the same way that, as nearly as I can understand it, Brecht wanted his audiences to stand back from and contemplate the events enacted on stage.

As Sarland says, Mayne "requires a degree of sophistication in the reader that would not normally be found in children of the same age as his characters. It is clear from the way he uses pace, dialogue, causal relationships, puns and wordplay that the last thing he wants is that the reader should be carried along on the tide of the narrative".

There is, in other words, an ambivalence about Mayne's work that disturbs his relationship with his child reader. And this is made more unnerving by a fracture between a narrative point of view that seems to want to ally the book with children, while yet containing narrative techniques that require the reader to disassociate from the story – to retreat and examine it dispassionately.

What Mayne may be trying to do – I say "may be" because I am not sure that he *is* trying for it – is not impossible to achieve, though it is very difficult indeed to achieve for children. I have no space to delve into the matter here, fascinating though I find it, except to say as a pointer to those who want to follow this direction for themselves: Alan Garner's *The Stone Book*, besides the other extraordinary qualities it possesses, manages to balance these paradoxical demands, involving the reader with the narrative while at the same time helping him to stand back and contemplate it. And Garner makes this participation possible for children at even quite an early time in their growth as readers, though the younger ones may require the mediation of an adult in order to enter into such a profound experience.

Taking sides can be crudely worked for, simply as a way of "getting the child reader on your side". Enid Blyton provides the obvious example. She quite literally places her second self on the side of the children in her stories and the readers she deliberately looks for. Her allegiance becomes collusion in a game of "us kids against them adults". Nothing reveals this more completely than her treatment of adult characters like the policeman Mr. Goon in *The Mystery of the Strange Bundle* (Methuen). The unfortunate constable's name itself – chosen by the author, remember – indicates Blyton's attitude to the man, to his office, and her stance as one of the gang, one of the children in the story. Let's play this game together, she says openly and unembarrassedly; let's have fun at the expense of the grown-ups; let's show them who's best; let's solve a mystery and have an adventure.

The very titles of her books reinforce this taking of sides. They act as an attraction to the book, raising in the reader expectations about the nature of the story to come that she never fails to satisfy. There are ten books in the *Mystery of* ... series, eight in the Adventure series, and twelve "about the Five Finder-Outers and Dog".

Incident by incident Blyton sustains her collusion with her implied reader, sometimes letting him have the edge on the characters by telling him what they don't yet know, sometimes letting the characters have the edge on the reader by withholding things it later turns out the characters knew all the time. And adults get the edge only so that they can be done down later by the narrator, her characters and her readers.

There is about her stories a sense of secrets being told in whispers just out of earshot of the grown-ups, a subversive charm made all the more potent for being couched in a narrative style that sounds no more disturbing than the voice of a maiden aunt telling a bedtime story over cocoa and biscuits. Ultimately Blyton so allies herself with her desired readers that she fails them because she never takes them further than they are. She is a female Peter Pan, the kind of suffocating adult who prefers children never to grow up, because then she can enjoy their pretty foibles and dominate them by her adult superiority. This betrayal of childhood seeps through her stories: we see it as the underlying characteristic of her children who all really want to dominate each other as well as the adults.

Richmal Crompton is quite as canny; she too allies herself strongly with her child reader.* But her work has a redeeming quality – one among others: her ironic treatment of William, the Outlaws and their adventures. A skilled short-story writer, she structures her tales with an elegance outstanding in its craftsmanship and finish. But above all she brings to children's reading that essential element they must discover if they are to grow beyond

*Of course, the William stories were first written for adults. But children soon adopted them, after which Richmal Crompton was never in doubt about her true audience.

the kind of writing Blyton's epitomizes. For without an understanding of irony, literature – beyond the merely plotful level – will never provide much pleasure and certainly cannot yield up its deepest meanings.

Once an author has forged an alliance and a point of view that engages a child, he can then manipulate that alliance as a device to guide the reader towards the meanings he wishes to negotiate. Wolfgang Iser provides a useful example, not from a specifically children's book, where such a manoeuvre is too rarely used, but from *Oliver Twist*. Iser cites the scene in which the hungry Oliver

has the effrontery (as the narrator sees it) to ask for another plate of soup. In the presentation of this daring exploit, Oliver's inner feelings are deliberately excluded in order to give greater emphasis to the indignation of the authorities at such an unreasonable request. The narrator 'comes down heavily on the side of authority, and can thus be quite sure that his hard-hearted attitude will arouse a flood of sympathy in his readers for the poor starving child.

What such manipulation of the reader's expectations, allegiances, and author-guided desires leads to is the further development of the implied reader into an implicated reader: one so intellectually and emotionally given to the book, not just its plot and characters but its negotiation between author and reader of potential meanings, that the reader is totally involved. The last thing he wants is to stop reading; and what he wants above all is to milk the book dry of all it has to offer, and to do so in the kind of way the author wishes. He finally becomes a participant in the making of the book. He has become aware of the "tell-tale gaps", the indeterminacies in a story.

8. Tell-tale gaps

As a tale unfolds, the reader discovers its meaning. Authors can strive, as some do, to make their meaning plain, leaving little room for the reader to negotiate with them. Other authors leave gaps which the reader must fill before the meaning can be complete. A skilful author wishing to do this is somewhat like a play-leader: he structures his narrative so as to direct it in a dramatic pattern that leads the reader towards possible meaning(s); and he stage-manages the reader's involvement by bringing into play various techniques which he knows influence the reader's responses and expectations, in the way that Iser, for example, described Dickens doing in *Oliver Twist* (7). Literature can be studied so as to uncover the gaps an author leaves for his reader to fill, and these indeterminacies take two general forms.

The first is the more superficial. These gaps have to do with an author's assumptions, whether knowingly made or not, about his readers. Just as we saw in the Dahl extracts (4) how a writer's style revealed his assumptions about the implied reader's ability to cope with language and syntax, so we can also detect from a writer's references to a variety of things just what he assumes about his implied reader's beliefs, politics, social customs, and the like. Richmal Crompton in common with Enid Blyton, A. A. Milne, Edith Nesbit and many more children's authors assumed a reader who would not only be aware of housemaids and cooks, nannies and gardeners but would also be used to living in homes attended by such household servants. That assumption was as unconsciously made as the adoption of a tone of voice current among people who employed servants at the time the authors were writing.

These referential gaps, these assumptions of commonality, are relatively unimportant until they become so dominant in the text that people who do not – or do not wish to – make the same assumptions feel alienated by them as they read. And this alienation affects the child just as much as the adult, once the referential gaps become significant.

Far more important, however, is another form of tell-tale gap: these are the ones that challenge the reader to participate in making meaning of the book. Making meaning is a vital concept in literary reading. Laurence Sterne refers to it directly in *Tristram Shandy*:

No author who understands the just boundaries of decorum and good breeding would presume to think all. The truest respect which you can pay to the reader's understanding is to halve this matter amicably, and leave him something to imagine, in his turn, as well as yourself. For my own part, I am eternally paying him compliments of this kind, and do all in my power to keep his imagination as busy as my own.

Of course, it doesn't all depend on the author; he can deploy his narrative skills brilliantly, "halving the matter amicably" with his reader. But unless a reader accepts the challenge, no relationship that seeks to discover meaning is possible. It is one of the responsibilities of children's writers, and a privileged one, so to write that children are led to understand how to read: how to accept the challenge. But more of that another time.

Let me offer the crucial gap in Sendak's *Where the Wild Things Are* (Bodley Head/Puffin) as example. In its pictorial as well as its textual art this extraordinary masterpiece is compactly authored. One might be forgiven for supposing at first sight that there are no gaps of any kind for the reader to enter. But not so; there is one so vital that, unless the reader fills it, the profound meaning of the book cannot be discovered. It is the gap which demands that the child reader supply the understanding that Max has dreamt his journey to the Wild Things, that in fact the Wild Things are Max's own creation. Once understood, that meaning having been made, the book opens itself to all sorts of other pleasurable discoveries which actually were clues to the meaning all along and which, once realized, present themselves as clues to yet further meaning. There is, for instance, in the first picture in the book, the Wild-Thingish doll hanging from a coathanger; and then, in the very next picture, there is the portrait of a Wild Thing framed and hung on the wall and signed "by Max".

Such guides to the reader may seem obvious to an adult, but children of four and five and six, who are the book's implied readers, make such a significant contribution and discover such details only if they give the book a willing attention of the same order as adults must give to filling the gaps in, say, Joyce's *Ulysses*.

Alan Garner's *The Stone Book* is built around three main images, each placed in precise relationship to each other so that they create two vital gaps which the reader must enter and fill before the potential meanings of the book become plain. Reiner Zimnik's *The Crane* (Hodder/Puffin) is as halved as Sterne could wish; Zimnik's tone of voice is so sensible, so matter of fact, so gentle and everyday, you can suppose the meaning(s) of his story must be so too. But in fact the book is heavy with possibilities and is not at all easy to plumb intellectually, though emotionally – as an increasing number of teachers are finding after introducing it to their nine-to twelve-year-olds – it is powerfully attractive.

9. *In sum* . . .

. . . and before we begin an exploration of one text.

I am suggesting that the concept of the implied reader, far from unattended to by critics of literature nowadays, offers us a critical approach which concerns itself less with the subjects portrayed in a book than with the means of communication by which the reader is brought into contact with the reality presented by an author: that it is a method which could help us determine whether a book is for children or not, what kind of book it is, and what kind of reader (or, to put it another way, what kind of reading) it demands. Knowing this will help us to understand better how to teach not just a particular book but particular books to particular children.

I have been trying to sketch in some of the more significant ways in which specific responses are provoked in a reader, the techniques that make up what Kenneth Burke in *The Philosophy of Literary Form* (Vintage, 1967) has called "the strategy of communication". This is achieved by major techniques such as I have described and by a variety of other devices such as what an author discloses to his reader and what he conceals, the way he signals his intentions, his evocation of suspense, the introduction of the unexpected, and the way he can play about with the reader's expected responses to the narrative.

All these create a relationship between an author and his reader, which I have used the word "tone" to denote; and an author, consciously or otherwise, reveals in his narrative, through the way he uses all these techniques and by other signals too, what he wants from his reader, what kind of relationship he looks for.

Now I want to examine some of these matters at work in one book, Lucy Boston's *The Children of Green Knowe* (Faber/Puffin).

III

10. Why "The Children of Green Knowe"?

For three reasons:

Mrs. Boston is a much admired and respected writer; her first children's book lends itself to my critical needs here.

Not only is she much respected, but she is historically important. *The Children of Green Knowe* appeared in 1954 and was one of the first of the new wave of children's books that marks the out-cropping since the Second World War. I think it intelligently argu-able that this book directly influenced a number of the writers who began work in the 50s and 60s. (In my view Philippa Pearce's *Tom's Midnight Garden*, Alan Garner's *The Weirdstone of Brisingamen* and the work of William Mayne owe a considerable debt to Lucy Boston.)

Mrs. Boston has said publicly some interesting things about her work, which provide an example of the kind of authorial self-comment I warned against earlier. During a talk given in November 1968 to the Children's Book Circle (a gathering of children's book editors in London who meet to discuss their professional concerns) Mrs. Boston said:

Is there a conscious difference in the way I write for grown-ups and children? No, there is no difference of approach, style, vocabulary or standard. I could pick out passages from any of the books and you would not be able to tell what age it was aimed at.*

Let's see. The opening of *Yew Hall* (Bodley Head), Lucy Boston's first book, and written for adults (or, to use her word, grown-ups):

Possibly it was their voices that made me decide that I could share my house with them, so that after having once refused, I repented and told them that they could come. He was a huge man, handsome like a statue in St. Paul's. His martial features and great neck suggest at once to the imagination the folds of a marble cloak drawn back across a superlative torso and looped over an arm to free the incredible giant legs in their marble tights. He was so near to the type classified as admirable at the turn of the eighteenth century

---

*Quoted from an extract published in John Rowe Townsend's *A Sense of Story* (Kestrel).

that his own personality might have escaped my notice if it had not been that his voice was as soft and warm in quality as a man's voice could possibly be. There was nothing feminine about it. It was like a breeze in the tops of a forest, and he gave the impression, that afterwards was amply confirmed, of having so much space to live in that he need never knock elbows with or trip over anyone else. Well might he be self-satisfied – like America he has no need of imports. A general comfort radiated from his bigness – a big heart, a big fire, a big meal, a big bed, a big pair of shoes; and, I suppose, we must also think of a big stick, a big clap of thunder.

Compare the opening passage of her first children's book, published the same year (see extract in [11] below): there are unmistakable differences in approach, style and vocabulary. *Yew Hall* has an urbanity that establishes very quickly a tone which implies a literate adult reader. The handsome statues of St. Paul's, the martial features and superlative torso, the type classified as admirable at the turn of the eighteenth century, America having no need of imports: this one paragraph is littered with references that expect a reader who can match the author's cultural and social background: the educated English middle class. The writing is confident, witty, slightly superior ("Possibly it was their voices that made me decide that I could share my house with them ..."), the kind of writing one would not be ashamed to be caught reading by one's butler.

What of *The Children of Green Knowe*? Who is its implied reader? Let's look at it under the headings suggested in II.

11. *Style*

Here are the opening paragraphs of *The Children of Green Knowe*:

A little boy was sitting in the corner of a railway carriage looking out at the rain, which was splashing against the windows and blotching downward in an ugly, dirty way. He was not the only person in the carriage, but the others were strangers to him. He was alone as usual. There were two women opposite him, a fat one and a thin one, and they talked without stopping, smacking their lips in between sentences and seeming to enjoy what they said as much as if it were something to eat. They were knitting all the time, and whenever the train stopped the click-clack of their needles was loud and clear like two clocks. It was a stopping train – more stop than go – and it had been crawling along through flat flooded country for a long time. Everywhere there was water – not sea or rivers or lakes, but just senseless flood water with the rain splashing into it. Sometimes the railway lines were covered by it, and then the train-noise was quite different, softer than a boat.

"I wish it was *the* Flood", thought the boy, "and that I was going to the Ark. That would be fun! Like the circus. Perhaps Noah had a whip and made all the animals go round and round for exercise. What a noise there would be, with the lions roaring, elephants trumpeting, pigs squealing, donkeys braying, horses whinnying, bulls bellowing, and cocks and hens always thinking they were going to be trodden on but unable to fly up on to the roof where all the other birds were singing, screaming, twittering, squawking and cooing. What must it have sounded like, coming along on the tide? And did Mrs. Noah just knit, knit and take no notice?"

The two women opposite him were getting ready for the next station. They packed up their knitting and collected their parcels and then sat staring at the little boy. He had a thin face and very large eyes; he looked patient and rather sad. They seemed to notice him for the first time.

The language in *Yew Hall* tends towards the Latinate. *Green Knowe* is much more firmly Anglo-Saxon. Rain is splashing and blotching, lips are smacking, knitting needles click-clack, not to mention Tolly's own list of participial verbs describing Noah's animals. This makes for a style not only simpler to read but far more active than a Latinate one, far more concrete in an everyday and child-appealing sense.

There is, however, as Mrs. Boston claims, no lowering of standard between the two books. *Green Knowe* is just as densely and richly textured – perhaps is even more richly textured – than *Yew Hall*. But the images and the words used to communicate them are quite different in the experiential demands made on the reader. At the crudest level *Yew Hall* requires familiarity with St. Paul's Cathedral, the late eighteenth century and the economy of the United States if one is to enjoy all Mrs. Boston has to offer. *Green Knowe* requires no such sophistication. You need only to have seen some rain, have been on a train, know something about the story of Noah and the Flood, and to have observed women knitting for the text to be completely open to you. After that you need only put at Mrs. Boston's disposal a sympathetic imagination and she leads you off in a very clearly signposted direction. Even from these three opening paragraphs we can see she is busy with sensual experience: the sight, sound, feel, and sense of things. It is a direction in which her story will take young readers a very long way.

For sure, then, the style of *The Children of Green Knowe* is much more accessible to a child reader, and comparison with the style of *Yew Hall*, which seems so much more confidently natural to Mrs. Boston – one feels it is closer to her own thinking voice – leads one to suppose its implied reader is a child. At the very least the style appeals to the child-in-the-adult, possessing that very tone of voice I earlier suggested is traditionally the English tone used in telling stories to children: direct, clear, polite, firm, uncluttered. And Mrs. Boston achieves it admirably.

We must discover whether or not the other aspects of her book reinforce the impression given by her style.

12. *Point of view*

Tolly is seven; remarkable for his age, a child of a very particular class. His father and stepmother are in Burma, the boy has been put into boarding school, left for the holidays with the headmistress and her old father, and then sent alone on a train journey to visit his great-grandmother, Mrs. Oldknow, who lives in a large old house. Throughout, the story is told from Tolly's point of view. Only occasionally is there a brief shift for some narrative purpose, as when the two women in the train "sat staring at the little boy. He had a thin face and very large eyes; he looked patient and rather sad. They seemed to notice him for the first time." Otherwise, the perceptions are all the boy's.

Even Mrs. Oldknow, so central a character in the story, is seen only from the outside. Her private thoughts and perceptions remain enigmatic, and influentially so: she occupies a somewhat mysteriously attractive place in the book. One wonders about her, and feels too a little daunted by her, a little afraid of her secret knowingness. The reader gets that impression from a subtly handled feature of the book. All along one cannot help feeling that it is Mrs. Oldknow who is telling the story. And probably the feeling would not be so strong were it not for the stories Mrs. Oldknow tells Tolly at night. They are about the children who lived in the house and died in the Plague of 1665. But then, the rest of the book is also about a boy in the house. Isn't the whole book therefore a story by Mrs. Oldknow? Has she, in fact, invented Tolly? Or isn't she, at the very least, telling his story, and doing it so well because she *knows* – can see into children's minds, as children so often believe some adults can, and tell what is going on in them?

So, though the story is told from Tolly's point of view – apart, of course, from Mrs. Oldknow's stories about the other, long-ago children – Mrs. Oldknow herself seems in control of it. These two things together stimulate a strong sense of alliance between Mrs. Oldknow, Tolly and the reader, thus placing the author unmistakably on the reader's side.

13. Taking sides

Before the story has gone far enough to establish the strong relationship I've just described, Mrs. Boston is signalling her allegiance. The opening paragraphs of the book reveal her sympathetic understanding of a small boy's response to the world about him, and in particular the world as it surrounds Tolly at that moment on the train. Every slight detail serves this end, from the clacking needles and the train being more stop than go, to the child-accurate observation of the rain and the flood and the train noise.

Then the two women take notice, and their conversation with Tolly sets him thinking about his circumstances. Now Mrs. Boston reveals whose side she is on unequivocally: Tolly being miserably shy of his stepmother, the kind Miss Spudd, who yet always calls him "dear".

When Tolly at last meets his great-grandmother, wondering if she is a witch and whether he will be afraid of her (the terrible business of meeting strange relatives), Mrs. Boston–Oldknow (for Mrs. Boston's second self must surely be Mrs. Oldknow) declares her allegiance openly: "What does one generation more or less matter? I'm glad you have come. It will seem lovely to me. How many years of you have I wasted?" A declaration of friendship, if not of love, which is reinforced by a further shift from adult-child allegiance to collusion no more than a page later:

At that moment the fire went *pop!* and shot a piece of wood out into the room. *Pop!* again.

"Buttons! Who said buttons? Poor Mrs. Noah." Tolly chased the sparks and trod on them to put them out.

"Why do you live in a castle?" he said, looking round.

"Why not? Castles were meant to live in."

"I thought that was only in fairy tales. Is it a real castle?"

"Of course."

"I mean, do things happen in it, like the castles in books?"

"Oh yes, things happen in it."

"What sort of things?"

"Wait and see! I'm waiting too, to see what happens now that you are here. Something will, I'm sure."

Something is being proposed here: at the least a game, at the most something more mysteriously magical, and it is to be an adventure enacted between Tolly and Mrs. Oldknow.

Next morning, the adventure begins: it involves Tolly's long-ago child relatives – whether as ghosts or not we hope to discover – household toys, garden animals, and Mrs. Oldknow. Being cut off by the flood simply asserts actually and symbolically the private collusive world inhabited by the boy and the old woman.

But the collusion is not just a means of disposing the reader to the book: its profoundest meaning depends upon the nature of the relationship.

14. Tell-tale gaps

Game or ghost story? More than a game and not just a ghost story. Each time we think that at last Tolly is indisputably seeing apparitions of Toby, Alexander and Linnet, Mrs. Boston withdraws confirmation.

A crucial scene comes after the snowfall. A tree's branches form a cave, which Tolly enters and there seems to meet and hear speaking the three ghosts; Alexander even plays his flute. But the scene ends: "Had he been dreaming?" And when Tolly creeps out of his snow-cave, "Somewhere in the garden a thrush was trying to whistle Alexander's tune." We are left wondering still.

Later Mrs. Oldknow leaves Tolly alone in the house and Boggis too is gone. Surely now the ghosts will emerge and they, Tolly and the reader can meet undeniably. But no. Despite the house being empty of others and dark coming on, so that the stage is set for a final exciting ghost-drama, our expectations raised for a climax (how many other writers have prepared us so before), Mrs. Boston will not satisfy us: "For some reason [Tolly] felt convinced that, until his great-grandmother returned, not so much as a marble would move in the house." She has employed a device similar to Dickens's in *Oliver Twist*: reader's expectations raised, and deliberately dashed. We are forced to wonder why.

Here is the amicable halving of this book; here is a tell-tale gap which the reader must enter if the book's true meaning is to be negotiated. Whatever is going on in the story can only be enacted between Mrs. Oldknow and Tolly. Nothing happens when they are apart. Together, their lives have followed a pattern. During the day, Tolly explores and plays, sometimes on his own, sometimes with Mrs. Oldknow, sometimes with Boggis, but always, however gently and subtly suggested, at the instigation of his great-grandmother. She, like a superlatively wise play leader, offers opportunities for Tolly to enjoy himself through experiences that enliven the world to him. He is led to look closely, hear clearly, touch sensitively, think imaginatively. The book is laden with instances in which Tolly encounters objects and, by sensing them and playing with them, imaginatively perceives the life in them.

These moments extend from the purely sensational –

In the fire the snow drifting down the chimney was making the only noise it ever can – a sound like the striking of fairy matches; though sometimes when the wind blows you can hear the snow like a gloved hand laid against the window.

– to extended passages in which Tolly's exploration of a room or a part of the garden or of a toybox is described in close and carefully imaged detail. The walk through the snow that leads to the snow-cave scene is one such.

Punctuating these descriptions of the day-to-day activities are four stories told by Mrs. Oldknow to Tolly at bedtime. This device suits the apparently naturalistic plot: Tolly is on holiday with his great-grandmother: the house and gardens provide his daily adventures; before bed he is given his fictional adventure. But these four stories are not just any stories: they are about the three long-ago children and their horse Feste, one story for each. Some critics – John Rowe Townsend in *A Sense of Story*, for instance – have felt this an awkward construction. To my mind it is not only a pattern that creates a satisfying rhythm in the book – entirely suited, as I say, to the plot's boy-on-holiday structure – but it actually makes the book's true meaning possible.

We are led to see things this way: Tolly and Mrs. Oldknow fantasize about Toby and Alexander and Linnet. Tolly may or may not actually see their ghosts, and enjoys the game. But the three long-ago children have undeniable reality only in the stories Mrs. Oldknow tells about them. There they live in their own right, not as spectres raised by Tolly and his great-grandmother, just as Tolly and Mrs. Oldknow have a reality in their own right only as characters in Mrs. Boston's story about them. Stories, Mrs. Boston is telling us, are the means by which we give life to ourselves and the objects around us. Stories, in fact, create meaning.

Strangely enough, in the very talk to the Children's Book Circle in which she claimed no difference between her writing for adults and her writing for children, Mrs. Boston also said:

My approach has always been to explore reality as it appears, and from within to see how far imagination can properly expand it. Reality, after all, has no outside edge. I never start with a fantasy and look for a peg to hang it on. As far as I deliberately try to do anything other than to write a book that pleases me, I would like to remind adults of joy, now considered obsolete – and would like to encourage children to use and trust their senses for themselves at first hand – their ears, eyes and noses, their fingers and the soles of their feet, their skins and their breathing, their muscular joy and rhythms and heartbeats, their instinctive loves and pity and their awe of the unknown. This, not the telly, is the primary material of thought. It is from direct sense stimulus that imagination is born...

Nowhere has an author so exactly stated her aims, and in few books has an author achieved her highest aims so certainly as Mrs. Boston does in *The Children of Green Knowe*. Through Tolly, guided by Mrs. Boston's second self, her implied reader is brought to grips with the direct sense stimulus that gives birth to life-expanding imagination. By any standard this is a fine achievement, all the more remarkable for the simplicity with which it is executed.

15. *Lucy Boston's implied reader*

Mrs. Boston makes no impossible demands on her child reader's ability to construct meaning from words. Her style is approachable, uncomplicated, specific rather than abstract. The first Green Knowe book is not long; its episodic and day-to-day rhythm punctuated by the stories-within-the-story makes it easy to read in unexhausting parts. Her alliance with her young reader is persuasive. The now almost old-fashioned middle-classness of Tolly's and Mrs. Oldknow's life (and Mrs. Boston's preference for it) is strong but not so dominantly obtrusive as to be a disadvantage. (The polite formality of the collusion between Mrs. Oldknow and Tolly is nowadays amusing. Even though they are playing a game, Tolly must always behave impeccably; he commits only one naughty act throughout the whole book: he writes on the newly whitewashed wall in Boggis's room, a wickedness allowed to pass without censure, of course, because it is done in a servant's room, not in the main house. Even Boggis, old retainer, wants to preserve the benevolent hierarchical social tradition, to the point of tolerating his daughter's indiscretion because it provides him with a male heir to his post. The book is deeply conservative and traditionalist; a political attitude which disposes children all the more readily to the story, for most children prefer things to remain as they always have been.)

All Mrs. Boston requires of her reader is a willingness to enter into the spirit of sensuous discovery. Given this, she deploys her craft very subtly indeed towards her stated aims. And that she is speaking primarily to children I have no doubt.

An Interview with Alan Garner

AIDAN CHAMBERS

An abridged version of this interview, which grew out of the ideas in "The Reader in the Book", appeared in the September 1978 SIGNAL to mark publication of one of the volumes of Alan Garner's *Stone Book* quartet (*The Aimer Gate*, Collins), a sequence of stories for children by one of Britain's leading authors. The transcript is now published in full as one instance of a signal way of talking about children's books.

The Reader in the Book

Let's see if we can clear some ground between us, before we come to the specifics of The Stone Book *sequence. If I were to give you the familiar words of Henry James, that the writer creates his reader as he created his characters, is that something that has any reality for you as a writer?*

No. I understand it intellectually but I don't experience it myself, never have. With the possible exception of *The Stone Book* itself of the four, but that is for a technical reason which started me to think along the lines of *The Stone Book* subconsciously quite early on in the process. That was through talking to Linda Davis about reading.

She's your editor.

Yes. But that was a long time before I knew I was going to do anything. That was general conversation between friends.

So the experience of both the event of writing a book, and particularly a book like The Stone Book, *or even in hindsight as you think back about the experience, the idea of making a reader inside the book has no meaning for you?*

276

No. And everything I say *about* writing is with hindsight. At the time there are conflicting emotions – usually there is only one emotion and that is to get the thing finished. The second emotion is not to think at all but to stop everybody else making a noise so I can listen to the voices in my head. To listen to the story and watch it happening internally. That's as far as *that* goes, but after the event and probably before the event of writing, there is a very strong busker I say-I say-I say feeling. I do want to stop people and grab them by the lapels.

You're aware of a sensation of speaking to somebody, are you?

Yes. Nobody in particular, just a sense of urgency to share an excitement that I don't understand within myself.

In principle, whatever the refinements of it might be, you would agree that, for you at any rate – I would say I think for most writers, if not all – the act of putting pen to paper is an act of wishing to speak to somebody, wishing to communicate something.

Yes. Although for technical reasons it's suppressed at the time of putting pen to paper.

Point of View

In that case, if you have no specific sense of an audience, no specific sense of the reader, how do you come to grips with the kind of problems that writing any narrative involves? Let me take one particular example, because I think it's probably the most pertinent both to writers who are consciously writing for children and to those who are not but who end up being published that way. And that is the problem of point of view.

If you look at The Stone Book *sequence, in each book the point of view is that of a child protagonist, of Mary, or Joseph, or Robert, or William, and everything is perceived through their minds and eyes. You only know what they know, you only hear what they hear. You don't see inside Grandfather, or Father, or whoever. Now, how did you solve that problem? How did that appear as a problem, or didn't it?*

Well for the last time – otherwise I shall be very boring – all this is hindsight and I'm just applying intelligence, but I am telling the truth. At the time the question for me is simply, what is the story? Now, I know it's not so simplistic. What happens is that, through a process of testing myself, I find, or create, the ideal form for that particular story to take. If it is to say "the clarity of the story is best expressed by eliminating all that is irrelevant to a child protagonist", then the story is seen through the eyes of a child protagonist. But I don't work it out consciously.

I understand. And you can argue from that that you're not intending to have children as readers of that story. You could simply say "This is a story which is about a child protagonist and therefore it's seen in that way." But there are other aspects of The Stone Book sequence which would seem to suggest that there were conscious decisions that directed the book towards children as readers as well as an expectation that adults will read it. Can we clear the point first of all of whether that was an intention or not?

It probably was. I can't honestly say that it was, except in a negative way. I certainly did not intend to exclude children. Now I have written in such a way, though not fiction. I have written in order to dissuade children sometimes.

When have you done that?

In *The Guizer.*

That's fascinating. And I would have thought in some respects in Red Shift.

Possibly. Now we've come to a technical point which is universal to everything I've ever written. I mentioned a busker. I believe strongly in declaring one's hand straightaway. Usually on the first page I say "this is the kind of book it's going to be". I think if you compare all the books, you'll see they have on their first page the essence of style, plot and – the indefinable quality that I know is in the book, is put on the first page. So that the reader can say "I want to turn over" or "I don't think it's worth going beyond the first page".

There are two things running now that are both very complicated and I don't know whether I can manage to keep them separated in talking to you but I'll try. The first one is that it would seem to me very difficult for any writer who is published on a children's list from the beginning – whether in the first book one intends that or not; and then each successive book comes out on a children's list – that however he may wish to stand aside from the deliberation of the audience, as he begins work on the next book he must live in the knowledge that it's going to be, or is likely to be published on a children's list unless he says, deliberately, "This is not going to be published on a children's list." That would seem to me to have a creative dilemma in it; it's another problem in the creation of the book: that is, the foreknowledge that it will be published for children. Can we clear up whether this is a pressure that affects you as you're writing: not as the words go on page, but in hindsight. Is it a pressure on you?

No. Not at all.

How do you relieve yourself of it?

This may be a matter of pathology rather than literary criticism. I think that to mess around with the question of writing for children all day would get me nowhere. There is probably a link between the twenty years – twenty-two years nearly now – that I have done nothing else but write and the first ten years of my life when I did very little but lie in bed. It is possibly a compensation for the loneliness of an only child who was paralysed. I am being very wise after the event now. But my interior world of childhood had no other criterion to measure it by, therefore I did not feel that what was happening to me was unusual. However, it was up to me to talk to myself. That may have resulted in my writing for children. It's the only intelligent thought I have on the subject.

Does that play back into the first thing I asked you about creating a reader? It might be better to put the question, is there a reader sitting inside you for whom you are writing?

Yes, me ... I don't want to make heavy weather of it but it is something that I can't answer otherwise – I think perhaps part of the reason for writing was to make myself live the life that in some way I was prevented from living as a child.

Writing for Children?

Let's leave that for the moment, because it will take us away from where I want to go, which is more towards the specifics of The Stone Book *than into general things. You did say something very interesting, which is that you virtually make a conscious statement on the first page which determines the reader you're going to include or exclude.*

Yes.

I would have thought this is very clear in The Stone Book *where, if one were making an act of cold critical analysis without discussing it with you, one would say there is a whole list of things which seem to make it a book which wishes to include children and wishes to include children of a quite early age. And those things would be: first, the point of view is a child's point of view and it would be quite possible to write that story from an adult point of view in a way which would exclude children from the reading of it; and in an attempt to say precisely the same things you would do it differently.*

Yes. But an adult point of view would not give me the ability to be as fresh in my vision as a child's point of view, because the child is discovering the universe and many adults are not.

So that in order to achieve the naivety of that text in its view of what is going on, you have to become the child-in-the-book. Is that what you are saying?

Yes.

And that would therefore not have any implication about who you intend as a reader; it's simply an attempt to achieve that artistic result?

Yes. Because basically the prose that I write is long narrative poetry, and that is one of the techniques of compressing the imagery.

I want to come to that later because it is a most significant part of the whole foursome – the whole four books. The second thing: immediately you look at the book you get (in all four, but I would have thought particularly in The Stone Book) *a sense of a very carefully limited syntax; you never go into highly complex grammatical form. The language – the vocabulary itself, the diction – is carefully controlled and yet it ranges over a vocabulary that most readers have lost, which is the vocabulary of the dialectical speech of people in Cheshire. One of the first words you get, in the second sentence, is "baggin", which immediately signals "Look out for –"*

That's it. That's a perfect example. If you're not going to read the word "baggin" read no further.

And yet it is set in a supremely simple English sentence: "A bottle of cold tea; bread and a half onion. That was father's baggin."

Yes. Its meaning is explicit: not only implicit, it is explicit: it's so clearly put.

Most people would say that's a classic sign of good writing for children. Authors attempt to achieve that because it makes the writing available to children, who can, we would say, easily understand the meaning.

The third thing one at once notices is that the entire story is concretely told; there is hardly an abstraction of diction in the book, and yet, of course, it's about highly abstract ideas. It's about universal truths. And they are very carefully worked for, are thematically stated by the father. There are two, for instance. The first when Mary's father has broken a stone, polished it, and revealed a green face with white flakes, shining like wet:

"'Tell me how those flakes were put together and what they are,' he said. 'And who made them into pebbles on a hill, and where that was a rock and when.'" [p.31]

The second comes when Mary has been under the hill:

"'What is it all?' said Mary.
"'The hill. We pass it on; and once you've seen it, you're changed for the rest of your days.'" [p.56]

You're right, but it wasn't done for a stylistic or philosophical reason. It's a result of my not writing the book in English.

You'll have to explain that, I think.

Of course it is written in part in modern standard English. It also is written in the North-West Mercian version of English. I'm using the word "version" because I don't want to confuse anybody by using the word "dialect". The importance of this is two-fold. One is that it concerns the first language of my own life. Most English people who are not from the middle classes are bilingual, although they learn to suppress the first language. As I did. It was twenty years before I could write like this. Therefore, there is the insertion of words – I'd like to say something on that unprompted in a moment. So it is North-West Mercian and English, and it is also the language of, effectively, the north-west rural working class, who are certainly not abstract in their activities. Therefore, they express themselves in a direct and concrete way.

I have not expressed myself in a direct and concrete way in order to write for a child – I have used this language, which is concrete and direct. I have approached the child in a way that I haven't written before: by bridging between English and my first language. I've done things, such as in the narrative parts, as opposed to the dialogue, where I have contracted verbs, such as *couldn't*, *didn't*. That to me seemed the only natural way to do it. So it's a very relaxed and un-teacher-like way of talking. I want to get back the richness and freshness of a language which was beaten out of me by teachers so that I could get on in the rest of the world.

That sounds a provocative statement.

I've used the word "un-teacher" not in order to make a statement about the relative merits of teachers and non-teachers, but because over the years I have noticed a lot of aggression manifest itself whenever writers and teachers come together. At first I just hit back and then I realized it wasn't slackening the blows on me and wasn't aiding the actual conversation. I have thought about it a little and I think that I may have a part, but not the whole, of the answer. It is that teachers and writers quite often make the mistake of thinking that they're handling the same material. They're looking at the language, they're looking at English, or "the novel" or whatever we're talking about, and they're on opposite sides of the same hill, looking at what they can see, and they are describing it. But they have mirror images, in a way. The teacher – however forward looking – is conservative, with a small "c", and has to be, because you cannot teach forwards until you have established something to teach from. Therefore, the teacher must teach what is. It must be a received text that is taught – a received language.

Now the writer, by the act of writing, adds to the total writing that is available in the world. And so there is the subtle difference that the writer, by writing, modifies the original material in some way. In other words, however conservative the writer is, by writing he is committing some kind of revolutionary act. The language changes as a result of that writing.

Most of the time I imagine the difference between teaching and writing doesn't show. But sometimes it does, and that will be the area which will attract the attention of the teacher, because the teacher will be interested and/or disturbed, and the writer will be committed and/or defensive. And, looking back over my unhappy experiences with teachers and theirs with me, I do find that we have appeared to be talking about the same thing, but we have not defined our terms to ourselves before we've actually spoken, and we've certainly not defined them between each other.

The way I have written in *The Stone Book* quartet has resulted in a form of language that teachers are almost committed to avoiding. A teacher must teach the received language and I am writing a language which is not received – I am changing the language. This is why some of the things that I appear to be saying – I personally rather than the narrator – could be seen to be slightly aggressive, such as, why let a child climb a church, or why use such "wrong" grammatical constructions. I'm not using wrong grammatical constructions. But I'm certainly not using received English.

Yes. I can understand that. For me one of the strong sensations – and I don't know one can argue it in any other language than that – as one reads the book is the sensation that you are deliberately wishing to recover a language which has become overlaid by what you are describing as the taught second language, the standard language you're getting in school.

Here is the most productive editorial work of any of my books, because the text has gone to Linda Davis, my editor, and when she's been through the text with her notes afterwards, if an idiosyncratic word has made her stop, my instinct has always been to remove it, because, having two languages, I have a weakness of not being able to pitch exactly for an outsider the quality of a word, and so I rely very heavily on editorial advice. That doesn't mean to say that I remove a word if anybody objects to it, but I have a tendency to. It has been a very creative editorial experience as well as a writing experience.

One of the things I wanted to ask you was how you achieved, how you worked for, what is an obviously carefully judged balance between the use of words like "baggin" and "raunge" – all those words which most people will either have forgotten or never heard. And yet you manage to achieve a balance which does not prevent either understanding or ease of reading. One goes along and the word's almost gone by before you've noticed it and yet you're aware of it. I've not seen it done quite with that skill before. I've not seen someone actually attempting to recover the demotic language quite as well as that, frankly. But certainly I've never seen anyone achieve that balance. Now, what you're saying is, then, that there would have had to be an outside opinion helping in the writing in order that it should be balanced?

Yes. Let's say, for instance, I pitch it 55%–45% towards North-West Mercian, towards dialect, and it ends up not 55% dialect 45% English, but 45% dialect 55% English. That crucial fulcrum is brought about by the editorial work, and I would say that if you find a nice balance in the book, that is equally to the credit of the editing.

There's something else about that which we may as well talk about now because it comes in relation to the diction, the words that are used which are drawn from the old demotic tradition. I don't come from the same area of the country as you do – I come from the north-east – so that some of the language is new to me. I've never heard certain words. I can't honestly recall "raunge" for instance. That's why it sticks in my head. But the tone of the speech, the emotional colour of the speech which establishes the relationship between the people – and particularly between the older people and the children – I remember absolutely from my childhood. It captures exactly that slightly sharp-edged tonal quality. You know it's a relationship of great affection but it seems all the time to have a cutting edge on it. Now, I have not seen that caught before quite so well in writing which attempts to catch it. D. H. Lawrence doesn't catch it, for instance.

Well, that is me and not the editor, because my editor is an American, therefore she would be quite unable to see that, she could not perceive it –

Quite. But is that something you consciously work for?

Oh, yes. And here's where I make a claim for the craft of writing. I have created the illusion of writing in two languages. I have written not a bastard language, but – if it works – I have projected into the mind of the reader the more important thing, which is an experience of that linguistic environment. Now that is done partly by my subjective listening to the genuine language – that is, recalling it – and partly by looking at it objectively as a language that has to be translated.

Having to be aware of the linguistic technicalities I find very difficult, because part of me is listening to my memory and the other part of me is the trained linguist saying "No, you move that sentence round that way." It's not genuine but the result is genuine. I think this is where Lawrence went wrong. He probably was doing the job of an anthropologist, or a linguist of some kind, but his real job was to convey what it was like to have been in that house at that time. I think his language obscures it.

Yes. Almost all the writers I can think of who have come out of the working class and who wish to re-create that atmosphere and that culture and that linguistic style, will almost always do it by phonetic spellings, by the use of punctuation. Now you don't do any of that at all.

No. But I have in the past. The reason I can say that's what Lawrence did is because I go cold when I think of what I myself have done. It obscures – well, phonetic spelling says it all. It's also incorrect.

I agree, but I'd like to hear your reasons for saying so.

Well. Phonetic spelling is condescending. Phonetic spelling is not good enough in its representation of the speakers. It is ugly to look at, bespattered with apostrophes. It is a sign of a writer alienated from his subject and linguistically unschooled.

But I think the primary objection to phonetic spelling is that it works against the whole reason for writing a story in the first place. The reason for writing, I would have thought, is to communicate an enthusiasm, a story, with as many people as possible, and phonetic spelling is a cheap way of making the writer appear to be communicating something when in fact he is obscuring it. In other words, by trying to reproduce the sound in a way that can be read by anybody who does not know those sounds – let's say, so that a southern Englishman can read what a northern Englishman says – the writer, if we use phonetic spelling only, will convince the southerner that the southerner's predisposition to reject the northern speaker was well-founded, because the phonetic spelling will misrepresent the speaker. It will not be a genuine northern voice speaking. It will be obscured. It will not be as clear as straightforward English would have been and perhaps straightforward standard, received pronunciation English would have been better to use than any phonetic spelling.

We're then left with a problem. If you're using received pronunciation English, how on earth can you communicate what the northern, western, southern, eastern or central speaker is saying? We're up against the craft question and I don't know that I have the answer for it. But at least I know the question exists and I've started to find out how to answer it by rejecting phonetic spelling – an attempt to reproduce the sound – by attempting to use a language form that is in no way opaque and is common to all speakers, but has, subliminally, the rise and fall, the cadence, the pitch, the structure, of the speech that is being represented. So the individual words – apart from the very carefully placed dialect words – the individual words are simple and understandable, but the way in which they are composed and balanced and the rhythm that this produces should register in some way as being unique.

It would be useful if you could say a bit more about how you achieve it without using phonetics. Are there skills that are necessary? Are there trainings that are necessary?

Every writer has to find his own way to do it. Mine happens to be that my background was my background. My education was that of a classical linguist; therefore I can apply, when necessary, the highly trained analytical skills of a classical linguist. So, I tend to write the thing down as I hear it – which is the subjective approach – and then to go back and quite coldly remove a lot of it and turn things round.

For instance, in the Cheshire dialect there are two verbs (this is only for instance): I must, and I mun. Now most people think that "mun" is the dialect form of "must". It isn't. A dialect speaker will use both words because they have different meanings. "I must" means "I ought". "I mun" means "I have no option but to". In *The Stone Book*, there is a narrative piece, "Then Chorley must have a church next, and a school". [p.14] There was no legal document to say that Chorley must have a church next; that is me allowing the idiom to creep into the narrative as well as into the dialogue. There are several times this happened, and in some cases I left it in and in some cases I took it out. I left it in when I was finding that I had done it naturally and that there was the strength of all dialect when it is strong. A dialect when strong says something that the standard language it exists in cannot say as well or succinctly. Almost the definition of a dialect word is one you cannot translate by a single analogue into the standard language.

I have a feeling, which I hope I'm never asked to prove, that most regional writing has achieved the very last thing that the writer would wish. It renders quaint the people he is trying to serve, and I would say that if *The Stone Book* sequence has done anything it has avoided that trap.

Yes. I would agree with that absolutely. I think the worst thing about most regional writing, whatever the intention of the author, is that it is condescending.

Yes.

Because it doesn't actually pay attention to what the language is really doing.

Quite. And I think perhaps a child's viewpoint may stop me from becoming condescending, because otherwise the child will get his ears clouted. I am a little in awe of the adults in the book when I'm writing it. Not respecting them because they're grown-up; but I do share the child's view of them.

But there's also something else, which is that there is an obvious affection and respect for the people and for their language.

Oh, yes.

But that wasn't always the case in your work.

No. That was a combination of technical incompetence and lack of clarity about the emotions at work in me.

I mean, was there a time in your writing career where you felt some disrespect for the very people you're writing about in The Stone Book?

No.

So it really was just a technical inability at that point.

Yes. Just incompetence.

The change comes between Elidor *and* Owl Service.

The change of clarity in my own emotions comes on a certain page in *Elidor*. You'll be able to find it for yourself. It wasn't a particular group or social class of people I was apprehensive about. It was the moment of growing up. The moment of realizing that it is a very savage world. And in *Elidor*, everything up to that particular page in *Elidor* has been my recognition of this but my refusal to see it in terms of humanity till then. It's always been fantasy and almost archetypal imagery. But in *Elidor* – I think possibly one of the strengths of *Elidor* is that the screw is tightened to the point where the nightmare is happening in a modern street, now, and there comes a moment when the children are running away from a semi-supernatural threat and they're crying for help in a suburban road and the lights are switched off in all the rooms and somebody can be seen on the other side of a frosted glass front door, reaching up to fasten the bolt, and one of the children in the *manuscript* shouts, "You lousy rotten bastards." In 1965 I met my first editorial inflexibility. I was not allowed to use the word "bastard". And from that time onwards it's been a steady trek towards *The Stone Book* sequence.

The Question of the Narrator

I want to pursue you on other things that we haven't even reached yet. I want to question you on something which the whole business of rhetorical criticism fetches up, and it allies itself with the Jamesian thing I began with, of the writer making his reader, in the same way as he makes his characters. Something which I do, frankly, believe objectively happens. I can well understand your hesitancy to see it happening but I think it does; psychologically I think it's an explanation of how – of what is going on when a writer's at work –

I don't deny your interpretation. I don't have a clear view of it.

Do you then have a clear view of what is allied with it in rhetorical criticism, which is the narrator of the book, who is not the full person of the author, but is almost a character as well?

Oh yes. Now there, if you'd started with that I would have said – that's the first time I've heard anybody say it so clearly. That is entirely what I feel.

Now I want to pursue that in The Stone Book. *The mistake one is likely to make about* The Stone Book *if one isn't careful is that the narrator is Mary. I don't believe the narrator is Mary. It is Mary's point of view in the first book, but the relationship with the narrator and Mary is much more complicated, I think, than that. Can you talk a bit about that?*

I'd rather answer questions, because you've touched the area of writing that I find most exciting and therefore the most frightening. It's where the heaviest responsibility lies and it is also what I understand to be creativity. It is the presence of the symbiotic coupling of the protagonist – let us assume for simplicity's sake there is one protagonist – it is the coupling of the mind of the author with the mind of the protagonist, allowing them, for the purpose of the clarity of this argument, to have objective reality on both sides. And this creates a third entity which I find mysterious in a most profound way.

And are you saying that third entity is the narrator?

Yes.

Yes. That's what I would say. It may be possible to come at it in The Stone Book *in one curious way. I'm struck all the time by the fact that in the second, third and fourth books the protagonists are boys and in the first book it's a girl. To be quite honest, I haven't understood why that had to be so, because every problem it solves could have been solved in another way. And I just want to make clear before I go ahead that this has nothing to do with who the narrator is; on the other hand, it may actually be the key to what I want to get at. Why did it have to be a girl?*

To begin with, all the characters are real people. I've changed some of the Christian names, but it is the emotional history of one rural family. By emotional history I'm saying that I have worked hard enough and long enough to be fairly certain that everything in *The Stone Book* sequence could have happened. I have no evidence that any of the plot of *The Stone Book* did happen, but emotionally that is the way they would have behaved. To begin with, Mary is the protagonist and it has to be Mary the girl because Mary was her name and she was a girl. But it is not as easy as that because there was a reason why I chose to start at that point.

The choice always lies with the author whenever he comes up with an ineluctable thing like that. Actually he makes it ineluctable. And I think this has to do with author-narrator relationship with the protagonist. Now, just let me make one point and again see if it helps us. It may not. I think the strange relationship that goes on between the narrator and Mary in The Stone Book *is almost like Mary's son looking back at Mum.*

That's very interesting. Because – here again I must give the writer his due. I have to stay with books until they are ready. I have to cook up a head of pressure inside me until the books appear to burst out because it's better to have them out than in. Now that means that in every book I do an enormous amount of, sometimes quite intellectual, work beforehand and then switch it off and let it just settle itself. In this case – because it was based on a particular family and their oral traditions and memories – instead of doing the intellectual research, what I did was to absorb the psychic shocks of that family.

What does that mean?

Instead of finding out, as far as possible, facts – which is what straightforward research is – I had to research emotions. Not in the way that a psychiatrist would, not in a therapeutic sense, not in a voyeuristic sense, but in the sense of standing there and not blocking those emotions, or the implications for emotion of a given set of anecdotes from within a given family. Because that family comes from my own primary and formerly abandoned culture. And so by "shock" I mean shock in two senses. I had to turn round and look at that culture and to understand it as opposed to ignore it or romanticize it; and to withstand its shocks. And then cope with facing the shock that those shocks created in me.

This is what gives those four books part of their unity and tension. You are aware that you are looking at a day in the life of a whole culture, each time, and it doesn't spring new-born. Those books are full of extra stories which don't, I hope, deflect anybody. It is a four-dimensional text, and that is because I was aware of the tensions within the family. An example would be that Mary grew up to have the job she wanted: she did go to work for Lord Stanley. The thing which makes her father drop his onion when she says that she wants to have all the pretensions, she did achieve. I have Mary's reading certificate. She was two years older than anybody else but she did make it in the end. She also produced an illegitimate son at the age of nineteen and that's the tension in the family, which produced the boy Joseph of *Granny Reardun*. That's why he was a "granny reardun". In the regional dialect of the north-west a granny reardun either makes a spoilt child or an illegitimate one – somebody reared by a granny.

In which case he has to go out and get himself a good ...

In which case this gives him, granny reardun, the edge which is never spoken of. The boy has really got a reason for wanting to better his grandfather, because he is totally alone. Now this is the skill of the writer, the writer must pitch that. It's like putting something into a dish that one's making. How much tabasco, how much chili pepper: you've just got to get it right.

We're slightly off the point of author–narrator–protagonist, and I would like to bring you back to it before taking up the fascinating issues you have just raised. The critical theorists are very unclear, I find. If one looks at the central textbooks – for instance, Wayne Booth's Rhetoric of Fiction *– you find that they seem to be saying that the author's second self – that is, the parts of the author who writes the book – is the narrator, that that's the person who is really telling the story. Now I don't think that's true. And what you're suggesting, when you say that it's the symbiotic coupling of the author with the protagonist, is that somehow this makes a relationship between the author and his implied reader, the person to whom he is talking, even though the author may not consciously have a picture of that person. You seem to see the narrator as a character, as someone different from yourself.*

Yes. This question, more than any other you've asked, makes me feel that I'm being got at. You're asking me to look at the back of my own head, you see. So I have to put lots of little provisos into this statement. But I suspect that the narrator is one of the major characters in any novel. An invisible character masquerading, at least in part, as the voice of the author. But the narrator is as carefully constructed and poised and balanced as any other ingredient of the novel, and is a work of fiction. By "symbiotic" I meant that the narrator needs the author, obviously, but the author needs the narrator in order for the author to be within the story and therefore in some way in control. But at the same time able to be outside the story, to do his important part of the job, of monitoring what has happened within the story as it is going down onto the page.

The only check I have against this as a theory is to ask the question "Who is the narrator?" in any given story.

I find that in *The Stone Book* it ties in with the change in narrative style, from the previous books, which have always been straightforward English, into this slightly relaxed style with contracted verbs and the regional cadences. That is not me putting on a cloth cap – I thought at one stage it could be. I'm convinced it's another character, within, but I don't know who.

An Aside about Meaning(s)

Is part of your irritation at the question anything to do with the possibility that the narrator in the book is in fact a mask behind which the author stands? And a question which asks what's going on in the narrator is a question that's probing the mask. Is there any truth in that?

I've never thought of it, as a question –

You see – if I can go on while you're thinking about it a little longer – the curious thing about stories is that they seem to be wanting to say something straightforwardly and entertainingly, when in fact they are ways of disguising meaning, for many reasons. The most obvious is the parables, which –

No, no. I'm going to stop you. They're not means of disguising. They're ways of limiting the constant drive on the part of interpreters to restrict the potential of the story.

That's just what I was going to say. Christ refuses to explain the parables because if he does that you'll accept only one meaning – the one the author gives you, and what He's actually saying is that these things have many meanings and the meanings you find are the ones that are rightly there for you.

I would say that if you had to isolate a single strand of storytelling that justifies the whole business of labouring and reading – writing and reading – it would be that storytelling is the one aspect of language that transcends normal communication. It does not communicate fact in the way straightforward historical or journalistic reporting should. It is far more than its words and therefore all storytelling is a form of poetry. I don't want to get bogged down in definitions of poetry, but I would say that to deny the viability of the paradox within a story is to ask that the story be reduced to a straightforward piece of reportage.

I wholeheartedly agree. I think we have to say two things. One is to make a statement: it is patently obvious that there are many writers – I would call them writers not authors – who use the craft of language to tell stories – they use the narrative form – to say things plainly. I would call them propagandists apart from anything else. Undoubtedly a lot of writers do that and undoubtedly a lot of children's writers do that. It's one of the worrying things about children's writing, that it's often not wishing to contain many meanings in the one story, but is trying to make just one meaning and trying very hard to make that meaning very plain.

Yes. But you see, if you get that kind of writer – and I'd like to say something about that kind of writer in a moment – if you get that kind of writer producing work, which then falls into the hands of the teacher who wants to make all plain, then we are dangerously on the road towards theoretical, moralizing, politicized writing and teaching.

Yes. I agree.

It's quite difficult enough to try to make the layman understand the difference between imaginative sustained writing and journalism without sounding as though one's making value judgements about the merits of creative writing compared with journalism. They are totally different operations which happen to involve human beings making marks on paper. Now the same applies to novel writing, to writing for children I would imagine, and therefore a lot of critics – I suspect that they're not the best critics, otherwise they wouldn't ask the questions – confuse the issue a great deal by comparing "A" and "B" and trying to find differences and similarities, when they should be saying "Why is 'A' writing in that form and why is 'B' writing in that form?" And only later asking if there's anything to be gained from comparing "A" with "B", because usually, in my experience, there's nothing to be gained at all, except a vulgar interest.

What you're implying is that, however it's done, one of the things you are striving to do in the creating of the story – whether that's conscious or unconscious, however it's arrived at – is to ensure that the story contains the possibility of many meanings.

It is an unconscious matter at the time of writing – I don't do it deliberately – but when I'm my own first reader I see that I did want to do it. And that is – yes – to enlarge the possibility of interpretation by presenting the story in such a way that it is paradoxically definitive in its statement, but infinite almost in its interpretation. It allows room for the reader to enter in and produce the unique and eternally re-created moment of the story when the reader is within the story. And this will vary with each reader. So that, as I've often found out, people can read a story, then ask the author a question that the author doesn't understand, because the author did not know that that question existed within the story. For him it did not, but it is a valid question nevertheless because of the chemical reaction between the reader and the story.

Over the years – assuming that, at least in this area, I do get better – I would say that the pattern through all my books has been that of developing simplicity at linguistic level, then at plot level, matched conversely with greater complexity of potential interpretation within the story. So that, with *The Weirdstone of Brisingamen* there is a great deal of florid language, a lot of loose as opposed to open ends, and not a great deal left to interpretation. It is what it is. And with the *Stone Book* sequence the things that happen are very simple but they're put together in such a way that it is possible for the reader to take it as a straightforward, ordinary story. And yet it is open to a great deal of interpretation. Which is not to suggest that in *The Stone Book* something has been perfected. What I am saying is that *The Stone Book* is a statement of some great proportion for me, if not for anybody else.

The Question of the Narrator again ...

All right. That satisfies me at least within this context. Let's go back to the first question to do with the mask of the narrator –
I'm unhappy about that mask concept, I don't think we've hit it yet. I don't feel that I am oppressed by being got at personally

because I've put up a mask, but I think perhaps we ought to leave that ...

Let's reject that then. Yes. Let's reject the mask. But I press you on this point because I do think it's one of the most fascinating things about literature as a whole. I mean you said – if I remember what you said a few minutes ago correctly – that one of the most important things about any piece of literature is the question of who is telling the story, who is the narrator of this book. And indeed that's what certain critics – particularly those of a structuralist stripe – would say. They'd say that the first question to ask of any story, of any fiction, is "Who is telling me this?" And one critic in particular, Barthes, would say that writing is most fully writing only when it prevents us from asking that question. I can understand what he means, though I know people who are very disturbed by that idea – they don't like it at all. So let's reject the idea of the narrator as a mask. Let's say that's not what it is and let me try and probe with you what it might be.

The paradox of fiction – of literature as a whole – is that it is the simplest way of saying the most complicated things and that we have no other better weapons to do it. Now I am saying – and you've been saying all through these conversations – that that's a very difficult job to do. It's much too difficult to be conscious of it. And one of the primary questions the critics see as they look at literature is, how do you resolve the question Whom am I talking to? Because all the time, on the one hand, you and other writers will say "Yes I want to communicate something" but, on the other hand and philosophically speaking, you don't have to ask the question "Who to?" So you might get out of it by saying "Everybody." But we all know that's not satisfying. Nobody conceives speaking to everybody at once; I don't believe they do – except perhaps megalomaniac politicians. I don't think artists do. And so two questions come up. Who are you talking to? How do you do it?

Now, is it perhaps that just as a story brings into itself multiple and profound meanings in the simplest way you can do it, and it's accessible to everybody, so a narrator is the invention of the author which allows him to speak to that person he can't begin to identify. The narrator does the mediating for him. Is that part of it?

Let's say that the narrator is the mediator and let me hypothesize a conversation that never takes place; the conversation between the author and the narrator, before the book is written.

Yes. Good.

I would say that the author addresses himself to the narrator and he says "I've got a very difficult job on my hands and I must speak to somebody and it's your job to do that for me." It's a one-sided conversation – in other words the author is creating the narrator. The narrator, I suggest, acts very much in the way that a filter acts for a camera. The cameraman realizes that he will not be able to produce a photograph or a film that represents what his own mind can see at that moment unless he puts, say, an orange filter on. The resulting photograph will not be an accurate representation of all the light that fell onto the film at that moment; it will be an inaccurate representation of the light that fell onto the film, but it will fall with a controlled inaccuracy, in such a way that the interpretation of the resulting film or photograph will have an actuality within the perceiver at least as great as within the man who exposed the film. So we have the strange medium of the film and then the print as a communicator between the mind and soul of the cameraman and the mind and soul of the person watching the film or viewing the print in another place, at another time. Time and space are transcended. The actual film, the medium, is at that moment irrelevant. The cameraman and the perceiver are at one, and the advantage at that instant is all with the perceiver, because he is given the chance to stand on the shoulders of the cameraman and see even further.

I suspect the narrator is a filter, eliminating glare from, and adjusting the tones of, the book.

All right. Now can we still call that the narrator being the mediator of the story between the author and the reader?

A character invisible in the role of mediator.

Yes. Right. I want to try and press a bit more a further confusion left lying about. I want to test out a possible answer to see what your reaction is as an author – someone who has both to experience this and then look back and see what happened. You're still left

297

with the idea that you are mediating to someone, and I think that's where the error creeps in.

This is where I start to feel oppressed again. As I said, I feel myself cornered.

Yes. And I think I know why. Well, I want to suggest what it might be. Let's go back to the idea which I found very persuasive that as a writer is writing it is not the man, the everyday person, who mends leaky faucets and repairs windows and pays bills, who is doing the job. It is some part of that man, which people have called the author's second self, who does that job. That is, when an author is at work the narrator is a construct of parts of himself. Now I find this, both from experience and just looking at it, philosophically persuasive. It gives me a clue to what might be happening. May it not be that the question "Who are you talking to?" is a nonsense simply because people see a particular whole man, boy, or woman sitting there being talked to, and that's not what is actually happening?

Except possibly a teacher who is in the classroom watching the individual child react.

But in fact what we're talking about I think is this. The author in his role as author mediates the story through the narrator. The narrator is a sieve, is a lens – you've used both those words attempting to describe how he acts – who, by his nature, talks to the reader just in the way that I would talk to you now, and would talk differently to your daughter Elizabeth or to the Prime Minister. I would perhaps even use different words, I would certainly use different syntactic constructions, I would talk about different ideas, and so on. Even the rhythm of my speech would change. And when you are writing your story, the narrator is the chap who causes that to happen, because he knows, not who you are talking to as a person, but those elements within anybody as a reader to which you wish to speak. So that the reader plays a role, just as the writer does. There is a reader's second self and it's the construction of that self, it is the make-up of that self, that the narrator is engaged in forming. He is signalling to the reader what bits of himself he has to use.

I hope we have a lot of tape left because you've opened up the door at last! I've been trying to get my hand on the knob and it wouldn't come to hand. The membrane that we're going through by asking that question, for which we've been footling around for hours, is the difference between straightforward analytical criticism and metaphysical supposition. We have to venture into metaphysics.

Yes. We do.

And therefore, from here on in I will beg so many questions and not define so many phrases and individual words that it may sound pretentious.

Yes, there is the reader to be created and I would suspect that just as I have been saying up to this moment "How can I know the child? How can I know the reader? Show me the child, show me the reader." – I say that in public. "What children?" – if I saw one ten thousandth of the people who read what I write I would panic because I can't stand crowds!

That's why you're a writer, not something else.

It's been brought home to me so severely with *The Stone Book*. I've had responses, for instance, from every kind of American. I have had responses from Finnish critics, who have been reading in English. From Japanese, from South Africans, from Australians, and so on. Responses of such personal intensity that I've been taken aback, in that they have all said in their different ways, "I have read about myself." And so I can make a fairly simple statement, which is that I discover that only when I am being at my most idiosyncratic and obsessively personal do I come anywhere near approaching the universal. And I find this a significant paradox, One that, I think, causes all the heat and no light when people start consciously to write for political means or social means and ends. Writing for children can be done, but I don't think it ever touches that question, and I think the children as a result are impoverished, because the story will not have many options.

That's right.

And we're back again where we were. So having gone over the threshold, through the membrane into metaphysics, let me stay there a while. Yes, the excitement for me as a writer is to get behind that objectionable question "What children?" and say "Yes, it is all children, it is everybody, it is the child in everybody." And to make my point without saying that I agree with the terminology I use, I would say that it's very close to the Jungian collective unconscious; that there are things in all human beings which are shareable, no matter what the background of the individual human being. And if the author is fortunate enough to combine his skills and his passion in such a way that he can single out those elements primarily, then the author will communicate totally at a level that he is not aware of. And I suspect that some of *The Stone Book* does that, otherwise a Japanese reader and a Finnish reader would have very little to say to a Cheshire author.

Yes, yes. I think we should leave it there, because I really don't think we can actually probe it more.

No. Except to say that there is a reader to be created by the author and the reader together. Just as there is a story to be created by the author and the reader together.

Yes. And the narrator, the element of the narrator in the book, calls forth from the real person – the whole person of the reader – those responses that are necessary to engage in the meanings that the writer is attempting to make.

Yes. Therefore, the narrator is in a strange dimension. He has to prevent the author from worrying about what's happening, from being aware too much of what's happening, without taking on an objective reality himself outside the book. Because the narrator does not objectively know anything at all. But he has to move between the author and the reader and the book. And, therefore, the narrator is a part of the author that the author decides will work subconsciously in order not to interfere with the difficulty of writing a book; and at a level which will communicate, as far as possible: at the universal level of understanding.

Tell-tale Gaps

In talking about the story being created by the author and his reader together, and in our long discussion of meaning, we touched on

*a particularly important point. That is what I've called the tell-tale
gaps in stories. I think they're as important, for instance, as the
way a musician will handle the absence of sound, or an actor will
use the pause. Now here it is a deliberate absence of making the
meaning plain, so that the reader must enter that gap and make
the meaning with you and if he doesn't – hard luck, and if he does
– the story takes off. It comes alive in a very convincing and a
powerful way. Whereas if the writer makes too much plain meaning
then he produces a banal book.*

Yes.

However great his theme.

Yes.

*Now, I just wanted to question how conscious you are of making
the gaps.*

Afterwards, very conscious.

Does that mean you go back and cut out?

Yes. I never put in – all revision is excision. I feel that the concrete
nature of the language of the rural working class of my background
has such a bonus, in the context of this conversation, that I could
almost never end the list of plusses. But to the point: its very con-
creteness stops me from going away into abstract philosophizing
because the people in that book would not do it themselves, so I
cannot. I have to stay to the point. I have to absorb the tragedy
or humour and give it its due weight and no more.

*We can work at this on two planes. One is the line-by-line small
gaps which you achieve, you are saying, by the fact that the people
from whom your characters are drawn would never have said more
than they do. They would have left you to make the meaning yourself anyway. And getting that right is a hard enough task, as you
have to be listening extremely carefully, you have to have a very
good ear.*

*But there is another kind of gap which is composer-controlled
not character-controlled. Take two which are in* The Stone Book; *
it's essential that you fill them, if you're to understand the story*

and appreciate it. One occurs in the scene on top of the weathercock and the other one is down below, when Mary is in the cavernous room. Now those, I would have thought, had to be consciously placed. They had to be consciously worked for in the rhythmic structure of the book. That is, the orchestration of the book leads to those points and if you, the author, get them wrong the book goes terribly astray and the reader will feel uncomfortable. You'll diminish what you're aiming for rather than achieving it. Now, for me they're beautifully and exactly placed. Let me ask first of all, was that consciously worked for? How did you shape that? Did you just feel it, or did you have to go back and arrange it?

I've come from a family of craftsmen and if I'm not a craftsman by now I never shall be and I do have a pride in my job. Yes, I do work at it: but through feeling, not thinking, not plotting.

But a craftsman will – my father, for instance, who's a joiner, will look at a wall and he'll say "O God! it's a sixteenth out." Now that's not a matter of working. It is a matter of received skills from long experience.

I've been writing for twenty-two years – this is a received skill. I don't consciously look at it and say it's a sixteenth out, but I know that it is exactly one sixteenth out on the page.

Right. Now. Is that a skill that you can start off with, or can it only be achieved by working for it? Can it only be achieved both by working for it in each individual text and also accumulating experience which helps you to do it better and better?

It's not either/or, it's both. It's the accumulation and experience enabling one to put it further and further behind at the back of one's consciousness and experience, so that you don't think about getting the wall straight, it is straight because you've been building walls for a long time. The shape is not worked consciously: it is felt. Conscious working, if it is needed, comes after the book is finished.

There's one more point about those two gaps and I would have thought all the gaps in all four books in the quartet. They are extraordinarily well judged for perceptions which quite young children can bring to them, just given a bit of attention. I mean they're a step ahead of where most kids are but they can reach out and get it. And that implies to me a consciousness that you knew you were doing it also for the reader, that you were deliberately including that reader – the child – in the book.

Well, your argument is such that I imagine you are right. Some protective factor was at work in me to stop me, so that I didn't pitch it under. I think it may be close to the analogy of lobbing something from the hall to somebody on the landing at the stair. You always have to aim higher than the person is. I think there's that; there's the trajectory of the story to bear in mind and if I think about it too hard I'll get it wrong.

But to summarize what you've said. There are two elements. One, I was working with an extraordinarily rich basic material. And two, I have what I hope is a proper pride in my job. The two are put together. Let us move it straight over into carpentry. If I'd been given a piece of oak as good as that twenty years ago, no carpenter would have let me near it; but now perhaps I'm learning to handle the basic material in the way that its grain suggests to me.

Yes, I will say that the material is an enormous gift, but also I have a long track record. I have been practising this skill for a long time and something surely must have built on it.

Yes. But I think you're answering a different question than the one I was getting at, so I must press you on it.

Go on.

What I'm saying is – to use the carpentry analogy – a carpenter could be given a beautiful piece of oak and he could make a piece of furniture which would be comfortable only for people of adult physical stature. Or he could prefer to make a piece of furniture equally beautiful, which would be comfortable also for a child to sit on, as well as an adult. And his skills could lead him either way, but he would have to make a conscious decision to do that. And what I'm trying to suggest is that you must have made a similar decision with The Stone Book.

Yes. And the craftsman surely is correct to say "If I have the choice between making something for a twenty-stone man only and something which will work for a twenty-stone man and a two-stone child, then the one that'll take both is better."

Yes. But we don't make all furniture to be comfortable for children. We make it mostly to be comfortable for adults and not for children.

That is not my concern. It really isn't. I have no interest whatsoever in what other people write, at the moment. I've got quite enough problems of my own without wondering about the place of what I'm doing in relation to any other constellations. That's the job of the critic, it's not the job of a writer.

Authors and Critics

Does that mean, then, you are prepared to accept the critic's investigation of what you do and take it at his word that that's what has happened? I mean, do you simply abdicate from saying that it was so or not so?

I would include the critic's interpretation. There are *my* reasons for doing something – I may not know what they are, the critic may elucidate them for me. Several times I've understood only when a critic has told me what I've done. That has happened about three times. And when a critic says something as if it was one of the tablets coming down from the mountain, it quite often is irrelevant to me. But that does not deny the validity of the critic's point any more than it denies the validity of the child's interpretation, because in this interstitial space in the story between the protagonist, the author and this third symbiotic unity of protagonist/author, there also has to be room for the imagination of the individual, and that creates anew the whole universe of the book. (And that is why – as a by-the-by – I don't understand how anybody can mark English.) If you are in a theatre and there are three hundred people in the audience watching Hamlet, there are three hundred and one Hamlets. And it's the same with a book. So the critic can inform me – I don't think I'm being self-protective here – the critic can quite often inform me where it's relevant and if it's irrelevant I put it down to his right to react chemically and uniquely.

How important is it to you as a writer that the critical atmosphere around you be lively and intelligent?

It's totally irrelevant except for the fact that I'd rather be in an environment that is lively than in one that is dead.

So that the presence of critics around you, talking about you, doesn't influence you, doesn't affect you?

Oh no. Because of the time lag between my writing what they are criticizing.

I was thinking of it as a future thing. That is, what they have said about what you've done in the past affecting what you're going to do.

No. If a critic writes something which I read today, it's irrelevant to what I'm writing today in the heat of the writing of it. I'm not talking about aggressive criticism. I'm saying that at the time of reading criticism it is about something that is in my past. And my present, although connected to it, has a stronger demand.

The other thing that interested me in what you said was your lack of interest in what other writers are doing. Is that what you meant to say?

Yes. I don't see that it has anything to do with me. I wouldn't dream of suggesting to another writer that he or she should do anything at all. Therefore, I may find it interesting, ten years later, when we have a perspective, to find that I did something which was being done by somebody else at precisely the same time. Now then, if you like, the social historian in me becomes interested. Why did two writers find it necessary to say that at that moment, without knowledge of each other?

But that's quite a different thing from being the writer at work. The conventional wisdom would be that artists are people who feed off each other, are sustained by each other, are part of a community who are, by their interest in each other, refreshing themselves, progressing their ideas, working towards a newness of form, and so on. All that kind of mix of ideas people mean when they talk about an artistic community. But what you're saying is that it doesn't affect you like that at all.

No. In fact I have strong views in the other direction. I feel that it is dangerous for writers to meet. I do not like the company of writers. That is not an antagonistic remark. I find it embarrassing to have to be in public with other writers. I think we come over as a rather pretentious bunch and – yes – they, writers, feed off each other, their egos rub up against each other and they just try to outdo the next fellow. No, I think that writing has to be, for me, an isolated process and I am only confused by somebody else's tensions. I don't feed off them. I'm confused by them.

The technical problems you are faced with when you're writing, many writers, I think it would be true to say, solve partly by reading a lot of the same kind of work. They're seeing how other people do it and taking bits and pieces that help them solve their own problems. Now that isn't so for you?

By the time I have read the textbooks that I need to read, I have no desire to open another book. I don't read novels. I simply do not read them.

Garner and the Greeks

How do you solve your narrative problems, then? What's the process you go through?

The simple answer is I just listen to it, but of course that's not the answer. I have to bear in mind that I was trained in understanding how literary effects were brought about. I was fortunate in that my training was not in English.

Why was that fortunate?

I find that most English graduates I speak to are now journalists, and they will admit – too many for it to be coincidence – that they wanted to be full-time writers, not journalists. I'm not saying that journalism is worse, it's just different. But they were aware of the corpus of English literature and they felt there wasn't anything left to say. That is both true and stupid, at the same time. I was trained in the schools of Latin and Greek. At the age of eighteen, I was also introduced as an extra subject to English. I found nothing at all that was relevant to me in twentieth-century novels, compared with the relevance that I found in Greek plays that were over two thousand years old. I remember wondering why that should be so, that somebody should have written in Greece over two thousand years ago in such a way that it helped me to come to terms with the way my girlfriend's mother was behaving.

But no novel that I picked up was relevant to me at all. When I actually settled down to write, I thought, "This is a very difficult job – so I may as well try to get it as near perfect as the best Greeks did, because it's not going to be much harder. It's going to be very difficult to write badly: it won't be much harder to write well." I tried to find out by going back to the Greek texts. It just happened to be Greek. Any language, I'm certain, would do it. The question was, what was it that made it universally relevant? The answer seemed to be that the man stayed with the story until it could be said in those words and no others and certainly no more: everything was down to the bone.

The modern novels I had rejected I found were being written by over-literate abstract minds for other literate abstract minds, and I had had enough of that. There was nobody saying to me "I love you." There was nothing really basic, nothing worked through, suffered, resolved. I found very little catharsis in the writing. Mind you, I didn't read a lot of it because my bias was towards the Greek. I knew where to go in my academic skills to find the quintessential nature of writing. So I'm not denying that it exists in English of the twentieth century. I'm saying that I knew where to get it more purely for me.

By my mid twenties I was aware (a) that it was difficult to write anyway, so it was worth hanging on in case you could write well enough to be very good; and (b) that there was something missing, and I couldn't find it. Another strand through all the books has been an instinctive searching out of the concrete culture that I had to be removed from in order to be educated. Which is raising a political point, but I think it's one that we don't realize often enough, that the first-generation grammar-school boy from a working-class home, especially if he's of high intelligence, is as much a social problem as the educationally sub-normal, and I think the whole family should be treated by the social services. By "treated" I mean that it should be recognized that there is a danger.

What is it that happens to them?

In my experience one of three things. There is a snapping of the elastic, and the emergent creative intelligence shrivels back into the restrictive narrow confines of the working-class culture, which has become narrow and restrictive by history and also by the widening of the horizon for that child. So the child suffers and becomes a bitter and cynical adult. That is the commonest form. The next one, which is a sort of bridge between accommodating oneself to both cultures, is to become an elitist in the worst sense, which means becoming a bigger rat than any other rat in the race and using all the cunning of one's background. The third way, which is the one I experienced, was to find that the elastic had snapped, but that I couldn't shrivel back into the family. My momentum was such that I shrivelled away from them. It was mutual. My family could not absorb me and I could not bear the pain of saying, in some way, usually emotionally: I'm sorry, I can't be what your preconception would have me be.

I can see all that operating in Owl Service *and* Red Shift.

Yes.

Is The Stone Book *sequence a kind of – the cliché would be "coming to terms with"; I'm going to use two other words – forgiveness and redemption of that?*

If I had used those words I think it would have been genuinely precious and pretentious. You've used them. If it's true, I'm very glad. That is certainly something that I hope has come from it. It was not the intent.

No. I can see that. But then partly it was the intent, because that's the eternal struggle in what you're doing.

You mean: why did I choose to do that?

Yes.

Why didn't I go and do something else?

That's right.

No. That is true. The reason for the choice was kept from me.

Yes.

I'm certain that that was what it was.

Yes. And if it hadn't been kept from you, you couldn't have done it anyway.

Quite.

The 1944 Act

There are so many hares running now that I'd like to follow up. I just want to follow one or two. First of all, almost as an aside, just to check someone else's experience on these lines, to do with the disaffected working-class boy, the educated working-class boy we've been talking about. Do you personally find that you feel at home with the main body of nineteenth- and twentieth-century English literature as expressed in the novel, when you read it?

No. I don't feel at home with anything after *The Tempest*. What I'm saying is that eighteenth- and ninteenth-century writing seemed to have nothing to say to the whole of me that had a rich texture, that was concrete. Eighteenth-century writing is full of Greek and Latin tags and the whole vocabulary has a Mediterranean bias, because the men who were writing knew that they would be read by other men who'd had a similar Mediterranean bias in their own education. So half of me had been amputated in one blow by that English neo-classicism of the eighteenth century. And the opportunity to reinstate a native English culture, which was given to my generation by the 1944 Education Act – I think the loss of that opportunity is one of the great tragedies of our century.

I'd agree.

It has not produced the celebration of the integrated joy of being able to translate the Agamemnon and to talk to my father. Now I am talking to my father and I am now forty-three years old and

I don't think I have ever had a genuine conversation with him in my life before, because my childhood was spent struggling away from those values. This is subconscious, but I can remember the actual genuine, at the time, fear that I was going to be pulled, not back, but I had a sense that I really wanted to go somewhere else emotionally. And only when I got where I wanted did I realize that it was meaningless if I could not also embrace what I had been, still was, and am.

Would it be true to say that the things you were attempting to come to terms with led you to write for children? That one of the reasons you began there was that writing for adults-only would have required from you a literary behaviour which would have been locked into the very tradition that had caused the fracture?

That's so plausible I'm suspicious of it, but equally my nose tells me that that is largely correct. I've never thought of it that way. I should think so. I think the nearest I'd come is saying that, from time to time, I'm probably writing for the child that I was. In other words I was probably trying to write for the human being at the moment when he was aware of both forces in equal balance, just before the rift.

And he's trying to harmonize the first –

The Language Again ...

He's trying to harmonize. I do think – I mean, it's why I do not write social realism: it would deflect me – I do think, and I will say it again, that the failure to cultivate all that has been opened up to the arts by the 1944 Education Act is something that we really will pay an enormous price for, because we've been cut off from our main stream for over two hundred years. I delight in Latin: I'm not knocking it; I'm not criticizing it. But it is not English. Nor is English debased Latin. English is a most articulate and powerful language, yet in its literature it draws on only a fraction of the energies. That's what hurts.

Here's an example: In the last book, *The Aimer Gate*, there is an enormous dramatic point open to me if I use a wider spectrum of language, and provided it doesn't show. (I will spend a little time on this because it is true for the whole structure of the book. All four books are structured this way.) I choose from North-West Mercian that which standard English will not do, but my own native language will do. And I use it with the skill of a writer, not with the skill of a straightforward native speaker.

The normal way of denoting possession "my" in the dialect is to say "me". Teachers teach children that "me" is incorrect. It is not incorrect. It is a dative pronoun. "Me book" is "the book that is to me", and it is used when the possession is not emphasized. Me dad, me book. But if you stress possession the dialect speaker will say "my" – my dad, my book, not yours. And the dramatic climax of *The Aimer Gate* is where a sunny uncle relationship suddenly has its focus switched and you realize: (a) Charlie is going to be killed, and (b) he is a sniper in the trenches. He's been going on to the protagonist child, Robert, that the child must get a craft, he can't just be an allsorts. There is no trench warfare. Uncle Charlie shoots the rabbits with his rifle when they come out of the corn. That moment speaks for all. He's an absolute marksman. Then he says, "There's me craft and there's my masterness." In two clauses, "me" and "my" together. Now if that's recognized by the reader, I've lost. If I've pitched it correctly, that line will make somebody cry, but they won't know why – they'll cry for the right reasons. It's Wilfred Owen's "War and the pity of war". Uncle Charlie's family craft-pride has made him become a killer. In war, the creative act is to destroy. The maker is a breaker. "There's me craft and there's my masterness" – in other words, he knows that he's a killer. He also knows he's going to die.

Now that is an example of something English could not do. It doesn't have the structure and the vocabulary to imply, in one sentence, what I have just said.

You mean standard English –

Standard English.

Based upon the Latin and the Greek.

Yes: but not only Latin and Greek. Another interesting thing about English is its balance, which is a balance not an imbalance, between the Saxon roots and the Latinate roots, and what happens when the non-literate concrete people, the rural working-class, get hold of a Latinate word. They give it an enormous richness. For instance, we would use, in standard English, the word "generous". Now, in Cheshire dialect it's a whole phrase which I think has great poetic beauty. They take the word "fluent", which is not Saxon, it's Latin, and instead of saying "he is a generous man" they say "he is a man very fluent in giving". Now that is to provide the Latinate word with a new meaning, a new angle on the word, which I think enriches English and our imagination.

Another lovely use, which gives strength to what's being said, and again there's no single word in English which does it, is the Latinate word "previous", used in dialect only to mean "out of place in coming forward". "You're a previous sort of a youth." I don't know of a standard English analogue for that, but if that was said to me I'd wince. And there's one word, which if my father ever used to me, I should never recover from, because I have only heard my father use it twice in my life and it is the ultimate criticism. It is putting beyond the pale. It is saying you do not have the basic human qualities required. If my father said to me "You are ignorant", I could never get back into grace.

Now I've given you three words which are Latin in origin – ignorant, previous and fluent. When taken by a concrete language and reapplied they gain a life which the 1944 Education Act seemed almost God-given to release into the community and it has not done so.

The Genesis of "The Stone Book"

Consciously, I could not write in order to do anything except finish the book, so the hindsight danger is to appear to have been very clever, but it is not deliberate.

The nearest I've come to writing in order to do something was, in fact, the germ that started *The Stone Book* as a one-off book. I had no idea that *The Stone Book* was going to beget others. I did not know there was a quartet until I was nearly at the end of *The Stone Book*. Through talking to Linda Davis, my editor, and hearing other conversations, I was aware that there was a problem over the nature of the material available for young readers today and that there was concern among teachers that readers were being lost because a child with the technical ability to read was being provided with material which insulted his intelligence and therefore he would quite rightly go and watch something on the television. So – as part of a simple general conversation – I did discuss it some two or three years before I had the basic drive to write *The Stone Book*.

When I was starting to write *The Stone Book*, I remembered the earlier conversations with great clarity; I thought, I must now forget those conversations because I am a writer. I'm not a technical linguist who can feed into the language the right proportion of difficulty, interest, and so on. I do not have that skill, or the training, or the background. But I did want to give the child as much room to expand as the child could take, without making the child feel that if he hadn't expanded far enough he was losing something.

Now this I think is the definition of a children's book. If a child can read with a totality of experience and the adult can too, that is a good children's book. Therefore I would say that *Lord of the Flies* is not a children's book, because I doubt if a ten-year-old can read the whole of the text without sensing gaps in his comprehension. This is not to criticize the author, it is to criticize the use of the book by other people.

I was faced with the fact that at the time, ostensibly, my editor and I were engaged on an educational project; it was as simple as that. And, I thought, Well, how am I going to do it? Then I did something instinctively. I went back to my own childhood for the first time, and I remembered that when I learnt to read, the act of reading was more important than the content. It was a physical act: I could feel the shape of the words in my mouth as concrete objects. And so I started to tell the story of *The Stone Book* in a vocabulary that I could taste – I could actually feel the words in my mouth. That was the simple level of doing it. When I looked back at the text, I see what the twenty years of writing had enabled me to do.

It is why, of all the work I've done so far, the only work which I would permanently want to hold on to is this quartet of four books, because what I set out to achieve, I surpassed. In other words, I did it despite myself. Because integration set in, and when I look back at the text it is far better than I, the organism, the trained male, could have done. Something else took place, and I can only put it down to the fact that at last I stopped being defensive towards my background. I did not have a chip on my shoulder. I had something far worse, I had one on my soul.

I also was very well read in a lot of abstract languages, so the simple language of *The Stone Book* is a complete trick, at one level. I chose a lot of the words because I wanted them to taste as I remembered their taste from childhood. That was my only criterion. But when I look at it I see that, incidentally, sections of *The Stone Book* obey rules which are demanded of poetry, both in medieval Welsh and in early English. Now that is something that you have to know even to understand. But I think that you can get it emotionally. In Welsh poetry there were certain rules which involved sequences of consonants and vowels which had to be maintained. Something similar was present in Old English. At the beginning of *The Stone Book* you can see how it works as a piece of poetry and also how it works for the teacher. I may have, almost by default, supplied the teacher with a reader. There are two paragraphs I'd like to use as an example, but what I'm saying is true in all four books:

The new steeple on the new church glowed in the sun: but something glinted. The spire, stone like a needle, was cluttered with the masons' platforms that were left. All the way under the Wood Hill Mary watched the golden spark that had not been there before.

She reached the brick cottage on the brink of the Moss. Between there and the railway station were the houses that were being built. The railway had fetched a lot of people to Chorley. Before, Father said, there hadn't been enough work. But he had made gate posts, and the station walls, and the bridges and the Queen's Family Hotel; and he had even cut a road through rock with his chisel, and put his mark on it. Every mason had his mark, and Father put his at the back of a stone, or on its bed, where it wouldn't spoil the facing. But when he cut the road on the hill he put his mark on the face once, just once, to prove it. [pp.13–14]

In the first paragraph there are links of assonance (such as "glowed" and "golden", "steeple" and "needle") and of consonantal sequence. "The new steeple on the new church glowed in the sun: but something glinted", is a sentence formed by contagion. It is this aspect that has affinities, with Old English and Welsh poetry, and it comes without conscious thought. If I tried to write like this knowingly the result would be a mess.

Something else happens in the second paragraph. "Brick", "brink", "bridges" are eased together by a word that isn't there. "Brought" is hiding under "fetched", which itself has been preferred because of the growing "ch, ch" of the working mason's hand: "church", "watched", "cottage", "reached". And so "fetched" instead of "brought". Then all is resolved in the word that is making the noise: "chisel".

If you'll look at the two paragraphs you'll see other examples.

As I've said, I found myself engaged on an educational project that I was not equipped to fulfil. Therefore, I was thrown back on something instinctive, which didn't fulfil it: it surpassed it. And enabled me to write.

And that, presumably, is the reason why it is a text you have to prepare very carefully for reading aloud. In that sense, it is poetic: if you get a piece of poetry wrong as you are pronouncing it, then the whole thing falls apart. Whereas that's not normally true of prose; you can re-interpret, you can give it different phrasings, you can give it different orchestration. I find with The Stone Book *you have to get it right and if you don't it's a terrible calamity and the audience know it is.*

And this relates to the enriching of the text by the dialect and why phonetic spelling just throws sand into the works. I became aware very late in life that the music, poetry and justification of any language or dialect is not in its vocabulary or phonetics, but in its cadence, the rhythm, the music of it all. And therefore, just as I came between Mary and the reader, and came between Mary and the narrator and produced this third point of view which you mentioned earlier, so I have come between the dialect speaker and the standard English speaker. I have tried to convey this in *The Stone Book* by drawing on both my languages to provide a third language, which although it may contain a lot of unfamiliar expressions, unfamiliar words, is never opaque. That is where the editorial help was so essential to avoid overfeeding of the language.

That is why if there's any editorial query, my instinct is to remove the word immediately, because I sense indigestion.

Writing FOR Children?

Of course, you're arguing a terrible paradox now, because I was struggling with you right at the beginning of the conversation to confess to some, however removed, attitude towards the child reader you're including in the book and now you're actually demonstrating how you've done it.

The paradox is valid. It's caused by my necessarily divided approach. I have to suspend judgement of what I'm writing, at the time of writing, so that the story is not cramped by me. Then, afterwards, I have to know exactly what it is I've done, so that the story is contained with clarity. It's hard to keep the two functions separate when talking about them after the event. But I still say that I don't write *for* children. The two paragraphs I've just analysed in *The Stone Book* may serve the technical requirements of a school book, but they are the product of criteria that recognize neither schools nor children, although the product itself may welcome them.

Can I just summarize it in order that you can check my summary. It seems to me you're confirming that in some remotely conscious way the forces which are working in you and which produce the kind of book you have written to date, without exception, speaks of your having a deliberate intent of including the child reader, if not as the prime reader then certainly as one of the readers you wish to have, and that the narrator is working for this as he tells the story.

Yes. All right.

Now that may not be Alan Garner working for it, but the narrator in every book you've done works for it.

Yes.

And I did want to ask you, in fact, whether you're ever conscious of attempting to get the reader on the narrator's side. Do you do things which will facilitate his entry into the book? If I could just go on for a moment, while you're thinking about it. I would argue that you do, in the sense that you obviously study your openings carefully, and as in an opening in chess, it is meant to bring your opponent into the game in the way you want him in. In The Stone Book *it has enormous elegance in that you use a syntax which is absolutely approachable and not difficult. You use a diction which is totally within the young reader's capacity, but you give him one word in the second sentence, "baggin", which is signalling that there are going to be linguistic references he's going to have to cope with. But within the context of the sentence it's totally clear what you mean, so that you've helped him there again, in a way that you would not have necessarily had to help a reader whom you assumed had your range of references, your education, your adult stature, your adult background – which is the assumption made throughout English literature not written for children.*

Yes.

Now, all those things taken together – the point of view, the style, the choice of subject, the choice of theme, the way the narrator creates, is created, or creates himself – says to me, this is a book, this is a writer who wishes to include children in his audience, whether he gets adults or not.

This is correct. That's a good summary. That is exactly what we have been flailing towards.

All right. I realize when the flow is on, as with the honey flow, you've got no time to think about it. You just go out there and get the honey. But when you've finished a draft you become your own first reader. You are looking at the book to see if it works in the way that you are the only person can know the narrator wished it to work. So then you're the reader who can check the narrator and that is an editorial process which you've very well described in this particular sequence as going on not only with yourself, as the writer, but with an editor who has to stand outside it and not know certain things in order to check certain linguistic uses. Now, at the point of being your own first reader, do you rework in such a way as to include in the text devices which will draw the reader in, which will get the child, as a reader, onto your side and will mould him into the kind of reader you want?

Yes.

Can you describe any of the techniques you used, or ways in which you've done that?

The ways in which I've done it vary. As I have had more experience I find that when I come to the stage of being my own first critic and editor and reader, more and more I find I've already done it. But I do remember thinking about techniques, and the result has always been less happy than when I write without thinking about them. So now I let technique look after itself.

Yes.

That, of course, is simply craft.

Yes.

And working for long enough. Now how is it done? Let's talk, just for a moment, about how it doesn't work. Because usually a negative is a good way into getting something positive. Well the cliché example is a bad stage play, where the first ten minutes is spent by people talking to each other about that which they already know. Okay?

Yes.

So how do you get across without making it obvious? That is a technical problem. And this is where, by writing a sequence of four books about a rural family in Cheshire, I feel that I've come closest to the Greek playwrights who showed me that there were standards. I have been able to have the self-discipline – and this is only my way of doing it – the self-discipline to hang on to a story until it was down to its minimum, until there was only the bone of the story, with no superfluous words or structures. I then find that the techniques are not techniques but are basic structural features. Now, an example of that.

In *The Stone Book* it is necessary to provide the emotional tension, which need never be described, because all I'm doing is providing a piece of drama. You have to believe that the people in the story have strong feelings. You don't need to know what has created those feelings. Now this is where I would include the adult and include the child. The child reader must know that when Mary's father and his brother are about to have an argument it is something that the adults remember, the build-up of adult tension, and Mary gets under the table and she sees both sets of feet, the twitching and the still. Now that is technique.

The social historian will know all about the partial emancipation of the nineteenth century and will be able to date that to within a few years possibly – say plus or minus five years, because the narrative mentions the innovations in the environment. The child will, I hope, not be put off by my description of the railway line coming. I just mention that she can see a train and the reason why father's so busy is because he's building so many houses. The reason there are so many houses is because the railway's come to England. Now that puts it between 1840, 1860. The child reader does not have to have a history lesson. In order to get on with the story I have built in information for the person who wants to read it at another level. And so the row between the stonemason and his cottage industry weaver brother works at the child level under the table and later the emotion I hope is such that it is natural for the father instinctively to try and dissipate the tension that was in the room, by explaining to Mary why he and his brother row. And he does it in a sentence or so, by saying he makes houses for the big masters who've taken William's living from him and William never sees the end of what he does; he's just a weaver and it all goes to market and he never sees it again. Whereas father cut that road, built that church. Now that's a perfectly good explanation for the child reader. It also raises questions about society which I don't think have been asked very often.

That is how I bring in the reader without spending pages of people telling each other that it is 1864. It's irrelevant. And so often I feel that inadequate writing is the result of not asking the questions in the right order before writing. I don't think the author has done enough work before switching off and just going and getting the honey – before going to get the story. The right questions must be asked very quietly and calmly and the irrelevant must be scrubbed with a ruthlessness that only professionalism can bring.

You must not indulge. You must not put something in because that's what Uncle Harry said. It may be a brilliant anecdote, but if it's irrelevant it's got to go. In *The Stone Book* there was stuff that I would have loved to put in, but the writer in me said no, that is irrelevant. In *Tom Fobble's Day* it doesn't matter to me that a child may not know that it's January 1941.

Tom Fobble's Day is especially interesting because it could be said that it's an autobiographical book, since the child protagonist is the age I was at that time, so I did draw on a lot of my memory. But that child is not me. It's a very irritating question, the autobiographical one, because it's so stupid. All the characters are autobiographical – all of them. I don't mean literally every character, because some characters exist in a book because the author isn't good enough to do without them. They are mechanicals. I'm not talking about those, I'm talking about the true characters, those through whom the essence of the story flows. And I do say that all those characters, all the primary characters, are autobiographical. Not that they are in their totality autobiographical; but each character contains a fragment of autobiography.

I'd better define autobiography. I don't mean confession of what happened to me. I mean that a given character, whether male or female, young or old, takes on the gender and the age as co-ordinates to place the character within humanity and within the book, in such a way that something that needs to be said can be said most efficiently. And the reason it needs to be said is because the author has experienced it. But it is not the author saying "I had a miserable time when I was twenty-nine – and here is a twenty-nine-year-old character." It is the author saying "I had an experience. It was important enough for me to remember as an experience and to bring into the story. And it is best expressed within the flow of the story by a twenty-nine-year-old male – female – recidivist – or whatever."

In *Tom Fobble's Day*, for instance, there is a reference to searchlights and bombers and guns, but nobody explains them. The only thing that matters to me there is that things are happening that the child reader, thank God, is no longer experiencing. I don't wish to make a social point. It helps the social historian again. What is universal – and this is the connection with the Greek playwrights

– is that of my own children (who tend not to read my books at all) the oldest, Ellen, is adult so she feels that she can actually deal with it. She has something very interesting to say about *Tom Fobble's Day*. What enabled Ellen, who'd never experienced war, to experience war – and she has said this – was the description of the awfulness of wet clothing in snow.

This is almost like switch selling. You take an aspect of life that is beyond the experience of the reader and you deliver it in terms which are entirely within the experience of the reader, so the reader accepts the description and recognizes, and says yes, that's exactly how it is. By a simple switch they "buy" the experience they cannot possibly have had. So, that is the technician in me, asking questions. How do I avoid a lot of description which is very much period writing – the nature of the light in 1941, the whole build-up to blackout, of being cold and miserable and having enough to eat but no joy in life? How does that come across? Is it essential for a child to experience it? What area? And the way to get through is to go to the universality of how a woollen balaclava helmet chafes the chin. It's as simple as that and very difficult.

Point of View Again

It has almost become assumed that in order to produce a children's book a child has to be at the centre of it, as protagonist and often, more and more, as narrator too – the first person of the story. Is it possible to write a children's book with an adult protagonist?

Theoretically, I have serious doubts. It would be very difficult for me to conceive of writing a children's story with an adult protagonist, if the setting of the story were the present day and the immediate environment of the projected reader – that is, in this case, Western Europe – because it would clutter up the emotional vision of the writer to such an extent that I think he'd be in danger of taking a bad photograph. Just as when we look at a holiday snapshot we see, to our horror, that there's a lamp-post growing out of Auntie Jessie's ear. We did not see that when we took the photograph, because our eye was selecting. But the camera lens does not select – the camera lens photographs what it sees. It is the job of the photographer to eliminate and make the camera photograph only what the brain sees. There's an analogy there which is very close to writing. If you put an adult as a protagonist, you have to eliminate the confusion of emotions, experiences and sheer mileage that that adult will have and the child will not have, that will put a rift between them. And you've got to do it somehow. I would say one solution would be to go to an environment that the child does not know. It would be possible to write with an adult protagonist in an exotic setting, or in another time. And this is where I think science fiction has a very strong hand to play, because you can have adult protagonists there. The ideas – again we are getting close to the Greeks – are stripped down to the basic questions, which the child knows all about but doesn't have the vocabulary for – why? and what?

Aren't all adult protagonist stories read by children, whether set foreign or science fiction, actually folk tales?

But yes. They're all coming back to – we're in dangerous water here because I'll have to use words that could antagonize people – we're talking about things like Jungian archetypes and a lot of jargon words that I want to avoid.

First-Person Narrative

You've never written in the first person have you?

No. I've often considered it. But I never have and I feel that for me – personally, and I must stress that this is only a personal opinion – it would destroy that third point of view: the relationship between the narrator and the character and the child. The protagonist, the reader and the narrator. For me it would flatten out the texture of the story. I may change my mind. I've thought of it over so many years and I can never find a reason for it. It seems to me to narrow the options by saying "this is what happened" instead of saying "is this what happened?" I like to leave stories open-ended and there is something narrowing and confining for me about the first person. I can see that it can be used by another writer positively. Instead of saying it is narrow and confining he would say it is concentrating and focusing. But I think my reason for it is that as a child the only time my father ever tried to read to me was a total failure because it was *Robinson Crusoe* and he never got beyond the third page – somewhere round there – because I kept saying "you didn't".

I would hesitate to presume to suggest reasons you haven't thought of for yourself, but might one of the reasons why you haven't used the first person be that you are extremely keen – and again we're not necessarily talking consciously – that the true nature of the adult characters should be available to the child in the book. Available to both the child protagonist and the child reader. The only way to achieve that is in the third person. You can't do it in the first person. Is that true? I just want to go on to make the point that one of the most impressive features, to me, about The Stone Book *sequence is the richness of the adult life you pack into such a small number of words. I mean, these are stories of about seven and a half thousand words, so that the quartet is in all less than a third the size of a normal novel. And yet the adult characters are much more alive as people, and not just people seen through a child's eyes, than they are in many adult books. Is it indeed an interest that you do have to present that fullness of life within the book?*

Yes. Just to round off the first-person business which you led in with. I don't know that I can say anything of any permanent objective value on the subject. I'll just say that I agree with you that for me it would be an inhibiting factor to do first-person narrative and for the reason that you said. I would say that is my strongest reason. It restricts my footwork. I think it's the process of enrichment that starts early on in my part of the job, which is to know as much as I can about the environment of the story.

Do you mean the physical place?

The Image of Childhood

Physical place and emotional equations that are at work – the forces that are at work between people. And then, I am ruthlessly selective – emotionally, not intellectually – about what I choose to crystallize in the totality.

In *The Stone Book* sequence it is possible to make the adults more readily available to the child, because within that culture and environment the child had a valid role. The child added to the subsistence of the family. Quite often one sick person could put the whole family's survival at risk. So the child, from birth, grew up to earn his keep, if it was only picking stones off the field. And therefore was more readily accepted into an adult community – although he would know his place. The pecking order was very strictly adhered to, but he was respected as a human being, not pampered as a toy. And I think from the pampering-as-a-toy attitude towards children we get this strange parting of the ways (which was not there certainly in Elizabethan England) where children, and doing anything for children, is taken as a totally separate and lesser activity. In the families that I've written about in *The Stone Book* the children knew their place, but they had their respect.

That explains to me one kind of understanding about the children in The Stone Book *sequence. I want to ask the question another way. It seems to me that children's books now, and for two hundred years have both reflected what adults think childhood is and in part have formed it. I think I would cite, for example, the first great children's book ever published, which is Edward Lear's* Book of Nonsense, *which came in 1846, as an oblique statement about what he thought childhood was. Lear didn't know he was making it, but he accorded them that ability, that perception, to know that these things were funny and that children would not misuse that fun. Thinking about childhood in that way would have been against the tradition of the way children were brought up. So it's a subversive book; it's changing attitudes towards childhood and changing children's views about themselves.*

Yes.

And what is allowed for them. Now, that's still going on. I would say – and I would be able, I think, to argue it given sufficient time – that The Stone Book *sequence presents a view of childhood which is in some ways reformatory too, that it presents a view of childhood that we still haven't taken account of now. It's different from the commonly held view. Can you talk a bit about that and your view of childhood?*

Not directly. I'll try. Childhood and books.

Well, literature (at the level that has been concerning us) is a creative and re-creative act for all who experience it. It has to be reformatory: it must expand the individual, so that he can assess the values of his time, confirm those that are relevant, modify where necessary, and reject the obsolete. This process can be helped as much by fairy tales as by avant-garde novels: the form doesn't need to be modern.

But literature itself must be dangerous – "subversive" was the word you used. And I feel that the creative tension, the danger, is leached out of books for children and replaced by pasteurized dogma, impeccably written in the nineteenth-century mode, elegantly produced, and bland.

That would tie up with the one example I happened to have in my head as I was putting the question to you. Which is that when I have read The Stone Book *to teachers there is always at least one person, and usually more, who objects to the scandalous way in which the father allows Mary to climb that ladder and then goes and puts her on top of the weathercock and spins her round.*

Dear God!

Right. But you can take it in another two ways. There is one sociological aspect of it, which I wondered was the answer you would give me, which is that the working-class – I'm sorry to make class points, because I hate them myself, but it is true – the working-class would not have protected, do not protect, their children in such a way, and would have connived at what Mary's father does. This is something that has never got into children's books because, on the whole, they're not written by people who have had that experience. And so they are protective of things they would draw back from. They would include a line about how you shouldn't do this on your own, for instance.

Yes.

Even if they climb the ladder at all.

Well, that's middle-class. That is the protection of the social species because we have only 2·4 of them per family.

That's right. Yes.

Whereas Mary had two sisters and four brothers.

Yes. But that's a sociological point, to start with. There is another point in it, though. Which is that one of the meanings in the book I would take to be the fact that you're saying childhood should be given the potential, should in fact be put at risk. And you wish both adults and children to know this. You wish them to take the risk. Is that reading too much in?

It is reading too much in, but I think it is a point that must be allowed. What worries me is that we could start deliberately to build risk in, which would be wrong. All I'm advocating is that risk should not be artificially suppressed. To impose risk would be simply to swap one dogma for another.

Risk was a natural part of my childhood, and had nothing to do with a lack of parental affection or concern. But I realize that this is a nicety that many adults don't understand.

There was an editorial dispute (*not* with Linda Davis) over *Tom Fobble's Day*, which reached that rare point where I had to insist that the text should not be changed. The editorial objection was that William went off to have tea with his grandfather without asking, or telling, his mother first. I said that the mother loves the child, and although it's dark outside and snowing, she isn't worried about him or wondering where he is. The working-class philosophy is, "If anything was up, we'd know soon enough," rather than the more protective, "Oh dear, what can the matter be?"

It sounds ridiculous when I describe it now, but at the time, finally, I had to insist.

There was also the matter of sledging at night. I was told that it was dangerous. I said that I was relating an activity, not promoting it. The argument got nowhere. It seemed that the editor was so concerned for child-safety that the dramatic and structural force of the sledging incident in *Tom Fobble's Day* hadn't been noticed. So I asked why – and the answer scared me, and still does.

The main objection to the sledging and to the failure of William to ask permission to have tea with his grandfather was that they were incidents that teachers and librarians might object to, which in turn might damage the sales potential of the book.

Now that's frightening. It's why I exclaimed when you told me about the reaction you get when you read *The Stone Book*. You're implying that the editor had recognized a fact of marketing life.

There are three principal human beings between a story and the child reader: the writer, the editor and the adult who makes the book available. If they go down like dominoes, if the adult can dictate to the editor and the editor can commandeer the author, then where is the story? Where is the child?

A few moments ago you made me experience in the particular a movement I've sensed generally: and that is a movement to turn books for children into tracts for authority. It's producing a literature, or an industry, that has little to do with life, but offers instead an inorganic, cosmetic cleanliness that one sees in totalitarian cultural enterprise, an example of which would be the self-removal of Nazi painting from the development of art.

Such dead-end mediocrity will attract the conformist and the derivative: you've only to look at the artists who come to power under a Hitler or a Stalin for evidence of that.

I wish I were overstating the case, but, by being an industry, by pandering to those unqualified to differentiate, children's literature loses its creative bite. And, without bite, literature can cope with nothing more substantial than gruel; and that's where a comparison is to be made with State Art.

Writing is a solitary act. To try to please others, or to join a school of thought, a movement or a group is to risk diffusion. It's my main reason for avoiding the company of writers. A writer should accept his isolation. Talk dissipates. In this long conversation now, I've spoken only of work that is behind me. I've said nothing about what's happening at the moment, or what may happen next, and if you were to ask I shouldn't answer. An incubator is a sealed unit.

If what I do is to be of any use it must come from me, however inept, and not from a gang, however gifted. The lesson of *The Stone Book* quartet will bear repetition. Only when I am at my most idiosyncratic and obsessively personal do I approach a universality. Or so it would seem. Anyway, I'm not going to chance it.

I would agree personally with all that, though I guess others would dispute aspects of it. I wish I had time to pursue it further. Without it, however, let me bring you back to the issue that began this part of our talk: your attitude to childhood. Maybe there are books which you read as a child which influence you now, or which you remember and which still affect you?

From my own childhood, what I value as much as anything is the iconoclastic publishing of two comics, *The Dandy* and *The Beano*, in the nineteen-forties. There, at comic-strip level, was the healthy questioning of all authority. And I'd like to think that in everything I do a little of the genetic structure of *The Dandy* and *The Beano* is passed on. What excites me most when I'm being my own first reader and critic is the finding of that strand.

The strand is identified always by the same two factors intertwined. One is: it's cheeky. It may not appear to be, but it is just a bit naughty, in some way. I'm appalled by it. And it is also totally balanced by a responsibility of craft and decision. The first sentence of *The Aimer Gate*, for instance: "Robert took Wicked Winnie off the wall and oiled her." At such moments I feel that the strict literary training that I had in the centre of Greek myth and tragedy is making the obvious but illogical leap to the chaos and iconoclasm of *The Dandy* and *The Beano*. The two worlds unite and I feel a current go through me and I know it's good. And so I would say, you know, to turn it into a quote, I would say that when I'm really flying, it's Aeschylus writing "Desperate Dan".

A Subject Guide
to Ten Years of Signal

The index which follows lists the authors and titles of all articles published in SIGNAL during the first ten years of publication, together with the principal subjects, authors and books discussed in these articles. The index is intended only as a broad guide to the full range of material published in SIGNAL during this period, and readers in search of more detailed information on the content of the magazine should consult the annual index published in the September issue each year.

References in the index are made to issue and page numbers, e.g. the citation 5/47–55 refers to pages 47–55 in issue number 5.

Hunt, Peter, articles by, 15/117–30;
19/12–21; 25/12–15; 28/9–25
Hutchins, Pat, 10/32–6

Illustration, 1/16–19; 3/67–80; 5/78–
83; 11/88–93; 13/10–15; 16/33–9;
19/45–50; 21/108–14; 28/26–33
INFORMATION BOOKS: A FEW
HOME THOUGHTS ABOUT THE
T.E.S. AWARDS AND ABOUT
TELEVISION'S EFFECTS ON
PUBLISHING (Moss), 25/25–9
INTERNATIONAL EXCHANGE?
(Amor), 29/103–8
International Research Society for
Children's Literature, 28/47–53;
29/103–8
INTERVIEW WITH ALAN
GARNER, AN (Chambers), 27/
119–37
INTERVIEW WITH ROBERT
CORMIER, AN (Chambers), 30/
119–32
INTRODUCTION FROM "THE
DRAWINGS OF MERVYN
PEAKE" (Peake), 1/16–19
IN WHICH METHUEN GIVES A
POOH PARTY (Moss), 22/44–7

Japanese children's books, 12/135–8
JAY WILLIAMS, 1914–1978 (New-
man), 27/112–17
Jennings, Elizabeth, 29/71–3
Jessica's First Prayer (Stretton), 1/
20–8
JOAN AIKEN (Townsend), 5/72–7
JOHN CHRISTOPHER: ALLEGOR-
ICAL HISTORIAN (Williams),
4/18–23
JOSEF LADA, ILLUSTRATOR
(Amor), 21/108–14

JOYCE AND COURT OLDMEA-
DOW: WINNERS OF THE
ELEANOR FARJEON AWARD
(Taylor), 21/139–42
JULES VERNE AT HOME
(Lowndes), 10/3–13

KATHLEEN HALE AND ORLANDO
THE MARMALADE CAT (Moss),
9/123–7
KEY OF THE KINGDOM, THE
(Greaves), 30/159–68
K. M. BRIGGS, NOVELIST (Moss),
30/133–9

Lada, Josef, 21/108–14
LEARNING TO READ: AN ESSAY
WITH SOME VICTORIAN EXA-
MPLES OF READING GAMES
(Tucker), 24/122–39
Leeson, Robert, 11/106–7; articles
by, 13/3–9; 14/106–8; 16/18–25;
20/55–63; 24/149–54; 30/151–8
Le Guin, Ursula, article by, 19/3–11
LETTERS TO TWO CHILDREN
(Potter), 8/74–80
Librarianship, 9/109–14; 12/162–3;
13/30–7, 38–41
Loeff, An Rutgers van der, 11/102–4
LOOKING FOR A PATTERN
(Williams), 16/3–11
Lord of the Rings, The (Tolkien), 6/
87–95
Low, Florence B., article by, 18/118–
30
Lowe, Virginia, article by, 24/140–7
Lowndes, Marie Belloc, article by,
10/3–13

MacDonald, George, article by, 16/
26–32

Index

Page numbers in italics refer to illustrations